★ 301 ★ SMART ANSWERS to Tough interview questions

★ VICKY OLIVER ★

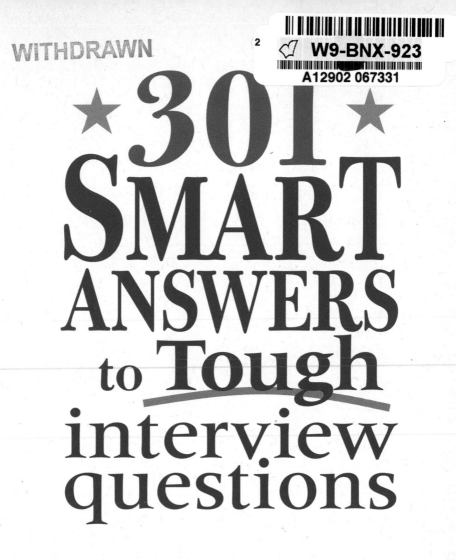

S sourcebooks

Copyright © 2005 by Vicky Oliver
Cover and internal design © 2005 by Sourcebooks, Inc.
Sourcebooks and the colophon are registered trademarks of Sourcebooks, Inc.

Published by Sourcebooks, Inc.
P.O. Box 4410, Naperville, Illinois 60567-4410
(630) 961-3900
FAX: (630) 961-2168
www.sourcebooks.com

Library of Congress Cataloging-in-Publication Data

Oliver, Vicky.
301 smart answers to tough interview questions / Vicky Oliver.
p. cm.
Includes index.
1. Employment interviewing. I. Title: Smart answers to tough interview questions. II. Title: Three hundred one smart answers to tough interview questions. III. Title: Three hundred and one smart answers to tough interview questions. IV. Title.

HF5549.5.I6O38 2005
650.14'4--dc22

2005008423

Printed and bound in the United States of America
VP   20 19 18 17 16 15 14 13

DEDICATION

This book is dedicated to my grandmother Margaret.
May she rest a little more peacefully,
knowing that I finally wrote something
in addition to advertising copy.

TaBLe OF contents

Professional Acknowledgments. vii

Introduction: How to Prepare for the Most Harrowing
 Forty-Five Minutes of Your Life: The Job Interview ix

Chapter 1:
 Start with the Basics: Answering the Easy Questions 1

Chapter 2:
 Give Us One Good Reason Not to Hire You 33

Chapter 3:
 You're Too Old, Too Young, Too Seasoned,
 Too Green, Too Female 61

Chapter 4:
 The Impossible Questions 91

Chapter 5:
 How to Ace the Personality Test 123

Chapter 6:
None of Your Business
(Or, Are You Really Allowed to Ask Me That?) 151

Chapter 7:
Good Cop/Bad Cop Routines in the Interviewing Game 177

Chapter 8:
Questions from Another Galaxy, Far, Far Away 211

Chapter 9:
So You Were Fired 239

Chapter 10:
Your Turn 269

Chapter 11:
If I'd Only Said X Instead of Y, I'd Be Hired
(Or, How to Change Your Answers after the Interview) 291

Chapter 12:
Special Situations 327

Conclusion:
How to Snag the Job of Your Life in Forty-Five Minutes. 355

Appendix:
Job Websites. 359

Index 363

About the Author. 371

Professional Acknowledgments

Writing is a solitary activity. But behind every successful writer is a team of people without whom the book would have never been made. My heartfelt thanks to:

Charlie Schulman, for believing in this project from the very beginning and for introducing me to "the second Charlie," Charles Salzberg.

Charles, thank you for always meeting me for lunch at a moment's notice to discuss random writer emergencies, and for introducing me to the indomitable June Clark.

June, thank you for your energy, drive, dogged persistence, and especially for introducing me to Bethany Brown.

Bethany, thank you for touching this book with your fantastic editing insights and for introducing me to the wonderful world of publishing.

INTRODUCTION

How to Prepare for the Most Harrowing Forty-Five Minutes of Your Life: The Job Interview

In today's "buyer's market" jobs are scarce, and hundreds of candidates compete for all too few positions. Companies have been forced to become incredibly selective as they sort through resume after resume from scores of qualified candidates. Due to other forces in the marketplace, glowing references do not carry nearly as much weight as they used to. As a result, the interview has become more like a final exam in college or even graduate school, complete with trick questions, curveballs, and ludicrously tough questions designed to shake out the applicant "plum tree" by deliberately putting candidates on the spot.

While the average interview still lasts for approximately forty-five minutes, it could well be the most harrowing forty-five minutes of your life. Interviewers no longer tend to ask "How well do you respond to pressure?"; they seek to determine it for themselves instantly, in your very first meeting, by mercilessly tossing you into a simulated pressure cooker situation.

How do you prepare for today's new, rigorous, psychologically draining interview? You need to treat it like the final exam (or trial) that it really is, and study for it.

The purpose of this book is to give you a quick reference guide to the 301 questions you are most likely to hear, and a way to answer them with intelligence, passion, and a certain flair that will help you best your competitors. Tips, brief analyses of why these techniques work, and helpful suggestions on how to rise above the pack will be peppered throughout.

Make no mistake: in order to prevail, you are going to need to trounce your competition. With all of the layoffs that have taken place during the past few years, it's entirely likely that the company where you really want to work will be interviewing people from several different levels to fill the position you seek. You could be competing against someone with three times your experience, or conversely, against someone who can do the job at half your salary level.

How do you get over the hump? How do you convince this organization that you are the ideal candidate for the job, and to hell with the competition? Here are the 10 critical steps that you need to take to ace your first interview, so that you can move on to your second, third, and fourth interviews (at which point, hopefully, they'll offer you the job already).

Top 10 Ways to Nail the Interview

1. Breathe deeply, and try not to panic. That was easy. Phew!

2. Try to set up your meeting for one full week (five business days) from the time that you first receive the call to come in. Your tendency will be to go for an earlier meeting to "get it over with." Do not yield to this instinct. You will need the time to prepare for your meeting. (Of course, if the interviewer insists on an earlier date, graciously accept it.)

3. Do your homework. Get on the Internet, and pull every article you can find about the company. Don't just read the articles; study and dissect them. Start crafting a "master list" of questions of your own about the company, based on the information that you unearth.

4. Go wider and deeper. Look up the company's website. Obtain past Annual Reports from the organization, and review them as if your life depended on it. Buy trade publications from your field; and brush up on what the company's competitors have been doing. Be certain to add some of this competitive information to the list of questions that you are preparing to ask in your interview.

5. Call any contacts that you have from the company, and start gently picking their brains about your upcoming interview. Ask your contacts about initiatives that are taking place in the organization right now; find out about the management structure; figure out where your interviewer is on the internal "totem pole." If you don't know anyone in the company, call any contacts you have in competing organizations to learn what they know about the company. Go out for drinks with them at night; treat them to dinner if necessary. Do not ignore this important step!

6. Review the questions and answers in this book thoroughly. Then, very importantly, change the answers a bit to reflect your own situation. (You never want to come off as "textbook"; rather you will need to be you, at your most charming self.) Add the questions and answers from this book that you feel you are most likely to be asked to the "master list" of questions that you are creating.

7. Write down your goal. Isn't that simply to get the job, you ask? Yes, of course if it is, but phrase your goal in a way that is very specific to the company. "My goal is to land a job as vice president of Customer Relations at the ADR Corporation, and to make $XXX,XXX a year." (You will know the perfect salary level based on the research you've already done on the organization.) Studies show that writing down goals helps people achieve them faster. Try it; what do you have to lose?

8. Review your "master list" of questions, answers, company history, and competitive insights every single day until exactly fifteen hours before your interview. Lock yourself in a quiet room in your house or apartment if you have to, and ask yourself the questions (and state the answers) aloud. This simple step, which so many candidates fail to do, can help you memorize your answers in advance. Won't that sound canned, you wonder? No, it won't. When you really know your material, you will actually come off as sounding far more "spontaneous" in an interview.

9. Decide, well in advance of your meeting, which outfit you will wear. This is to avoid any tough decisions at the last minute. Be certain that your outfit is pulled together and appropriate for the job you really want. Also, on the day of, make sure that you have showered, brushed your teeth, and have clean, well-kempt nails and hair. Carry a roll of breath mints with you just in case.

10. Then fifteen hours before your interview, force yourself to stop studying for it, and try to relax. Do yoga if you enjoy it, or listen to a favorite tune. Lay off the caffeine so that you can get a good night's sleep.

Realize that you are now the best-prepared job seeker in the universe, and use your wits and charm to add some *joie de vivre* to your all-important meeting.

CHAPTER 1
Start with the Basics: Answering the Easy Questions

An old adage tells us "there are no stupid questions." If only there were no stupid answers!

If you are tired, underprepared, or overly nervous when you meet your prospect, your chances of performing well decrease dramatically, and even "softball" questions can seem ridiculously challenging. So first, study really hard. And then, sleep really well. (If you have no idea why this is important, it's time to go back and read the Introduction of this book. And tsk, tsk for skipping it in the first place.)

There are five types of "back-to-basics" questions:

1. *Questions That Ask You to Walk a Mile in Your Interviewer's Cole Haans.*
2. *Questions about Your Dreams and Aspirations.*
3. *Questions That Blatantly Ask You to Sell Yourself.*
4. *Questions That Reveal If You've Done Your Homework.*
5. *Questions about Your P.W.S. (Preferred Working Style).*

Do a really great job at answering these, and sometimes, you may even make it to round two of the interviewing process without having to field any of the tougher questions.

What if you've been out of the Interviewing Game for a while and simply feel rusty? Read the Q&A's that follow; work out your own answers to the same questions; and invite a job-hunting buddy over to practice with you. You'll have more fun studying, and your answers on the day of your interview will be considerably sharper.

What separates a great answer to an easy question from an answer that is only marginal? Details, details, details. The questions may be easy, but being superficial about your answers (because you're anticipating tougher questions down the line) is never a good idea.

Questions That Ask You to Walk a Mile in Your Interviewer's Cole Haans

Sometimes, the hiring gods are with you. You walk into an interview, looking exactly like the type of person that "belongs" at the company, and your interviewer also happens to be in a supremely good mood that day.

A great first impression is made in an instant. When this is the case, your interviewer may ask you, in so many words, to put yourself in his shoes, and convince him to hire you. If you are lucky enough to find yourself in this situation, first, relax, and then, resolve to knock your interviewer's socks off. Nothing's going to stop you from landing this job!

1. If you were hiring someone for this position, what qualities would you look for?

A. I would look for three main talents, Alex:
1. The ability to solve problems;
2. The ability to nurture strong working relationships; and
3. The ability to close deals.

A candidate who possesses all three qualities would make the ideal associate new business director.

Let me tell you a little bit about my background. I "grew up" on the account side, and for seven years, helped companies like Revlon and Stoli Vodka solve big problems—such as how to position themselves in an increasingly fractured, competitive environment. Revlon, which for years had been the number one cosmetics company, was nervously watching its market share erode. Stoli was in a similar situation, due to Absolut's strong presence in the marketplace. I helped Stoli launch some new flavored vodkas, and the company soon regained valuable market share. Stoli rewarded me by offering me a job working on new product development. And I switched over to the marketing side for the next two years.

In marketing, having good people skills was mandatory. I had to beg vendors and suppliers for more shelf space. I had to chat up bar, restaurant, and hotel owners, and convince them to prominently display our vodkas.

I also wined, dined, and played golf with CEOs, CFOs, and owners of all different types of companies. So I know that I will be extremely resourceful when it comes to attracting new business to your company.

What Interviewers Want

Interviewers are only human. Before they will commit to a long-term relationship with you (by getting you on staff and giving you health insurance), they want to know what's in it for them. Here are the top three things interviewers look for:

1. Problem-solving skills. Bring up case examples that prove you know how to solve problems.

2. Good people skills. The ability to foster good working relationships is a vital business skill. Discuss situations where you worked well with others, or where bosses entrusted you with more responsibility, based on your past performance.

3. Closure skills. The ability to get things done. Mention those times when your good judgment or ingenuity helped you close a deal.

While you certainly can't be "all things to all interviewers," it may help to identify one or two qualities that you possess from each of the lists that follow. When you are asked questions about your skills, try to focus your responses to demonstrate that you have these qualities.

Problem-solving skills	**People skills**	**Closure skills**
1. clear thinking	1. flexible	1. good judgment
2. logic	2. agreeable	2. excellent follow through
3. creativity	3. good listener	3. energy/passion
4. ability to synthesize facts, compare & contrast, draw conclusions	4. articulate	4. resourceful, good at breaking through insurmountable blocks
5. generate solutions that are profitable because they meet a current need, identify a new need, or are so fresh, they are irresistible	5. team player	5. pattern of personal achievement
6. originality; the ability to think outside the box	6. charismatic/ inspirational/ motivational	6. results orientation
	7. trustworthy	

2. What would you like me to know about you that's not on your resume?

A. Well, Pat, I have the right mix of interpersonal and work-related skills to be a successful commercial real estate agent. A lot of people think that being a good saleswoman is simply a matter of being outgoing. But this is only part of the equation. You also need to be able to solve real problems for companies.

What if the space that you're showing isn't in the ideal neighborhood? You've got to persuade your prospect that the value of the property will overcome the inherent drawbacks of the location. What if the commercial space doesn't have as many windows as the company's current property? You have to help your client envision a different way to carve out the space, if only to muffle the complaints of the top executives. You need to be able to think, not just in terms of square footage, but also in terms of "profit per foot" for the company in question.

Above all, it's critical to seal the deal. For the past four years, I was among the top five closers at a large, commercial real estate company.

Why This Technique Works

1. You tackle problems with ingenuity.

2. You've proved that selling space goes way beyond price per square foot. The least the company can do is "give you some space" with a nice window office, where you can prominently display your fancy new business cards.

3. Let's say that I offer you a job. Please tell me how the company will benefit.

A. I am an expert on LED and rotational signage. I have been selling huge, LED signs to stadiums for the past five years. This has involved not only a great deal of technical expertise, in terms of understanding the technology that goes into our product, but also the ability to compare and contrast our offering to others that are less expensive to implement and maintain.

I've had to convince large groups of people, who are not technically inclined, to spend the money for a quality product. I always promise them tremendous service on both the front and back end, and then follow through. As a result, my clients have been very pleased with my performance.

Your company will benefit from my expertise on three counts: 1) I will train your sales staff how to close on deals more quickly and profitably, 2) I will share my extensive contact base with your company, and 3) I will reorganize your service department to be more "hands on." Then, your customers will give your company those glowing referrals that will lead to even more new business.

Why This Technique Works

1. You're the expert on rotational signage.

2. You've promised your interviewer new business if he will simply sign you on.

4. Why should I hire you?

A. Well, Martin, as we've been discussing, your company's website could probably benefit from a complete overhaul. For a first website, it's not bad...It covers all of the pertinent information that you want your customers to know about your business. But I agree with your own assessment, and feel that your website could be more inspired. You need some technical help with links, and I know how to come up with the key words and phrases that will bring a lot more web traffic to your site.

I think that a more creative flash opening, along with some music and graphics will keep customers on your site longer. It would be helpful to have something there that was continually updated in real time, perhaps some company news, or even games that would reward people for learning more about your services.

I've created twenty websites for all different companies, and one of them is in a similar line of business. I'd love to show you that website, so that you can get an idea of what's possible for your company. Can we hop onto your laptop right now?

Inside Information

Men seem to think that the "Why should I hire you?" question is challenging, and something of a blow to their egos, whereas the identical query seems to bounce off of most women without leaving irreparable damage. This suggests that there is something in the tone of the question that men intuit. Perhaps men sense a certain edginess about it, almost as if the interviewer were asking, "What makes you think that you're good enough to hire?"

5. You go to a store and give a $10 bill to the clerk to pay for a $9 item. When you get home, you realize that you received $20 in change. Do you go back to the store, or do you keep the money?

A. You go back and return $19, explaining their error to them.

EXTRA CREDIT

Questions about ethics are being asked during interviews with increasing frequency. Why raise any doubts about your morality? With the recent scandals that have occurred at some of the world's most prestigious accounting firms, don't even joke about keeping the money that falls out of someone's pocket!

Questions about Your Dreams and Aspirations

Of all the conceivable questions that you could be asked, these are perhaps the most basic. But your answer has to do a lot more than simply cover off on the basics. It needs to be thorough enough to make your interviewer treat you like a serious contender, and inspired enough to make your interviewer wish to get to know you a lot better. That's right. A really great answer will encourage your interviewer to ask you even more questions.

6. Can you tell me a little bit about yourself?

A. Certainly, Mark. I grew up in Rochester, where, as you know, the Kodak company has always had a huge presence. My fascination with photography started at the age of five, when my older sister took an amazing picture of me swimming in our parents' pool. By the time I was eight years old, I was spending an hour a day in a dark room, experimenting with retouching. Then, when I turned eighteen, I moved to Manhattan so that I could major in Photography at the School of Visual Arts. At the time, it was one of the only respected art schools on the East Coast. But at some point later on, I decided that I was really more of a business person than an artist, and so I started repping commercial fashion photographers, which I've been doing successfully for the last ten years. While I was working during the days, I completed my MBA at night. And I really think that the fact that I have both a BA in Photography and an MBA from a great business school makes me the ideal candidate for a management position here at Kodak.

Why This Technique Works

1. You've drawn a line between your childhood all the way to the present, proving that you were born to do this job and have spent your entire life working to achieve your destiny. Way to go!

2. Your two degrees prove that you're one of those rare individuals who is both creative and business-oriented, two traits that will serve you well in your future career.

How to Pack for Your Interviews

Pack light. If you show up carrying a lot of physical baggage, your interviewer may assume that you're also lugging around the emotional kind. But pack thoroughly. You need to be prepared for any contingency.

When you really want to impress a certain interviewer (which is any interviewer that you happen to meet), here are the ten essentials to pack into your briefcase or handbag:

1. Your cell phone (which will remain OFF during your meeting).

2. Directions to your appointment—including your contact's name, phone number, address of the office, and floor.

3. A few extra copies of your resume.

4. One pen and one small pad of paper (so that you can jot down notes after your meeting).

5. One roll of breath mints. (Just do it, okay?)

6. One comb.

7. One small mirror (or compact) for last-minute inspections before entering the office building. Nothing wedged between your teeth? Excellent.

8. One lint brush (in case the last people in your cab happened to be bringing their pet ferret to the vet).

9. One folding umbrella (to avoid arriving wet and wrinkled).

10. One picture ID (so that you can get past security in the lobby).

Inside Information

No matter what field you are in, you need to be passionate about the reason you like it. It's not a day job; it's your career. This is your calling. You were put on the planet to do this. Even if you work in a field where cynicism runs rampant, you must come off as a True Believer. You are the disciple of your profession, a future leader waiting in the wings. Don't be ordinary. Dare to be extraordinary.

7. Can you describe your dream job?

A. This is my dream job, Mara, and that's why I approached you about it in the first place. I am excited about the prospect of helping your promotion agency upgrade and fine tune your loyalty programs. I believe that rewarding repeat customers with movie tickets is a killer idea, and I can't wait to bring it forward to the Coca Colas and Dr. Peppers of the world.

8. What are your short-range and long-range goals?

A. My immediate goal, humble as it may sound, is to "start at the very bottom" of your talent agency. I will do anything it takes to get my foot in the door here: type contracts, organize files, make phone calls on your behalf, make coffee, scout for athletes, contact coaches—you name it, and I'll do it. I have always felt that being an agent is the world's best occupation, and I will devote myself to learning your business from the bottom up.

I am a very quick study, and have been the personal assistant for Marlene Summers for the past two years. Even though much of my job entailed setting up personal appointments and dinners for Marlene, whom, as you may know, founded the Ladies Network, I found myself much more drawn to the occasional task that I would be asked to handle for her husband, Charlie Summers. Charlie started as a professional wrestler, and sometimes he would ask me to review his contracts, contact his agent, and negotiate small points for him.

My long-range goal is to "grow" into a talent agent in my own right. But as that's probably years down the road, right now, I'm keen to start as your "assistant agent slave." Charlie and Marlene know that this is my burning desire, and they wrote a letter of recommendation for me, which I brought today to share with you. (Then, pull it out.)

EXTRA CREDIT

Know your place, and embrace it enthusiastically. It will magnify your attractiveness to employers exponentially.

Q. What two or three things are most important for you in a job?

A. I have to believe in the core vision of the organization, and I really respect yours, because, as far as I can tell, it's very much on trend. Over the last few years, thousands of companies have had to make deep cuts in their staffs. This has lead to a situation where "outsourcing" has become a way of life. Entire departments are now outsourced, and of course, your firm is meeting the need, brilliantly. You are supplying over fifty companies with talented labor, on an as-needed basis, for far less money than it would ordinarily cost. Fortunately, I'm a pretty good juggler. I get real satisfaction from bouncing from one project to another. The nature of your business virtually guarantees that this will be the case, and I'm really excited about the possibility of working here.

10. How do you set and manage goals?

A. My first life goal was to figure out my strengths, and, by the age of sixteen, I had decided that I was logical, articulate, resourceful, and enjoyed solving problems. These strengths led me to pursue a double major in political science and history at Dartmouth. Directly afterwards, I went to law school.

I started as an associate at Brimble, Brimble & Brimble, but couldn't take the ninety-hour weeks. So, after a couple of years, I moved over to the corporate side, and became the in-house counsel at CGH Systems. After three years at this post, I decided that I was really more suited to a job in business development. CGH encouraged me to make the switch, and for the following three years, I helped the company look for acquisitions. I find that business development enables me to use all of my natural talents, and it's my goal to continue to pursue my calling at your firm.

EXTRA CREDIT   Discuss the acquisitions in depth. Show how they helped CGH Systems embrace its corporate mission, grow, and make money.

Tale of Three Cities:
Tenacity, Felicity, and Electricity

If you have tenacity, you'll find that most interviewers will return your calls, schedule meetings with you, and generally pay attention to you.

Felicity is luck. And as Thomas Jefferson once said, "I'm a great believer in luck, and I find the harder I work, the more I have of it." So work diligently at finding a job, and anticipate that one day soon, you'll get the lucky break that you deserve.

Electricity is chemistry. Interviewers are attracted to candidates who possess both tenacity and felicity.

Questions That Blatantly Ask
You to Sell Yourself

To some extent, you are always being asked to sell yourself on a job interview.

This is important to remember when certain questions appear to yank you away from your primary goal. What makes the following questions a bit easier than most is that there is no agenda on the interviewer's part, other than learning why you feel like you're the ideal candidate. Some common, winning themes that you will want to bring out in your answers are:

1. The ability to bounce back from career setbacks (if you've had any).
2. Results, results, results. Never hold back on good strong results!
3. What you do in your spare time (or during working hours) to make you an A-player rather than a B-player.
4. Your ability to handle pressure, including adversity.
5. Your desirability.

Remember this always: YOU are your strongest advocate!

11. What is the most difficult thing that you've ever accomplished?

A. I changed the corporate culture of the company where I was working. When I first arrived, there was a poisonous atmosphere. Everyone kept their doors closed all day long. To put it mildly, there was no *esprit de corps*. I decided to do something fairly radical. I sent out a memo to the entire staff saying that, effectively immediately, the company had an open-door policy. For about a month afterwards, I would case the halls. If I discovered that someone's door was closed, I would take it as an invitation to enter that office without knocking. Inevitably, there would be at least two people inside gossiping. I would ask them to talk to me about whatever the problem was, and they were very forthcoming! There were two great results of the open door policy. The first was that I had a chance to find out what people's issues were with the company. And the second was that everyone started leaving their doors open, and morale definitely improved 100 percent.

12. Can you tell me about a recent achievement that you're proud of?

A. The "Ireland NOW!" program that I implemented boosted package tours by 30 percent. The program encouraged Americans to rediscover James Joyce, and other local Irish legends, by making a pilgrimage to Ireland on Bloomsday, which is June 16. Thousands of travelers wrote letters complimenting the program, and telling us how much they had learned from their journeys. And the positive word-of-mouth that the "Ireland NOW!" program received boosted advance bookings for the following summer by 50 percent.

When you are asked this type of question, talk about results. Use hard numbers wherever possible. This is your opportunity to shine.

13. What do you like to do on the weekends?

A. I spend one full afternoon every weekend catching up on general interest publications, such as the *New York Times* Arts & Leisure section, *Business Week, Esquire, GQ,* and *Vogue.* I find that doing so keeps my finger on the pulse of popular culture, and helps me come up with marketing ideas for our line of home décor products. I also read the trades, of course, but I find that once a trend is reported there, it's already played, and I'd rather spot trends on the upswing.

For example, a couple of years ago, I detected a trend towards minimalism, and, as a result, recommended a whole line of "white on white" paints, furniture, and accessories for the home office that boosted our brand sales by 30 percent. I also scour yard sales during the weekends, because I can often tell what's about to be "in" by the stuff from the attic that people are throwing out.

Read everything. Even dry research reports may contain pearls of wisdom. Ignorance is inexcusable.

14.
What special traits do you have that make you well-suited to this job?

A. I'm punctual, organized, get along well with people, and am supremely diligent. I also pore over every word of the research reports that we receive. There is so much information, all around us, that can help us do our jobs so much better, if we simply bother to read it. You would be amazed at how many times I have been able to sell through an idea simply by referring to some fact, or little gem of knowledge, that I unearthed about one of our products or one of our competitor's.

15.
Can you describe a time when you felt under pressure to perform? What was the outcome?

A. Certainly, Marcia. As an associate at DHK, I used to travel to board meetings with my boss, Cara Gordon. One day, Cara couldn't attend an important meeting, and she sent me to cover for her. I sat in a board meeting of an electronics company, and became very concerned that they weren't following best practices. There were a number of accounting discrepancies that I noticed, and so I practically assaulted the CFO with question after question!

When I returned to the office, I reported my suspicion to Cara. As a result, we ended up doing more due diligence on that company than we had ever done before. And it turned that my hunch was absolutely spot on.

Our company walked away from that investment, and I was rewarded with a huge bonus that year, even though our numbers were slightly off.

You Don't Have to Be Super-Trendy to Profit from a Trend

It's got nothing to do with the length of your hemline, the width of your heels, or the height of your hair. Keeping an eye on trends helps to keep your ideas fresh-squeezed, rather than stale and recycled. How do you spot a trend? Read every single newspaper or magazine that you can get your hands on. Keep your eyes, ears, and mind open. Start paying attention to "crossover" fads, e.g., those inner-than-in trends that surface in two places at the same time. Does a current TV show remind you thematically of a new movie that's coming out? Does a new art exhibit have the same color palette as the cover of your favorite magazine? Did you happen to notice the same eclectic appetizer listed on the menus of three restaurants in your neighborhood? Congratulations! You know a good trend when you see one. Your powers of observation are excellent.

16.
Please tell me about a time when you had to work independently.

A. In my last job, I sold T-1 lines to companies. For various reasons, my first territory wasn't very responsive. So, I started canvassing different neighborhoods, and finally located one that was an up and coming dot-com center, our very own "little Silicon Valley of the south." I asked my bosses if I could pursue this new territory; they blessed the idea, and I ended up being the top telecom line salesman that year.

Why This Technique Works

1. When sales didn't come with the territory you asked for permission to find a new stomping ground.
2. You found a new area that turned out to be the gold mine of silicon.

17.

What, in your opinion, is your most outstanding achievement so far in life?

A. I've always been happy that I managed to complete my college thesis. I was juggling five classes a semester, a post on the student council, a job at the campus movie theater to help pay for books and housing, and still, somehow, I found the time to write a thesis about why the economy tends to improve during election years. I graduated with honors from my university, even though I was overcommitted on all fronts. I think that I probably respond positively to stress, which I believe should help me do very well in this field.

Why This Technique Works

1. You've used your college experience to show that you already have "real life" experience.

2. You mentioned that you cope with stress particularly well, and, in more and more businesses today, unrelenting stress is a way of life.

18.

Where else are you interviewing?

A. I've been interviewing at the three top, bulge bracket investment banking firms, SDL, MNP, and VJK. But I would much rather work for your boutique, because I feel that I will probably have a chance to learn more here, much faster, than at a larger firm. I read that your company gives first-year associates a great deal of responsibility when it comes to servicing clients.

I would so much prefer to get this on-the-job, "real life" training from your firm, rather than the textbook, classroom training that most of the big firms provide. Can you tell me more about some of the projects that your first-year associates have been working on?

EXTRA
CREDIT

It's fine to use a word like "boutique" as long as the company where you're interviewing considers itself one. Otherwise, you may wish to refer to it as a "smaller company" or simply, "your company."

Questions That Reveal If You've Done Your Homework

In today's competitive environment, there will be several perfectly qualified candidates vying for the same position. Therefore, in the first few rounds of the interviewing process, interviewers are generally looking to *eliminate* candidates, rather than hire them. What is the single biggest reason that candidates don't get called back? Let's call it "lack of preparation." Candidates who reveal that they haven't done their homework are quickly bypassed for those who have.

If you have studied the firm, you will certainly ace the questions that follow. If you haven't, you will be politely ushered to the door with a vague promise that "we'll get back to you." Brush up on the company, and you won't have to hold your breath, waiting endlessly by a phone that refuses to ring.

How to De-Stress for Success

Stressing how well you handle stress is an effective job-hunting ploy, especially if you are going for a job in a high-stress field. If you've been in the field for a while, you already know if it's considered stressful. If you haven't been, here are some adverse factors that usually lead to a great deal of on-the-job stress:

1. A workaholic corporate culture, resulting in a consistent pattern of workdays lasting ten hours or longer.

2. Interoffice competition on assignments, particularly if bosses directly compete against those whom they are supervising.

3. Ambient loud noise at the workplace, due to uncarpeted floors, lack of privacy, tolerance for blasting music, or acoustical imperfections in the walls and ceilings.

4. A perception, either real or imagined, that the business is "glamorous." This leads to unbridled competition and a cutthroat atmosphere (which is so unglamorous).

5. Loss of current clients for whatever reason, creating severe internal pressure to win them back, or to attract new ones.

6. Growing pain caused by winning new business, and having too few people on staff to handle it.

7. Unforeseen changes at the workplace, such as pending layoffs, or new bosses, partners, and teammates coming on board.

8. A revolving door atmosphere, based on everything listed in point #7 occurring more than once every two years.

Most of this information is easily accessible if you keep up with the trades. So, if you know for a fact that the corporate culture of a company is stressful, and stress doesn't happen to stress you out, it's a good idea to bring it up on your interviews.

19.

Where do you predict that this industry is going in the next three years?

A. I think that we're going to see the cell phone business rapidly take off. In my view, the cell phone is quickly evolving into the perfect 24/7 business and entertainment center. On the business front, it's already a necessity, connecting people to their colleagues and clients 'round the clock. Why send an email, when you can use your cell to page people, text message them, or leave a message in real time?

But recently, the cell phone has also started to become a portable entertainment center. You can now use it to take great photographs, giving you another superb excuse to pull yours out and play with it during the day. And in Europe right now, people play video games on their cell phones.

It wouldn't surprise me if you could play tunes on your cell in just a couple of years. At that point, you'll be able to connect to any business-person in the world, day or night, and keep yourself entertained while you're waiting for him to call you back. How is your company taking advantage of this trend?

20.

What do you like about advertising?

A. I like the fact that one simple idea, generated by an art director in a tiny cubicle, can reach out and influence millions of people. The biggest thrill of my life has been "catching" a stranger on a subway or bus reading an ad that I wrote that appeared in a magazine. The power of a simple, compelling idea is unmatched. When you tell the truth about a product or a service in an interesting way, it really touches people.

What if the future of a business looks bleak? Acknowledge it, but temper your pessimism by telling your interviewer two things that you would do to forestall the inevitable. If the business looks bright, tell your interviewer why that turns you on. From Wall Street to Main Street, optimism makes interviewers bullish about hiring candidates.

21. You majored in philosophy. How did that prepare you for this career?

A. I think that philosophy is probably the world's least practical discipline! So the short answer is, philosophy *didn't* prepare me for a career in architecture at all. But it did force me to become philosophical about my prospects, and I basically decided that, unless I wanted to become a teacher or a writer, I desperately needed to get a second degree that was more practical. After two years of trying to figure out what to do with my life, I visited Chicago one weekend, and was absolutely spell bound by the gorgeous architecture all around me.

I came home, applied to architecture schools all over the country, and was accepted by one of the best. I've never looked back...this is definitely the career that I was meant to be in. I brought some blueprints today of a new condo development that I've been designing. May I show them to you now? (Then, pull them out.)

Beware the Jovial Interviewer

When an interviewer seems to be particularly friendly or jovial, he may inspire you to let your guard down. Do not succumb. While you want to establish a feeling of camaraderie, take care that you don't reveal things about yourself that are so honest, they could actually hurt your chances of landing the job. Here are three things *not* to say, even if your interviewer seems like the nicest, friendliest, most understanding person on the planet:

1. I have visions of retiring from the business in the next five years.

2. Now that I've paid my dues and proved myself, I'm looking for a job that's a bit less taxing, hours-wise.

3. My husband is up for a job in Toledo, Ohio. I don't think he'll get it. But if he does, that might impact how many years I would stay here.

22. What have you done in the past year to stay on top of this competitive environment?

A. Well, Clara, along with reading the trades and the *Wall Street Journal* religiously, I also stay up-to-date with news clips from CNN.com. Beyond that, I've started conducting weekly store checks on my own. There really is no substitute for walking through the aisles of the drugstore, and taking a good, hard look at which products command shelf space, and which ones get lost in the clutter.

EXTRA CREDIT

Tell your interviewer about a brand new product that got your attention.

Questions about Your P.W.S. (Preferred Working Style)

Flexibility, and the ability to go with the flow is one predictor of success in any field. Think about it. You may prefer to work alone, but if you are flexible enough, you will manage to do well in a team environment. The same thing is also true in reverse. If you're really a team player by nature, but happen to be easygoing, you will succeed in a "do-it-yourself-er" culture where people are expected to self-manage. However, *telling* an interviewer that you are "flexible enough to deal with any corporate culture" sounds wishy-washy and false, unless defended with some hard evidence. A better idea is to research the firm in advance, find out what they're looking for, and position yourself accordingly.

23. Do you prefer working alone or in teams?

A. Well, I am an independent type, and so I like to brainstorm first on the directives, and then go off for a little while to mull over how to fulfill them. I've always been very interested in executive headhunting, and feel that, under your guidance, I will make a big contribution to your company. From what I understand about the position, you and Paul Wiley will call a weekly meeting to discuss the new job leads and candidate requirements. Then, I will sit down, meticulously comb through our candidate pool, and arrange to meet several job seekers who fit the "specs." After that, of course, I'll do my utmost to place them! I also anticipate that this job will entail some cold calling, to expand our pool of candidates and identify more leads. I happen to know a lot of people on both sides of the management table—job hunters as well as employers—and I look forward to sharing my leads with both you and Paul.

Alt. A. I am a really good team player, and appreciate having the resources of a fantastic team all working towards the same outcome. I feel comfortable in groups, and enjoy team activities, such as brainstorming, name generation, coming up with strategic platforms together, and identifying new trends in the marketplace. In my last job, I worked for a famous branding identity company, and some of our meetings would last for days and days.

I would just roll up my shirtsleeves with the rest of the team, and we would sit, closeted in a conference room, with a gigantic pad of paper, magic markers, various toys, and tons of newspapers and magazines, discussing corporate identity issues until everyone felt comfortable that we had arrived at the right solution. I know that your company is also structured around a true team concept, and would love to hear more about it.

24. What motivates you to put forth your greatest effort?

A. When people really count on me to pull through for them, I am at my peak in terms of my performance. As an assistant planner, I have four bosses, and I get along famously with all of them. Still, one week over the Christmas holidays, all four of them took their vacations at the same time.

During that week, I ran focus groups by myself, came up with strategies for several of our clients without any supervision, and had an insight about the retiree market that became the backbone of our new fall marketing plan. I love being a team player, but that week on my own proved to me that when push comes to shove, I am capable of pulling projects through with my own resources.

EXTRA CREDIT
Share your insights about the retiree market. Ask your interviewer which markets his company is targeting, and impress him by spontaneously coming up with an idea for one of them on the spot.

25. Who was your greatest role model?

A. In my very first job, I was a salesgirl at Bloomingdale's. They rotated the sales staff, and I was moved from the Men's Department to the Bridal Registry. The manager of the Bridal Registry, Patricia Hillson, was a true inspiration. She really believed in my potential, and could sense that I was keen to learn how she went about choosing china patterns and flatware. After the store officially closed at night, she would spend hours with me explaining why she had chosen a particular line.

Approximately a year later, Patricia went on maternity leave for a couple of months and temporarily promoted me to run the department in her absence. By the time she returned to work, three of the china patterns that I had chosen for the store had become bestsellers. I was then officially promoted to Junior Buyer, but in Children's Wear. I owe my quick rise into management completely to Patricia, and she has remained a good friend and mentor ever since.

Why This Technique Works

1. You have given credit where credit was due, showing that you're gracious and the type of person who fosters good working relationships that last.

2. Your mentor will give you a glowing recommendation that will help you win the job.

Classic Flub Answer to the Easy "Role Model" Question

As a woman in the field, I have often found it difficult to find real "role models." Fortunately, I have always been self-reliant, and somehow managed to get promoted four times in my career without a lot of help from the inside.

Why This Technique Fails Miserably

You come off sounding like a "Lone Ranger." Why should anyone hire a Lone Ranger when there are hundreds of polite, team-oriented candidates clamoring for the job?

Thank God It's Monday

You spend more time at work than with your spouse or significant other. You may as well love what you do. If you don't, then you should really seriously consider changing careers. Feel like it's too late for you to career hop? It's not. If you are currently employed, think of changing your career in terms of baby steps. What tiny, baby step can you take today that will help you achieve your dream job tomorrow?

1. Volunteer for a cause that will help you build up the necessary skills for the new job that you seek.

2. Enroll in a class that meets once a week at night.

If you were fired from your last job or were laid off (and felt relieved about it), take the opportunity to do something proactive today to achieve the career you really want.

26. When can you start?

A. Tomorrow. *(If you're currently not working.)*

Alt. A. Two weeks from tomorrow. *(If you're currently employed and somewhat junior.)*

Alt. A. I can give my notice tomorrow and start in three weeks. *(If you're currently employed and somewhat senior.)*

Alt. A. Four weeks from tomorrow. *(If you're relocating to a new area to take the job.)*

Top 10 Tips for Being
a Brilliant Interviewee

1. Be polite, organized, and enthusiastic.

2. Plan interviews around your prospect's schedule, rather than your own. (Try to give yourself enough time to study the company thoroughly in advance, but be flexible.) And never turn down an interview because you have a class that day, are meeting with a personal trainer, or because it's your day to pick up the kids.

3. Do your homework. Research the company thoroughly (even if you already know absolutely everything about it).

4. Ask contacts for the inside scoop on the company and, if possible, about the personality of your interviewer.

5. Smile at your prospect, and shake his or her hand. The gracious interviewee lands the job.

6. Avoid canned answers to questions. Take the answers in this book, change them around, play with them, and really make them your own.

7. Nix slang words such as "like," "gee," "um," and "wow" from your interview spiel. Valley Girl–speak automatically subtracts, like, major IQ points.

8. Follow the news. There could be a story about the very company where you're interviewing.

9. Don't leave the interview without asking your prospect at least three questions. (See chapter 10.)

10. Follow up with a thank-you email or letter within three business days after your interview.

That's a Wrap

1. If you are asked to put on your interviewing "hat" (or walk a mile in your interviewer's shoes) and tell him why he should hire you, take the opportunity to wow him—with your problem solving ability, interpersonal talents, and closure skills.

2. The answers to questions about your dreams and aspirations need to be thorough and inspired. Don't be afraid to wear your heart on your sleeve and ask your interviewer, point blank, for the job.

3. Does your future employer want to hear about your accomplishments? There is no place for modesty in the executive suite. Stress your ability to handle pressure, your desirability to other firms, and results, results, results.

4. The fastest way to get eliminated from consideration is to be poorly prepared. So do your homework—on the field, the competition, the specific company where you are applying, and if possible, the particular interviewer who is meeting with you. He will evaluate your job suitability based on the way that you handle the interviewing process. Prove that you deserve the job by acing your interviews!

5. If anyone inquires about your "preferred working style," it probably means that he wants to figure out whether you are more introverted and independent, or extroverted and team-oriented. While it's important to be flexible, it's difficult to prove that you are, without tangible evidence. A more intelligent idea is to research the company, find out how things work on the inside, and position yourself as the "solo star" or "team player" they are seeking.

CHAPTER 2

Give Us One Good Reason Not to Hire You

This is a perennial favorite of interviewers. They love to ask candidates to essentially "unsell" themselves by probing for their weaknesses. During the late 1980s, a lot of job-hunting books counseled candidates to "turn their biggest weakness into a strength." Unfortunately, thousands of interviewees followed this advice verbatim, and started giving canned answers to the question. One of the most popular answers at the time was: "Well, I'm really a workaholic" (strongly implying, of course, that the candidate would slave deep into the night for the firm, night after night).

Interviewers began to hear the same answer from candidates roughly ten million times, and so today, this type of question has evolved. It's now phrased in a way that is much more difficult to answer because it requires the one trait the question was designed to elicit in the first place: honesty. (Meanwhile, if you do happen to be a workaholic, these days you're expected to count that trait as one of your strengths!)

There are five types of "give us one good reason not to hire you" questions:

1. *Tell Us Your Biggest Weakness.*
2. *Let Us Tell You Your Biggest Weakness.*
3. *You've Jumped Ship Too Many Times Already.*
4. *You Won't Fit in Here, Because…*
5. *You'll Be Miserable Here, Because…*

When you are confronted with this type of question, first answer the question honestly. Then smile, look your interviewer in the eye, and give him an even better reason to hire you!

Tell Us Your Biggest Weakness

This question continues to unnerve even very experienced interviewees. Today, there are all sorts of new twists to the question, making it even more of a conundrum. Still, with a bit of practice, you can turn it around to your advantage.

27. **What is your biggest weakness that's really a weakness, and not a secret strength?**

A. I am extremely impatient, which, of course, superficially, could be considered a strength because it means that I'm a quick study. But I honestly believe that being impatient is also a real weakness on a number of levels. I expect my employees to prove themselves on the very first assignment. If they fail, my tendency is to stop delegating to them and start doing everything by myself. To compensate for my own weakness, however, I have started to really prep my people on exactly what will be expected of them. I give them the full scope of the assignment, and then various "check-point Charlie" dates for them to discuss where they are on it. At my last job, for example, I was the project manager for a sweepstakes promotion for one of our clients. There were business managers, lawyers, and writers on my team. I broke down all of the tasks into manageable chunks for each employee, then gave them timelines of when they needed to circle back to me. It worked brilliantly—the process helped everyone get the job done, on time and under budget.

Why This Technique Works

1. You're being honest by giving a real weakness and not a secret strength.

2. You're demonstrating how you turned your weakness into an effective management technique that lead to a successful outcome.

EXTRA CREDIT Ask your interviewer if he or she would like a reference from one of the people you managed, and/or give the outcome of the sweepstakes project. How much money was generated by it?

28. Can you give me an example of when you disagreed with your boss or coworker and how you handled it?

A. My boss was punctual, organized, and fantastic with the day-to-day details of running the business. And I really learned a tremendous amount from him. The only thing that I felt he might have lacked was the "pie-in-the-sky," "let's-take-the-blinders-off" gene. I thought that, maybe 15 percent of the time, our team's efforts might have been better utilized brainstorming on how the business would evolve, so that we would be better prepared for the future. I mentioned the idea of brainstorming to my boss only twice, he seemed to feel that we didn't have the resources to engage in this type of activity, and so I just buckled down and helped him manage the department the way that he wished.

EXTRA CREDIT

Don't pick bones with bosses who aren't there to defend themselves. If you are asked about a disagreement that you had with a former boss, make the bone of contention sound tiny. Show how you swallowed your pride, instead of choking on it.

 I see from your resume that you worked at CC&L for four years, and that's terrific. But I also noticed that you weren't promoted during that time. Why not?

A. CC&L is a great company, and thanks in part to my team's contributions, they are doing very well these days. But that wasn't always the case. When I first arrived, the company was strapped financially, and it really wasn't making its margins. I worked for a dynamic boss, Clive Richardson, and he organized our team to help CC&L do the necessary belt-tightening. During the first two years that I worked there, people were being fired left and right, and just hanging onto my job was a feat.

Once the company began to turn around, Clive was offered a terrific job at a rival organization. It took CC&L six months to replace him, and when they did, my new boss was eager to bring in his own people from his former company. Once again, I tenaciously hung on to my job, and, even though I was long overdue for a promotion, I really didn't think that the timing was right for me to broach it. Many of the people who were in HR left once the new regime was in place. And I couldn't think of one person who was still on staff (besides me) who could vouch for my performance!

However, I made it my mission to prove to my new boss that I was talented and should be kept. A couple of months ago, I finally approached him about a raise and received 20 percent. Given what our company had been through, I was ecstatically happy to get the money and the pat on the back.

Why This Technique Works

1. You've proven that you're ambitious, but also practical. Your circumstances demanded a lot of patience, a virtue that you evidently possess.

2. You used your interview to bring out an impressive fact about you: namely, that you were rewarded financially by a boss who was looking to cut current staff members.

30. What was the name of the supervisor who let you go? What is your best guess as to what she would say are your strengths and weaknesses?

A. The name of my supervisor was Muffy Prister. Muffy often told me that I was a dedicated and hard worker with a lot of drive. She also said that I had "a great deal of talent," but that Prister, Porter & Pimble was probably not the right environment for me to showcase it. PP&P is a terrific, traditional, old-school firm, but not a place for relatively young people with visions of finding the next new thing. Muffy also wrote a reference letter for me, which I brought with me today to show you.

EXTRA

CREDIT

Refuse to play the blame game. Even if you know for a fact that your ex-boss has a terrible reputation in the industry, blaming her for your failures can only make you look bad. Among bosses, the instinct for self-preservation runs deep. So never badmouth your former employer, or your prospective employer will worry that you might do the same thing to him down the road.

Letters from Ex-Bosses: Your Best References?

If you are let go, always try to get a reference letter from your former employer. It will give you a good idea of what your ex-company is likely to say about you when they are asked for a reference. But read the letter very closely before bringing it with you on your interviews. Is it genuinely positive, or somewhat vague, damning you with faint praise? Is there any sentence in it that one might be able to read two different ways?

By law, former employers are allowed to say very little about your on-the-job performance. But with a letter in hand, a future employer might try to tease out more information from your former boss than she would ordinarily. If the reference letter is weak, you may be better off owning up to the fact that you had problems with your ex-boss, leaving the letter at home, and giving some of your former colleagues' names out as references instead.

On the other hand, if the letter is glowingly positive, by all means bring it with you. It may prevent your interviewer from calling your former boss (which is probably a good thing).

31. I play golf with Samuel Rosenshine, and he told me that when you used to work for him, you were edgy and nervous. Is that true?

A. I used to feel intimidated by Samuel, and I suppose that I acted out when I was around him. But I will confide something interesting about him. Samuel is the only person that I ever worked for who suggested that I see a shrink. And believe it or not, I decided that Samuel had a point! So, several years ago, while I was still working for him, I went and found a terrific career shrink that I have continued to see once a week. She helped me work on my personality and smooth out the rough edges. How am I doing right now? I don't feel like I'm acting nervously...am I?

Why This Technique Works

1. You answered a very difficult question with charm, even throwing in some self-deprecating humor.

2. You referred to the person that you've been seeing as a "career shrink" rather than a psychiatrist, a subtle but savvy distinction.

Follow the Rules, But Don't Be a Slave to Them

Let's get one thing straight. On most interviews, you should *never* bring up the fact that you see a shrink (or take meds). However, special circumstances require special measures. If you need to prove to someone that your personality has changed for the better, referring to psychiatric counseling, group therapy, or a self-improvement class that you took to correct the problem may be a good idea. And it's less of a risk than acting hurt or insulted that your interviewer asked you the question in the first place.

32.

Your headhunter told me that you are looking for $XXX,XXX. I don't have a problem with that amount, but it does seem a bit low considering how long you've been working in the field. Why is your salary requirement so low?

A. Well, Stan, as they say, "more is always more." But I would be happy with $XXX,XXX because I have been freelancing for the past two years, which has thrown me off of the raise every eighteen months continuum. The truth is: freelance rates are determined from a completely different budget than the hiring budget. So it's possible to make very little money freelancing at one organization, and then turn around and triple the amount at the next consulting gig. By requesting $XXX,XXX, I am really just asking for what I was earning at my last full-time job.

But you should know that, even though the amount is on the low side, I am actually far more experienced now than I was when I was working at LL&R. At my salary, I'm a great value, and I'm hoping that you will pick me up now—while I'm still "on sale."

 EXTRA CREDIT

Offer to provide your interviewer with references from the places where you have been freelancing.

Let Us Tell You Your Biggest Weakness

This type of question can be even tougher to deal with than questions where you're asked to reveal your own biggest weakness. In a veiled manner, the interviewer is telling you that there is a lot of competition out there, and that, in her opinion, you're a long shot. First, always be sure to answer the question that's asked, then move the conversation on to a higher plateau.

33. This ad agency is a TV shop. But I see from your resume that you have far more experience handling print. You're weak on TV compared to other candidates. Why should I hire you for the job and not someone else who has the credentials that we're really looking for?

A. That's an excellent question, Bob, and I'm delighted you asked me that. I have worked in advertising for ten years at some of the smaller, creative boutiques that don't handle TV on as regular a basis as the big, global shops. But one thing I learned from these ad agencies is that print and TV are only mediums. The real thing that we offer clients is our ideas. And a strong, solid, award-winning idea will work just as beautifully in TV as in print. So while I may have fewer TV spots on my reel as other candidates, hopefully you'll agree that my ideas are stronger than theirs. Hire me for my ideas, and when you do, I promise you that they will translate seamlessly into TV.

Why This Technique Works

1. You've shifted the paradigm from what you don't have to what you do: ideas.

2. Instead of getting flustered when your interviewer identified your weakness, you complimented him for asking you the question. (Flattery will get you everywhere.)

34.

I noticed that you didn't attend college. This isn't necessarily a drawback, but it is unusual. Why did you decide not to go to college?

A. When I graduated from high school, I really just wanted to be out working in the real world. I had completed an internship at the *New York Times* during my junior year, and with this credential, I was able to land a full-time job as a copy boy at the *Newark Star Ledger* directly after high school. Within two years, I was given a beat covering court news. I had several full-length feature stories published by the time I was twenty-one, and I simply decided to stay in the field. I appreciate that a liberal arts education is a good thing, and occasionally wish that I had taken time off to complete my academic studies. But had I done so, I never would have found the time to develop my full portfolio of articles and clips. And I hope that you will consider me for this job as features editor, based on my proven track record.

EXTRA CREDIT

Don't believe everything you hear. When an interviewer tells you that something unusual about your experience isn't "necessarily a drawback," it probably is. Try to identify your Achilles' heel before your interview, so that you can bandage the wound in advance—with good, strong, indestructible logic.

35.

Why didn't you finish college?

A. At the time, that is, when I was all of twenty years old, I was expected to declare a major. I enjoyed all of the classes that I took equally, and couldn't decide if I should major in English, history, political science, philosophy, or comparative literature. At the college that I attended, there was no such thing as a "general liberal arts major." I understand that a lot of colleges now offer this for students in my predicament. At any rate, the whole decision-making process threw me into a bit of quandary, because I really felt that the major I chose would have major implications for my career choice.

I went home that weekend, sat down with my parents, and discussed my problem with them. My mother encouraged me to take a year off to help me find myself. Of course, what ended up happening is that, during my sabbatical, I fell in with a very talented group of documentary filmmakers. The first documentary that I worked on was submitted to the Sundance Film Festival. And caught up in the excitement and glamour of the documentary film world, I never went back to college.

Never Lie on Your Resume

How often do recruiters fact-check resumes? All the time. Perhaps twenty years ago, you might have been able to fudge the facts about your education on your resume, but today, you will not be able to get away with it. So don't even attempt it. If you didn't go to college (or business school), and most of the candidates you are competing against did, just explain your rationale, without becoming defensive about it. Confidence always beats insecurity. And real-world expertise always wins out over scholastic achievements.

Inside Information

If an interviewer is concerned that you are overqualified, avoid discussing your salary until *after* you've persuaded him that you are perfectly qualified. Don't downplay your experience, but concentrate on demonstrating that you still have a lot to learn and greatly desire the position.

Bottom line: Get the job offer first. You can always reject it if the money is terrible, or negotiate for more once the company really wants you.

36. Our HR department didn't do their homework on our candidates, and for their error, I apologize. But from the experience that you've cited, I fear that you are overqualified for this position. There's no way that someone with your expertise would accept a job for $XXX,XXX, is there?

A. Let's discuss whether or not I'm "overqualified" first, and then you can decide about the money. I would love the opportunity to work at your company because you have a wonderful management team in place with a stellar track record. I feel that I would grow and thrive in this atmosphere. I also believe that, even though I have a lot of experience under my belt, there is still much for me to learn. For example, I am keen to find out more about your team's successes with the SRG project. Who masterminded it? And did SRG continue to do as well in the third quarter?

You've Jumped Ship Too Many Times Already

Back in the good old days (circa 1962), it wasn't all that unusual for someone to land a job at an organization and happily toil away there for the next thirty years. Due to recent management shakeouts in all kinds of different firms, however, those days are over. As a result, questions about job-hopping are on the rise. Remember that it's not necessarily a bad thing to have jumped around a bit. For one thing: it shows that you're eminently desirable.

37. You have changed careers before. Why should I let you experiment on my nickel?

A. Did you know that most people change their careers eight times during their lives? So, actually, since I've only changed careers three times, I think I'm behind the eight ball, at least statistically. (Be sure to crack a smile, so that your interviewer will also.)

As a career-changer, I believe that I'm a better employee because I've gained a lot of diverse skills from moving around. These skills help me solve problems creatively.

My first job as a teacher gave me the patience to explain the same set of facts, in different ways, to people who might resist them. My second job, working for an accountant, gave me a facility with spreadsheets and numbers. My third job, working in the circulation department of a magazine, helped me understand how to translate complicated numbers to ad agencies with limited amounts of money. All in all, I feel that my varied background makes me the ideal candidate for ad sales director at your magazine.

By working in circulation, I've picked up a lot about marketing already. And the fact that I've switched careers a couple of times proves that I'm a very quick learner.

EXTRA CREDIT Make sure that your resume is skills-based, rather than traditionally chronological. It will make it easier for your interviewer to agree that you have the skills to handle the position.

38.

Given your checkered past, do you really feel that you're cut out for this field?

A. It has been an interesting journey. But every time that I decided to walk away from our field, something would happen to convince me to stay. Last year, on the cusp of pursuing a completely different career, I ended up winning an award and being written up in the trades. I'm very interested in working at your company because it's small, thriving, and encourages independent thinking.

39.

Your resume seems to have a lot of holes in it. It seems like you've taken a lot of time off in between jobs. Why on earth should I hire you?

A. I am happy that you're giving me the opportunity to address that, Alex. There are three gaps on my resume. After my second job, I returned to school full-time to get my MBA from business school. I figured that doing so would make me more employable and give me a better shot at the lucrative management positions I desired.

After two more jobs on the investment banking side, I decided that I really wanted to find out "how the other half lived." I quit my fourth job to raise a small management fund, specializing in utilities and large retail chains. Unfortunately, the utilities market went south shortly thereafter, and the recession didn't help large retail chains either.

But I didn't want to leave my partners in the lurch. So I told them that I was eager to work for a venture capital fund, gave them a year to replace me, and even helped them find a new partner.

EXTRA CREDIT

Tell your interviewer that the fact that you've worked both as an investment banker and a venture capitalist makes you twice as qualified for the position that you seek. Discuss the relationships that you've fostered on both sides of the business, and explain how your well-placed contacts will help you bring new business to the firm.

40. I can see from your resume that you have moved around and changed jobs a lot. Do you get bored in a job quickly and find yourself wanting to move on?

A. Not at all. I embrace new challenges, certainly, but the reason that I job-hopped was to bring my salary up to a living wage. My parents never helped me out financially, and I needed to move jobs a bit just to pay my rent! But now that I'm on track financially, I'm looking for a position where I can grow on the job. I'm very excited about the prospect of working for your company, because I know several people here who worked really hard and were recognized for their achievements. Above all, the thing that I am really looking for at this point in my career is an office that will become my home.

EXTRA CREDIT

A star shines brightly on all objects in its path. So by all means, if you know some rising stars in a company, mention their names to your interviewer. Let some of their "star power" rub off on you.

You Won't Fit in Here, Because...

With hundreds of applicants vying for all too few positions, many interviewers experiment with a particularly pernicious form of the "Give Us One Good Reason Not To Hire You" question. Namely, they will tell you right off the bat why they think that you won't "fit in" with their corporate culture. If you want the job, it's your job to change their minds. When asked this type of question, don't despair. Just politely point out to our interviewer why you will make a brilliant addition to the team.

41. You grew up in the Midwest, went to school in the Midwest, and have spent most of your working life out there. We are totally open to hiring people from the Midwest, but I worry that here on the West Coast, business doesn't operate the same way. Since we are two hours behind Chicago and three hours behind New York, our office hours are usually quite late. Also: we take our clients out for very late dinners, frequently "clubbing" with them until all hours of the morning.

A. It sounds like a great deal of fun—and "fun" was perhaps the one key ingredient that was missing from my last job, which is why I moved out to L.A. in the first place. I've always been a night owl, and I really enjoy taking clients out on the town. I look forward to bonding with clients over very late dinners, instead of incredibly long lunches.

Alt. A. Actually, I'm no stranger to late office hours and even later client dinners. At my last firm in Toledo, we wined and dined our clients three nights out of four. We also had business in London, which is five hours ahead. I'm excited about the fact that your company sounds so similar to my last one, because I know that I will fit in here smoothly.

A Special Warning to Creative Types: The Ferragamo Shopping Bag Is a Dead Giveaway

If you happen to be a "creative person" such as a copywriter, journalist, writer, art director, or designer, you will need to bring your portfolio on job interviews. This poses a special problem if your interview is during the workday; namely, how do you hide your portfolio while you're trying to discreetly whisk it out of your office building?

Hint: Stuffing your portfolio into an oversized shopping bag is not the correct solution. Either drop off your book to your interviewer's attention before you arrive at the office that morning or hire a messenger to deliver it for you the day before. The new boss at work may make your skin crawl, but it's unfair of you to automatically assume that he'll never be able to figure out what's in your shopping bag. You're creative...so why not be creative about hiding the fact that you're looking for a new job?

42. Half of your job would require managing a team of people in Phoenix. As the key contact person on the account, you would need to fly out there every four or five days, only to turn around and fly back here. You will be permanently on the "jet-lag" diet. Reviewing where you've worked in the past, I doubt that extensive travel was part of your job description. Why should I hire you over other candidates who have proven that they can handle the rigors of airplane travel?

A. Well, for one thing, I've never done it before, so I'm not burned out on it yet. At this stage in my career, traveling a lot on the job sounds pretty glamorous. I consider myself a great long-distance manager, and in fact, I did manage a team in Paris for a couple of years at my last job, although this required only a few longer trips every year. Above all, I have the management qualifications that you need and the desire to expand my experience and take on the challenge. I am a high-energy person, so I am certain that I would be able to balance the "jet-lag" diet with the new American cuisine that's the rage in Phoenix these days.

Why This Technique Works

1. Intelligently, you recognized that business travel takes a toll, quickly burning out those who do it extensively. Meanwhile, you're fresh and ready for your career to take off.
2. You turned your interviewer's remark about the "jet-lag diet" into some playful repartee. Start counting your frequent flyer miles!

 You live an hour and half away from the office. Most nights, we stick around until 9 p.m. How will you ever be able to survive working here?

A. Other people join health clubs to de-stress and unwind. For me, my commute home is my "quiet time" to relax. I love taking the train. No one disturbs me, and the ride up to Rye, even late at night, is gorgeous. At the end of the day, if I still have work on my desk, I'll just take it with me and finish it on the train. And if I don't, I'll use the time to catch up on a couple of newspapers, listen to a favorite CD, and think about tomorrow's challenges.

EXTRA **CREDIT** Sometimes, saying less is more. When you are asked about potential risks and disadvantages, just pick one risk to discuss. Position this risk as "very small," then turn it around to show why it's actually a big advantage.

How to Quit Your Day Job (as a Volunteer) and Promote Yourself to Staff

1. Pick volunteer jobs that build the skills you will need in your chosen profession.

2. Be a volunteer "cheerleader" (so the staff of your favorite charity will shout your praises to future employers).

3. Put together a portfolio of references from your volunteer work, all positive letters and emails that you received about your projects, plus any press clips. Did you write a brochure for your school's reunion or take photographs for a school poster? Include it.

44. Between the fundraising that you've done for your schools and the events that you've organized for your causes, you have a great track record as a volunteer, Greta. But working for the profit world is very different than the not-for-profit.

A. That's exactly what appeals to me about working for your company, Marvin. With a 50 percent participation from three of my schools during non-reunion years plus two charity events that I organized that received national press attention, I know that I have great people skills. I believe that I've honed the ability to listen to others, hearing not just what they're saying, but also what's just beneath the surface of what they choose to talk about. This listening ability, the "people gene" that I possess, will make me a terrific focus-group moderator.

45.

Why do you think you are qualified for this job? It's not like you have any previous experience.

A. Well, Sarah, I have a great deal of life experience. Coaching Little League on the weekends shows my ability to relate to people at all different age levels. I have also become very involved in the PTA, which often requires calming down irate people. Finally, I helped my school launch an internship program, spearheaded by both the parents and the alumni. This took management skills, people-assessment skills, and genuine persistence. So all in all, I think that I have the ideal qualities to become an HR manager at your firm. Are there any other skills that you feel the job requires? I have a long track record as a volunteer, and I'm pretty certain that my strengths correlate with your company's needs.

46.

I know that Mary interviewed you and was very impressed with your credentials. But she doesn't have hiring authority. I'm the person who makes hiring decisions, and I feel that we could really use more juniors around here, and fewer mid-level people such as yourself.

A. First, let's talk about your needs in the organization. From what you just said, it sounds like you have the budget to do one of two things: either hire several juniors, or someone more at my mid-range level. Here's what I can bring to the table that no junior could:

1. The experience and dexterity to do tasks right the first time without a great deal of supervision. This would free up your time to focus on the big picture and supervise the juniors that you have on staff.

2. A gut instinct for what will work and what won't. I think this talent takes roughly ten years to refine, so I doubt that even a very talented junior would have it.

3. The ability to manage juniors, that is, if you ever need any help with it. I like and respect young people, and in my career, I have often been given the opportunity to bring them up to speed.

EXTRA CREDIT

1. Offer to give your interviewer the names of several of the juniors whom you managed in the past.
2. Then call them up and gently remind them of how much you helped them advance in their careers!
3. Circle back to the first person you met with, Mary, post-interview, via phone. But take care to be discreet. Do not repeat what her boss said about her, but do tell her the gist of the rest of the conversation. She may be able to help you identify other selling points in your favor, based on what's been going on at the company recently.
4. Send both interviewers brilliant thank-you notes.

You'll Be Miserable Here, Because...

"Misery loves company," we've been told a thousand times. And to some extent, it's true. Many times, when an interviewer seems like he is trying to convince you not to come on board, it's because he secretly hates working for the organization. Or there may be a corporate culture that tolerates whining and complaining, and he's just venting his frustrations. But just because he's soured on the experience doesn't mean that you should. Optimism lands jobs, whereas pessimism becomes a self-fulfilling prophecy.

47. I know the company where you're currently working, because I used to work there. It's small, tightly knit, and highly dysfunctional. We're also small, tightly knit, and highly dysfunctional. There will be absolutely no improvement in the quality of your life, and from what I can tell, your salary, title, and benefits would all be the same. Why do you want to leave your company to come work here?

A. Well, it certainly sounds like I have the right qualifications to come on board! In fact, it sounds like I'm a perfect fit. Very seriously, I think that one always needs to look for ways to continue to learn and grow. Your company may have a remarkably similar corporate culture to my company, but I will still be facing new challenges here that I haven't experienced before. You have a whole different roster of clients, plus some great employees. Mostly, Peter, I'm looking forward to working for you. I've heard that you are a tremendous problem solver and a great boss. That's why I intend to switch over to your team.

Why This Technique Works

1. You've answered a difficult tickler with poise and some humor.

2. You've used the flattery card, but you haven't maxed out on your limit.

48. What do you view as your risks and disadvantages with the position we are interviewing you for?

A. I think that with the home office located halfway across the globe, there is a very small risk that one might not have the chance to interact with the key decision makers as often as might be ideal. On the other hand, teleconferencing, email, faxing, and having a 24/7 work ethic will go a long way towards bridging the gap. I'll be devoting myself to making certain the teleconference meeting every Wednesday at 11 a.m. is productive and effective. And if there ever is a communication breakdown with the key decision makers, I'll be delighted to hop on a plane and sit down with them in person.

How to Mix the Perfect Interview Cocktail

3 parts experience

2 parts intelligence

1 part charm (can substitute humor or playfulness)

Stir briskly. Pepper with three to twenty-three custom-blended answers. Garnish with five sharp questions of your own.

Share this cocktail with your interviewer for a callback interview. (But be sure to lay off the real cocktails until *after* your meeting.)

49.

You come from a gigantic global organization with networks on every continent. We have a grand total of a hundred employees in three local offices. I'm concerned that you will not find the resources here that you've had in the past.

A. The great thing about working for a huge company is that when it comes to pursuing new business, you definitely have the resources that you need. The bad thing is that you are put in a little box, where you're only allowed to do one job, and so it's very difficult to break out and learn new skills. I am keen to take on the challenge of moving to a firm that's vibrant, growing, and where I can master new skills every day.

50.

You have been an entrepreneur for the last five years, running your own company. So you're out of the loop when it comes to reporting to people. Please address how you would feel about presenting your ideas to several bosses who would need to have final approval over your proposals before letting you run with them.

A. As an entrepreneur, I had to report to several different stakeholders. First, I had to share my vision with my partners. If they approved it, I had to pitch it to vendors. After I got the vendors to buy in, I had to persuade my clients that it was a good idea. Then, of course, there was our company's accountant, lawyer, and, ultimately, the board of directors. I am very good at taking a concept and running it by a large contingent of people with several different agendas. I think it will be a joy to report to several bosses who will be on the same page when it comes to making this division profitable.

51.

On your resume, it states that you have management experience. Do you realize that you wouldn't be managing anyone at this company? And how do you feel about that?

A. Let's face it, Pauline, the old days are over. Hierarchical management structures have gone the way of Betamax. And those who can't adapt to change will become extinct. It's true that I have managed people in the past. But what is managing all about, really? It's about organizing due dates and deadlines, and it's also about having good, strong people skills.

I know how to motivate groups of people to get things done in a timely manner. This is a skill that will serve your company well, even though your management structure is flat, loose, and dynamic. And if it turns out that everyone around here is a self-starter, that will be even better for me. Because I'll have a lot more time in my day to get my real work done.

52.
Can you see yourself working for several demanding bosses in different teams at this company? Your time would not be your own.

A. Yes, I can definitely see myself happily juggling the demands of several different bosses. I don't want my time to be my own! I fully expect to put in the time, pay my dues, and learn from the best in the business. I am organized, productive, and very efficient, which most of my bosses have sincerely appreciated. Can you tell me a little bit more about who I would be working for and the structure of your organization, so I can show you that I'm the best person for this job?

53.
Are you sure that you really want to work here? I mean, you seem pretty talented. And take it from me, there are firms out there that are a lot better.

A. Well, I'm sorry to hear that you don't exactly love it here. And I want to get back to that in a moment. But I've always wanted to work here because your company has a great reputation, wins clients, gets written up in the trades consistently, has a charismatic CEO who is always quoted in the *Wall Street Journal*, and manages to do well year after year, according to your company's Annual Report. Still, I'm curious about your experience…what are some of the frustrations that you've encountered?

Is Acting Like a Pollyanna a Bad Thing?

No, it's not.

FACT: People would rather hire happy, agreeable people than unhappy, disagreeable people. Cynicism is an incredible turn-off in the Interview Game. So pump up the enthusiasm and put on your "happy face." Don't be afraid to use words that will express your joy. Remember always: work is love.

Why Change Is Good

Studies show that the ability to "embrace change" is one of the biggest predictors of success. You must always persuade your interviewers that you are able to adapt and flow with change (even if you don't believe it entirely). We live in a computerized, high-tech world where business operates 24/7. Changes that used to take years to enact now happen in nanoseconds. In the shark-infested waters of the corporate world, the ability to deal with change is today's Darwinian survival mechanism.

Did you used to have a secretary at your old firm who would handle all of your correspondence? Don't expect to have one at your new company, unless you are at the very top tier of the organization. Even if you are, chances are excellent that you will have to share her with at least three other people. Do you still use a Filofax? Leave it at home and talk about your Palm Pilot instead. Better yet, pull out your new, spiffy BlackBerry.

54.

Judging from your experience, your next "jump" would be to managing director. But there is already someone here who is managing director, and she was just promoted recently. In fact, you would be reporting to her. Could you work here enthusiastically, knowing that it might be years until you would reach that position?

A. I would relish the opportunity to learn from someone with such a great track record. I'm not even on staff yet. It would be presumptuous of me to already be looking down the road, worrying about when I will get promoted! But I will tell you one thing: I'm very excited about working for someone who's a rising star in the organization. In fact, that makes me want the job even more!

55.

You have had some very fancy titles in the past, such as "vice president" and "executive vice president." However, at this company, we took everyone's title away from them about two years ago. There was just too much "title inflation" around here. How would you feel about coming on staff without a title?

A. What is your title? I mean, I know that you're the owner, but do you have another title?

Why This Technique Works

1. By inquiring about your interviewer's title, you've successfully started a dialogue about titles, rather than immediately caving on the point.

2. You now have a chance to figure out what your title should be.

Get the Title to Which You're Entitled

Often, when companies claim that their people "don't have titles," in reality, they do. They just don't have the same old titles that you've heard a thousand times before. When confronted with this type of question, it's important to find out the *exact* titles of the people who are interviewing you. Ask them for their business cards. You don't want to come off like an old-fashioned title maven, but you also don't want to give up a title that it's taken you years to get, just because this company supposedly "doesn't have titles."

Remember always: ask, and ye shall receive. Nine times out of ten, there will be some newer, fresher-sounding title that's the equivalent of your old title. Find out what it is, and negotiate for *that* title.

That's a Wrap

1. If you're asked about your biggest weakness, first explain why it is a real weakness. Then turn it into a strength.

2. If your interviewer tells you what your biggest weakness is, acknowledge her concern, but then give her one compelling, "puncture-proof" reason to hire you.

3. Are you a career-changer? Emphasize how the skills that you've mastered from all kinds of different jobs make you the ideal candidate for the job at hand.

4. Nullify all of the reasons why you won't "fit in" at a company. Be enthusiastic, passionate, and charming.

5. Misery loves company, but companies hate misery. Don't get sucked into the: "you'd be miserable working here" vortex. Be a Pollyanna if you have to. Even people who see the working world as half empty prefer to hire optimists.

CHAPTER 3

You're Too Old, Too Young, Too Seasoned, Too Green, Too Female

Most executives will confront the age barrier at some point during their careers. The age barrier is an obstacle—invisible to the naked eye, but still very much a reality—that prevents candidates who are otherwise perfectly qualified from getting the jobs they deserve.

When the applicant seems "too young," sometimes it's because the interviewer had to pay her dues the hard way and believes others should as well. She may bristle at the influx of graduate students who might be up for very lucrative jobs in their early twenties. The age barrier also cuts the other way, of course; it has been responsible for preventing scores of early retirees from reentering the workforce.

The gender barrier is sometimes referred to as "the glass ceiling," but it can also be compared to a moat guarding the front door of the executive suite, because it manages to stop a lot of women from ever setting foot inside.

There are six most common—bordering on illegal—barriers to employment:

1. *You're Too Old to Work Here.*

2. *You're Too Young to Work Here.*

3. *Our Clients Are Looking for a Certain Type of Person (Not Your Type).*

4. *Clearly, You've Got Other Commitments, So...*

5. *We'd Love to Hire a Woman, But...*

6. *We'd Love to Hire a Man, But...*

Equal opportunity is the law of the land. But that doesn't mean that it is truly practiced in the hearts and minds of every employer. Here's how to tear down these walls of resistance, and break through the barriers that prevent successful interviewees of any age (and both sexes) from getting hired.

You're Too Old to Work Here

Interviewers are usually aware that if they even hint that a candidate won't work out because she's "too old," a legal nightmare will ensue. In-house lawyers have warned HR managers, along with everyone else on staff responsible for hiring decisions, that discriminating against someone because of her age is patently illegal. As a result, age discrimination has gone underground, where it's generally couched in language that's more "politically correct." Questions such as "Most of the people we have working here are babes in the woods. Do you really think that you'll feel comfortable here?" and "Don't you think you're a little light on 'life experience?'" often reveal an interviewer's secret prejudice, but being prepared with a compelling answer can help you overcome it.

56.

In our company, people skateboard through the hallways, blast music from their computers, and work 24/7. We're totally open to hiring working moms, but at the same time, I'm a little concerned that you won't fit in here.

A. I think that your concern is valid, and I really appreciate the opportunity to address it, Stan. First of all, I have three kids who skateboard around our house nonstop. One of them also plays electronic guitar till all hours of the night, and believe me, at this point I consider it "white noise." I am thoroughly capable of screening out all kinds of disruptions and focusing on the work. Secondly, the fact that I am a working mom forces me to be more efficient. Because I don't do my work with headphones in my ears, you'll find my reports well-organized, clear, and typo-free. Why work 24/7, when you can work for ten hours a day, finish everything on your plate, and deliver an excellent product? At the same time, I want you to know that if you ever give me a project that requires me to stay until all hours of the night, I will come through for you. That's what babysitters, nannies, and husbands are for—covering for me when it's going to be another late night at the office.

EXTRA CREDIT

Follow up with an example from your last job where you stayed until 3 o'clock in the morning to complete the project.

57.

You have all the qualifications that we're looking for, Sheila. But the person you'd be reporting to is fifteen years younger than you. Do you think that could be a problem?

A. The way that I see it, Jay, age is more of a mindset than an absolute, chronological number. I watch movies that are targeted to fifteen-year-old girls. Does that mean that I'm really fifteen inside? No, of course not! On the other hand, I tend to read autobiographies that are popular with seniors. While the magazines that I enjoy, like *Business Week* and *Inc.,* are definitely written for men in their thirties and forties.

In the pursuit of knowledge, I always try to identify experts, and I'm quite open to learning whatever they can teach me, no matter how old they are. I'm greatly looking forward to meeting my new boss and learning everything I can from him.

EXTRA CREDIT Mention a previous boss of yours who was only a couple of years younger than you (if true), and stress how much you learned from her.

58.

Are you telling me that, now that you're forty-something, you would be willing to start at an entry-level position just to get your foot in the door here?

A. Sometimes you need to take a step backward to move your career forward. Starting in an entry-level role would allow me to learn your business from the ground up. I would have the chance to interact with customers, suppliers, and retailers, picking up essential product knowledge along the way. The career that I've been in is so different than yours that

I would love the opportunity to start over again in your field. The salary cut would be well worth it, because in a sense I would be paying your company to relaunch my career.

59. Marianna expressly requested a "junior- to mid-level associate." You were probably at that level roughly ten years ago, right?

A. Yes, I was, but then I branched out on my own and started a new company. I'm happy that I tried it, because I learned with absolute certainty that I missed working at a big firm like yours. I really enjoy working in a team atmosphere. I have a good eye for design, and a gut instinct for merchandising and pricing. But with my own company, I often felt like I was spending more time shipping boxes than doing anything else!

Life is too short and we all work too hard to have zero fun on the job. For a start-up, my business was pretty successful. But I wasn't having any fun running it day to day. I want to get back to doing the things that I love. If that makes me a mid-level associate for now, or even a junior, I happen to think the move is well worth it.

Is It Possible to Go Back in Time?

In the executive suite, most people do their best to propel their careers forward. But sometimes, breaking into a particular company may require taking several steps backwards. Your salary, title, and responsibilities may all be scaled back. As long as moving backwards doesn't dent your ego so badly that it leaves a chip on your shoulder (which can really throw your career out of whack), the experience can often help you realign your career correctly.

If you took a sabbatical from the corporate world to start your own business, be cautious about how you position the move. A lot of companies are gun-shy about hiring entrepreneurial types.

The Law

There are several laws that are intended to prevent discrimination in the workplace. Following is a very brief summary. The U.S. Equal Opportunity Commission (EEOC) enforces these laws. For more information, go to Ask Jeeves on the Internet, and hit "Equal Employment Opportunity Commission (EEOC)."

1. *Title VII* of the *Civil Rights Act of 1964*—prohibits employment discrimination based on race, color, religion, sex, or national origin.

2. *Age Discrimination in Employment Act of 1967* (ADEA)—protects individuals who are 40 years of age or older.

3. *Title I* and *Title V* of the *Americans With Disabilities Act* of 1990 (ADA)—prohibits employment discrimination against qualified individuals with disabilities in the private sector, and in state and local governments.

4. *Civil Rights Act of 1991*—provides the right to a jury trial, limited damages for emotional distress, and punitive damages in cases of intentional employment discrimination.

60.

You have a lot of expertise in interactive marketing, but you have no experience in traditional marketing. What makes you think that you can make the jump?

A. I think that's an excellent question, Paul, and I'm delighted to address it. Traditional marketing has huge lead times, millions of marketing dollars behind it, and often no tangible results. Can you ever prove that a particular marketing push worked in terms of sales? In a word: no. By contrast, interactive marketing has almost no lead time, relatively little money behind it, and immediate results. You automatically know when something is working. Does someone punch the button to find out more information, yes or no? I feel that, in a certain way, this makes interactive marketing more "responsible" to the bottom line. And to do well in the field, you have to be disciplined about figuring out what turns on customers, and be willing to make the necessary tweaks that the marketplace demands. This ability of mine—the skill to coolly analyze the facts and make adjustments—is something that would benefit *any* marketer.

On the other hand, traditional marketing reaches and influences millions of people. Its potential powers of persuasion are staggering. I can bring something new to the way your company does business, while your company helps me build skills. It's a "win-win" all the way around.

Inside Information

"Win-win" interviewing strategies win jobs. So never sell your previous experience short. Look for ways to draw a line between the experience that you have and the experience that the company needs. Emphasize your ability to solve problems, organizational aptitude, and willingness to learn on the job. Golden handcuffs can only imprison you if you let them. Bust out of yours.

Don't Be a Legal Beagle

Brush up on the antidiscrimination laws in the workplace if you're interested, but don't read the Riot Act whenever you feel like a company's policies may be discriminatory. (The company will assume that you're a troublemaker, and won't offer you the job.) You're far better off taking a deep breath and answering your interviewer's questions with poise and maturity (if you're supposedly "too young" for the job) or with poise and youthful vitality (if you're supposedly "too old" for the job). Of course, if you feel chronically uncomfortable in an interview, it might be a sign that the job just isn't right for you. And there's no law against letting a company know that you're just not interested.

61.

You've retired twice already, Ira. Why should I hire you over someone who has worked steadily in our field for the past ten years?

A. I grew up thinking that the whole point of working was to make a big pile of money while I was still young enough to enjoy it. My plan was to earn the money, then kick back, and just spend it for the next thirty years. And for a while, Frank, my life went exactly according to the plan.

I retired for the first time when I was just fifty-five. My wife, however, had other notions. She's an accomplished painter and, while we have always been close, she never had any intentions of taking time off from her landscape painting to travel with me all over Europe. So after about six months of tooling around the continent by myself, I got bored, came home, and really wanted to work again.

I did so very happily, until I had a triple coronary bypass operation last year. This forced me to sit down and reevaluate my priorities. I decided that I would try to retire again. But the exact same thing happened. After a few short months, I was bored out of my mind!

However, this time around, I had a startling epiphany: work is the thing that keeps me alive. I'm not working to live. In fact, it's just the opposite. I'm living to work. In a nutshell, the reason that you should give me a job over someone who's been working steadily is simply this: I've had my "aha" moment while that person hasn't yet. There's nothing else that I'd rather be doing on the planet, Stan, than working for you.

Why This Technique Works

1. When asked an unfair question about your age, you've proven that you're younger at heart and more vibrant than other job seekers.

2. You've blended your working life and your personal life into a compelling story that can't fail to move even the most jaded interviewer. You'll be working again, full-time, very shortly.

How to Defy the Twin Forces of Age and Gravity

Most baby boomers today feel like they are ten years younger than they really are. Take advantage of the trend, and turn back the clock on old-fashioned notions about middle age and the right retirement age. Here are three proven ways to subtract ten years before your very next interview.

1. Take the year that you graduated from college off your resume (there goes four years!).

2. Wear control-top panty hose (if you're a woman). This automatically subtracts seven pounds (aka "middle-aged bulge").

3. Use two firming creams (one for your body, one for your face).

Now, examine yourself closely in a full-length mirror. Do you look younger than you ever have before? Excellent.

You're Too Young to Work Here

In the last few years, companies have been forced to scale back their entry-level hiring. Fewer recruiters than ever are visiting colleges to scoop up enterprising graduates. Training programs have been cut en masse. This doesn't mean that you can't get a job right out of college, only that you will need to be particularly adept at answering the following "You're Too Young To Work Here" questions.

62. Your passion and enthusiasm for working here are admirable, and, frankly, I wish we had more employees around here like you. Your academic credentials are also impressive. But I worry that there is no substitute for life experience, and there, unfortunately, you're a little light.

A. Book learning is no substitute for honest-to-God work experience, which is why I am applying for this job. My scholastic record, mostly A's, is simply proof that I love learning. With your guidance and mentoring, I will learn the ropes at your company faster than others on your staff. I need this job. You need someone with passion, drive, and the will to succeed. Let's seal the deal and make it official.

EXTRA CREDIT Gently remind your prospect that your salary base is a lot lower than everyone else's on staff. You're a real steal: a Jaguar for the price of a Buick.

63.

Do you see yourself staying and growing at our company, or leaving in two years to go to business school?

A. I might go to law or business school in a few years, but I'm 99 percent certain that I'll choose one where I can go at night. So there will be absolutely no break in my stay at your company. I've been interviewing at several of the smaller biotechnology companies, but I would much rather start at a big firm like yours because I know that doing so will expose me to several disciplines. If you hire me, it's my intention to stay here for many years to come.

64.

I understand that you attended a leadership program at your college offered by Procter & Gamble. Why would you rather work for us than for them?

A. The leadership program was outstanding, and it was one of many things that I did to build my resume during school. I also interned at the student union, ran for president of the student council, and worked at the Concert Club. I think that for a graduating senior, I have a very strong foundation in both business and management. And I look forward to learning a great deal more about marketing on the job.

Why This Technique Works

1. You successfully skirted the "P&G vs. Us" question, and focused instead on what you will bring to the organization.

2. You've picked up several of the business skills that you need to succeed before you've even landed your first official job. Clearly, there's a window office in your future.

65.

From your resume, I notice that you interned for a small investment banking boutique. Did you pursue a full-time job offer with them? What happened?

A. Yes, I did very well at my internship, and I had originally assumed that I would come on staff once I graduated from college. However, BB&L drastically cut back the number of new hires they were planning. As fate would have it, they will not be hiring any of the interns they had last summer. I loved working at BB&L, and I brought some references with me today to show you that my job performance there was stellar. Still, in some ways, I consider this new turn of events to be a lucky break for me, believe it or not.

I've always had dreams of joining a more prestigious firm like yours. Your company's training program is the best in the business, and I know that if I come and work for you, I'll be on the correct track for my career ambitions.

How to Turn Lemons into Lemonade

1. Position all setbacks as lucky breaks instead. The negative event, whatever it happened to be, was in fact a boost to your career, because...

2. Act as if you are genuinely pleased about the occurrence. So often the things that happen to us aren't necessarily "good" or "bad" in the absolute. We assign values to events based on our own pre-conceived expectations. Rather than assigning a negative value to something unexpected, turn it around into something positive and career-enhancing.

EXTRA CREDIT

Don't be commitment-phobic. If you just graduated from college, you don't have to decide about grad school for several years. But why make the company think that you're scared to commit? Always tell the company where you want to work that if they hire you, you will be loyal to them forever.

66.

Unfortunately, Chris, you're competing for this job against a couple of people who have real work experience under their belts. Did you receive any awards, honors, or achievements in college? Did you ever hold a class office?

A. I did not receive any awards, but I did hold several leadership positions at school. I was a paid teaching assistant for French class, which helped me gain some vital business skills. As a teaching assistant, it was my job to take very detailed notes about the lectures so I could help students who were having difficulty mastering the material. This skill will come in handy when it's my turn to take notes at client meetings, and then write up detailed conference reports with action steps.

I was also a student dorm counselor during my junior year at school. Whenever a student was having trouble with his peers or courses, he would share his distress. I would listen to his issues, and suggest ways of breaking through his blocks. I know that a lot of candidates probably claim that they have great people skills, but my university recognized mine.

What are the three Ps of performing at your interview peak?
1. Look presentable.
2. Sound polished.
3. Stay positive.

67.

Jane Wilcox has been working here for thirty years. While she's a terrific boss and very open-minded, I think that she might prefer to work with someone a bit closer to her own age.

A. I think that one's age really comes down to one's mental maturity. I may be young, but I'm incredibly precocious. I will buckle down and organize Jane's schedule. I will be pleasant and professional to everyone who needs to meet with Jane. But when necessary, I promise to be a rabid bulldog who will protect Jane's time fiercely, so that she can get the work off of her desk. When do you think that I can meet with Jane? I've heard so many terrific things about her, and I would be thrilled to meet her in person.

Inside Information

Using a $5 word like "precocious" is a lot more impressive than saying: "Gee, I'm really mature."

68.
We're looking for a mature, seasoned pro. Frankly, from your voice over the phone and those letters that you wrote to us, I expected to see someone with some graying temples.

A. Thanks for the compliment, Robbie. My blonde hair I owe entirely to Clairol. But I owe my general maturity to the fact that I actually have a great deal of experience in your field. I was first promoted to middle management when I was just twenty-five, so I got a head start in terms of learning how to solve problems. Let's talk a little more about the special challenges that your operations department is facing now, so we can brainstorm together on possible solutions. From the article in *Crain's New York Business,* I am familiar with some of the issues in your department. But I would love to hear more about them directly from you.

Why This Technique Works

1. You used some gentle, self-deprecating humor to rise above a potential obstacle.

2. You quickly followed up with an impressive fact about how others took a risk on you when you were even younger.

Act Like You're Confident (Until You Really Are Confident)

Some bravura goes a long way to having others perceive that you have confidence. Sometimes, simply by willing yourself to be confident, you will come off as far more polished than you really feel inside.

Absolutely Age-Proof Female Interview Uniform

1. One fantastically fitted, flattering skirt.

2. Beautiful, expensive panty hose.

3. Meticulously polished shoes.

4. A jacket that wraps it all together—preferably in a color other than black.

Why not in black, you ask? Because every serviceperson in the country wears outfits that are black. (But you're going for a job in the executive suite, right?)

Our Clients Are Looking for a Certain Type of Person (Not Your Type)

Stereotyping happens in an instant. You walk through the door, and before you can sit down, *gong!*, your interviewer has already rejected you, based on nothing more than the way you look. This is a snapshot prejudice; and no doubt about it, it's chronically unfair.

But let's face the facts. Along with being illegal in this country, "prejudice" is a very ugly word. And precious few interviewers will ever admit to it openly. Instead, the prejudice is often blamed on a client, or another third party, who isn't there to refute the charge. This secondhand prejudice can be quite difficult to conquer, even when the interviewer secretly agrees with you that it's unjust. Learn how to confront prejudice in the executive suite by studying the answers that follow.

69.

At CYT, we have an Equal Opportunity hiring policy. But at the same time, our show covers the beauty and fashion industries. Can you address how well you would fit in with the corporate culture?

A. Well, I'm not a model, and I hope that's not a requirement for dealing with people in the beauty and fashion business! I'm terrific at scheduling and juggling people's hectic timetables. I also follow all trends in the women's fashion publications, read "*Page Six*" religiously, along with *Vogue, InStyle* magazine, and *W,* and have tons of ideas for how we can scout for new talent for your show. I'm on the "A List" at many of the new clubs in town, so I feel confident that I can quickly befriend the up-and-coming stars that we wish to bring on as guests. Lastly, years of going to the gym have strengthened my arm muscles. So when it comes to helping the producer set up camera equipment, I'll be the assistant producer of his dreams.

Why This Technique Works

1. You let your interviewer know that he should review your candidacy without prejudice.

2. Then you cited your skills with panache.

70.

We love women at this company, but our clients are [pick any nationality other than American that is a male-driven society] and so we were thinking of hiring a man for this particular job.

A. Why is that, exactly? It seems to me that I am probably more qualified to handle this position than anyone, man or woman. I graduated cum laude from my class at the university, and I'm fluent in four different languages along with English—which I understand is somewhat unusual among applicants. My father's career as a diplomat took our family around the world seven times, and I even spent my junior year abroad in the Far East. So I am very familiar with the customs and the etiquette that would be expected of me. I would need far less training than an American man who grew up here and has never traveled outside our borders.

EXTRA CREDIT Go further. Recount a story about a particular foreign custom that you observed, and how it impacted you. Did your family ever entertain foreign diplomats? Tell you interviewer about it.

71. Our clients feel more comfortable with ethnic writers. After all, their products are targeted to the ethnic market. So, while I would love to recommend you for the position, I'm worried that our clients will feel uneasy about us hiring you.

A. Well, Margo, it's true that I'm not African American or Hispanic. But does that really mean that your company won't consider me for the job? I sincerely believe that being a great writer requires one major skill beyond being able to string sentences together, and that quality is empathy. I think that, rather than looking at my skin color, your company needs to consider whether or not I can empathize with our target market, and the answer is certainly yes. My advertising campaign for L'Oréal's line of hair mousses increased sales in urban markets by 65 percent. I also suggested the concept for a line of ethnic lipsticks to the marketing and sales staff of MAC—and it's performing brilliantly in focus groups right now. I have always identified with ethnic causes, and attended the kick-off party for a new urban radio station in our area two weeks ago.

I would hate to think that a company such as yours, which helps market ethnic products, wouldn't hire me simply because I don't meet a certain profile. Why don't you test me out for a month on a freelance basis, to see how well I perform on the job?

Why This Technique Works

1. You've hinted that "racial profiling" is wrong, without coming out and blatantly stating it.

2. The company is scared to hire someone who isn't ethnic. You've given your interviewer a way to save face: she can test you for a month and see how well you do on the job.

Warning Signs That a Company May Be Prejudiced

1. The company is sexually lopsided—either one way or the other.

2. The company has roughly equal numbers of men and women at the lower- and middle-management levels, but at the top tier every single executive is male.

3. Everyone on staff happens to be from a particular nationality (not yours).

4. You hear from a reliable source that the company is facing a class-action lawsuit.

5. A total stranger stops you in the hallway of the company, takes one look at you and says, "You're applying to this company? Gee, you're brave."

How to Confront Secondhand Prejudice in Person

By law, employers are not allowed to reject (or hire) someone based on her skin color. Still, prejudice continues to rear its ugly head in many corporations. And attributing prejudice to a third invisible party is still commonplace at many companies who should know better.

When you are the person who's being discriminated against, here are five ways to break through the barrier:

1. Avoid using highly charged trigger words in your interview, such as: "prejudice," "racial profiling," and "quotas." Be polite and as politically correct as possible.

2. Stress that you have the skills that you need to do the given task. Don't be shy about citing emotional skills, such as "empathy," "listening ability," or "being proactive."

3. Talk about results. Discuss sales figures and positive letters from happy customers and pleased clients. If you don't have good, strong results to share, mention other activities that you've done that will prove that you're the right person for the job.

4. If a headhunter is representing you, fill her in on all conversations that you have with your potential employer. Your headhunter may be able to appease his concerns.

5. Never, repeat, *never* refer to the company's "prejudice" in any follow-up communications that you have with your interviewer. Choose a different topic to write about in your thank-you email. Take the opportunity to bring out other strengths about you that didn't surface in your initial meeting.

6. Once you're offered the job, it might make sense for you to sit down, write a "pros and cons" list, and decide if you really want to take it. Don't automatically assume that the prejudice you detected was only on the part of the interviewer. If it is a company-wide phenomenon, you may have one completely unfair strike against you from day one.

Seriously think about whether it's worth taking the job under these circumstances.

72. This is a professional, aggressive, cult-driven place to work. Tensions with our European leadership run rampant. You've always worked in American companies where the culture was very different. What makes you think you'll succeed here?

A. Actually, several of the companies where I worked were cult-driven. At PLP, we lived, talked, and breathed athletic wear. The work environment was cutting edge, but also cutthroat. Myles Masterson was our cool, calculating, Machiavellian CEO, and everyone adored him.

It's Not a Job, It's a Cult

These days, cults have gone surprisingly mainstream. No longer do they have to involve piercing (or other forms of body immolation). In fact, from Silicon Valley to Wall Street to the suburbs of Connecticut, the "cult culture" has become the new rage at many companies. Here's how to deal with the "company-as-cult" phenomenon.

1. Don't be intimidated by questions that suggest that there is an "Us" versus "Them," and that because you worked at a more traditional firm, you must be one of "Them."

2. If you are asked how you would fit in with a work cult, position your last place of business as its own special cult, even if it was the most by-the-book company in the universe.

3. Remember that all companies are societies that are somewhat closed to the outside world. They have special, codified ways of doing business. They have pecking orders. Heck, they're sort of like cults...

Clearly, You've Got Other Commitments, So...

With so many anti-discrimination laws on the books, it's almost unbelievable that in the twenty-first century, women are still being asked questions that imply that they will not be able to juggle their personal commitments with the requirements of the job. But these questions continue to be asked with alarming regularity. Here's how to answer them effortlessly, to land the job that's rightfully yours.

73. How will your husband feel when it's 10 p.m., and you're not home again for the fourth night in row that week?

A. He will think that it's business as usual. My last three jobs, where I almost never got home before 11 p.m., trained him well for these contingencies. He has approximately fifty-nine take-out menus, plus my cell phone number if he gets lonely. In our field, it's no secret that there really is no substitute for hard work. You can't be frightened of the long hours or try to resist them, because we need to make ourselves available to our clients 24/7. We're in a service industry, after all, and the big difference between those who succeed and those who fail is their ability to service those who are paying the bills with professionalism and good humor, no matter what hour of the night it is.

Last year, on Christmas Day, one of my clients called me. I was making stuffed turkey for thirty-five friends and family members. My client had a lot of questions that she needed to clarify; the phone conversation lasted for over an hour, and the turkey was a little overdone, but still edible. I will be here for our clients on Christmas, Passover, and even Flag Day.

Why This Technique Works

1. Your interviewer implied that you needed to be a workaholic to handle the job; you deftly persuaded her that you are one.

2. You brought the conversation around to a personal story that demonstrates that in your mind, business always comes first. Start clearing your calendar...you're going to land this job!

74. I applaud your efforts at trying to reenter the workforce, Adrianne. But an awful lot has changed about the business in the last six years. Why did you take so much time off from work, and why do you wish to get a job now?

A. When I first had the twins, my husband was working 24/7, and I really needed to be there to raise the kids. He was launching a new company with a completely different business model, so money was very tight, and we couldn't afford any help. But during those six years, I really missed working, and my husband and I both agreed that, once the kids were in first grade, it would be only fair for me to go back to doing what I loved. Fortunately, I kept my hand in the business during those years by consulting for several of my ex-clients. With your permission, I would like to share some case studies with you now. They're good examples of what I helped my clients achieve during that time. (Then simply launch into your case studies!)

EXTRA
CREDIT

If an interviewer begins a question with the words "I applaud," it generally means he doesn't. And it's your task to craft an answer that will make him stop wringing his hands and hire you already.

Never Be Afraid to Tell a Business Story

Everyone loves to hear a good story, interviewers included. So whenever possible, tell a compelling story about something that you learned on the job. Here are the elements that any good business tale about you should include:

1. Likeability. You're the hero (or heroine) of the tale, so you will need to come off as likeable.

2. Conflict. Every worthwhile protagonist needs an obstacle to overcome. The obstacle can be anything from a particularly unsympathetic client (who forced you to discuss business on Christmas Day) to some form of self-deception ("I thought I'd make a big pile of money while I was young, and then simply kick back and spend it for the next thirty years.")

3. Resolution. What happened?

4. The Moral. What you learned from the experience, and how that makes you a better job candidate today.

The best business stories often involve some self-deprecating humor. Did you spill coffee all over yourself while being interviewed by the chairman of the board? Did you trip over a chair while making a killer presentation to a group of shareholders? Be sure to let your interviewer in on the humorous details. He'll be doubly impressed by your accomplishment and your pluck.

We'd Love to Hire a Woman, But...

In some ways, gender discrimination is like a stubborn virus. It can be contained, but so far, anyway, it has not been stamped out. In fact, with gender discrimination being deemed illegal, it tends to surface in a new, particularly virulent form. Namely, an interviewer will tell you what a drag it is to work for a certain person because he's one of the "good ol' boys," the kind who fosters a working environment that's semi-hostile to members of the female sex. Unfortunately, the reason the interviewer is telling you this is almost always because, on some level, it's true. And he's simply trying to convince you to self-select out of the candidate pool. Unless you're fairly certain that working in an atmosphere like this will make you ill on a daily basis, use the techniques that follow to help put your interviewer's fears to rest.

75. Steve likes to foster a jovial, "boys' club" atmosphere around here. Everyone on his team plays pinball after hours in our creativity lounge, and softball together on the weekends. We would love to get a woman in his group, but honestly, I'm not sure that his group is any place for a woman.

A. It sounds like it would be a great deal of fun to work here, Maurice, and it also sounds like Steve's group could use a woman or two. I am a master at pinball and foosball, if you guys ever want to expand your game collection. Seriously, tell them to watch out…because I can take on any man! I could get into weekend softball, too. I'm kind of a sports junkie, so please don't be fooled by my skirt and heels. Now, on a more important matter: I think that having a woman on the team will help round out its collective personality profile, making it more appealing to your end-clients outside the organization. Some of them are undoubtedly women, and they have probably wondered why Steve's group doesn't have any.

Why This Technique Works

1. You sound like you're easygoing, enjoy having fun, and are the type of woman that would fit in well with "the boys' club."

2. You followed up with a smart reason for why the company should expand Steve's group to include women, without sounding like you're uptight, strident, or on a feminist march.

76.

Ever since that article, "The Ten Worst Companies in the World for a Woman to Work" came out, we've been struggling to even things out around here and hire a couple of women. And you seem like you're perfectly qualified. But this company isn't exactly women-friendly. The guys are just joshing around, but they make crude jokes and noises; sometimes they use bathroom humor, and, on a more serious note: nobody in top management is a woman. Do you really think that working here would be fun for you?

A. Well, Kirk, I have to confess that I'm used to it. So the answer is a resounding "yes." I have four brothers, two of them are older, two are younger, and as the middle child, I was teased mercilessly for my entire life. I haven't experienced the type of fraternity environment that you described on the job yet, because, let's face it: it's not 1955 anymore. But I have dealt with the situation at home very adeptly, and I still love my brothers!

Alt. A. "Ten Worst," huh? There's nothing I like more than a good challenge. Bring it on!

EXTRA

CREDIT

Don't give your interviewer an easy reason to eliminate you from consideration. If you're a woman who's applying for a job at a boys' club, find ways to show that you're "one of the boys" and will fit in seamlessly. Hey, how about those Knicks?

How to Break into the All-Male Fraternity (If You're a Woman)

In the late 1980s, the prevailing feeling was that to prove that you were "man enough" for the job, you had to dress like one. This lead to the rise of shoulder pads, which became a mandatory part of female office attire. Fortunately, for everyone concerned, this unflattering fashion has become deservedly unfashionable in the intervening years. You don't have to bulk up anymore to break into the frat house. But it doesn't hurt to come off as the type of woman who feels supremely comfortable around men. Think about the way you behave with your closest male buddies, and act that way in your interview. Over-prepare for your meeting, so that you can arrive feeling super-knowledgeable and relaxed enough to enjoy yourself.

We'd Love to Hire a Man, But...

Certain industries are heavily dominated by women. And a particular company may have an alpha-femme vibe to it. When this is the case, it can sometimes be hard for a male candidate to be taken seriously. If you happen to be the "wrong sex" for the boss in question, your interviewer may attempt to politely dissuade you from pursuing the job. Here's how to counter his concerns and land the job anyway.

77.

You'd be working for Samantha Quincy. And she's notoriously tough on her male assistants. Several of them have quit in frustration. Why do you think that you'd be any different?

A. I think that it's a huge mistake when job applicants automatically assume that an entry-level job will be easy. I expect just the opposite. Given the caliber of your organization, I anticipate that everyone who's working here will have rigorous, exacting standards, Samantha Quincy included.

This is my dream job, and, as you know from my countless emails to you, I've had visions of working for your company ever since I was seventeen years old. I will do everything I can to make certain that I perform at my personal best because I want to stay here for many years to come. I look forward to the challenge of pleasing Samantha, even if she is very tough on me. From everything that I've read about her, I know for a fact that she is absolutely brilliant. Samantha has a tremendous amount to teach the right person, and I am her willing student.

EXTRA CREDIT

Offer to provide your interviewer with a written reference from one of your female ex-bosses. Or better yet, give him her phone number, so that he can call and hear her cite your praises.

78.

It may sound weird, but I've never worked for a woman in our field. I suppose it really is the "all-male bastion" that people claim. But you would be working for a woman. Do you think that fact will change the way you feel about coming on board?

A. Gus, we're several years into the new millennium…it's interesting to me that you haven't worked for a woman yet. I did at my last three jobs, and I found the experience to be exhilarating. I've noticed that some of the clients that I've had in the past really appreciate having a balanced team presenting work to them. If the boss is a woman, it makes sense to have a guy like me underneath her. I just think that it helps clients and partners recognize that we are modern and up-to-date. My previous experience taught me that I can learn just as much from a woman as a man, and I respect the women in our field enormously.

That's a Wrap

1. If your interviewer feels that you're "too old" for the position, counteract that impression by proving that you're young at heart, vibrant, and willing to take several steps backwards (if necessary) to align your career on the right path. Condense your life story into a compelling sound bite that will touch your interviewer.

2. Does your interviewer think that you're too young for the job? Emphasize your love of taking on new challenges, intense loyalty to the organization, and extracurricular activities that taught you real-life business skills.

3. If the company tries to reject you based on the way you look or your skin color, stress your empathy, listening ability, or diligence at the interview, but choose a different tack for why you deserve the job in your follow-up communications.

4. Did someone suggest that you have other, more pressing commitments (than the job)? Demonstrate how you are coping with them brilliantly.

5. If a chauvinistic, anti-female bias exists at the company, strive to show that you love working for men, and will fit in comfortably with the all-male club.

6. Are you a man who's looking for a job in a company that really wants to hire a woman? Bend over backwards to prove that you have no issues with women in positions of power. You are "gender blind," and can learn just as much from a woman as a man.

CHAPTER 4
The Impossible Questions

Impossible questions are questions that really have no correct answer. They can be logic-based or mathematical conundrums that tax your brain cells. Or they might be questions designed to test your common knowledge. Whatever form they take, they're called "impossible" for a reason. These questions are purposely designed to fluster you and catch you off-guard. And interviewers ask them to see how well applicants perform under pressure.

To tease out the same information, a nice (or inexperienced) interviewer could just as easily ask a candidate to "describe a time when [he] had to work under a deadline and there wasn't enough time to complete the task." (Apparently, this question is asked during Microsoft interviews. It's a piece of cake compared to seemingly more random questions that really put the applicant on the spot.)

There are five types of "impossible questions":

1. *"Pop Essay" Questions.*

2. *Questions That Have No Correct Answer (But Require Logic to Answer Them, Anyway).*

3. *Ethical Questions with a Twist.*

4. *"Pigeonhole Yourself" Questions.*

5. *Questions That Send You to Confession (Or Oprah).*

When you are asked an impossible question, the key thing to remember is that your answer is usually not half as important as the way in which you deliver it. Poise, confidence, and some humor will take you far when confronted with these questions.

"Pop Essay" Questions

In college and grad school, pop essay questions pop up constantly. These days, they're also popular in the executive suite, where candidates are definitely graded on a bell curve. When you are asked this type of question, don't worry about giving the "right" answer, as much as defending your answer. The important thing is to be thorough about whatever answer you do give.

79. What is the best-managed company in America?

A. Probably not Enron or WorldCom. In all seriousness, I have been very impressed with Apple Computers. In recent years, they invented both the iMac and the iPod, brave new inventions in a jaded world. The iMac defied all expectations by coming out in retro,

Populux colors at a time when other computer companies were simply making beige boxes. That took real courage. The iPod was also marketed in a way that was counterintuitive but brilliant. Record companies were screaming at anyone who would listen about the perils of downloading. They were even threatening lawsuits against students who were downloading. Meanwhile, the iPod decided to celebrate the joy of downloading your favorite tunes.

EXTRA CREDIT

Stay on the cutting edge by keeping up-to-date on current events. Listen to AM radio talk shows once in a while, go watch an interesting documentary, take an active interest in the world around you. Doing so will vastly improve your score on all Pop Essay Questions.

80.

If you could be any product in the world, what would you choose?

A. That's a very interesting question, Sarah, and one that I've never actually thought about before. If I could be any product, I think it would have to be a Motorola flip-top cell phone. The flip top helps to screen out the noise of traffic and other pedestrians so that you can handle business from absolutely anywhere 24/7. The fancy screen keeps you up-to-date on your emails and text messages, so you're never late with your correspondence. Plus the cell phone comes in a jazzy silver color, which, for some reason, reminds me of elegantly streamlined German engineering.

EXTRA

CREDIT

It doesn't matter which product you compare yourself to as long as you have a little fun with it. So act like you're having fun (even if you wish the interview would just be over).

81.

If you were running a company that produces X and the market was tanking for that product, what would you do?

A. I would search for new markets for the product while I spurred the engineers to change the product to make it more marketable to its original core audience. Let's take Verizon's text-messaging service as a case in point. I've never worked for Verizon, so this example is purely hypothetical. But I do know that in Japan, text messaging was the rage for about four years. Everyone was text messaging each other all the time.

Now, text messaging has become fairly popular here in the States. But what's happening in Japan? People have started using BlackBerry en masse, because it's so much faster than text messaging. Let's face it: you don't have to keep hitting the same key over and over to arrive at the one letter that you want. Eventually, I predict that here in the States text messaging will also become far less popular, because we live in the Information Age, where speed of transmission rules all.

If I worked at Verizon, I would be seeking new markets for their text messaging product right now. Maybe it should be positioned as "a simple way to tell someone that you love her," more like a Hallmark card than a serious business tool. Who might be interested in a product like this? Retirees with a lot of time on their hands. I might try marketing text messaging to grandparents as a way to stay in touch with their loved ones. Perhaps we could cut seniors a price break if they signed up for text messaging when they first bought cell phones. Simultaneously, I would also be talking to the engineers on staff, and picking their brains about ways that we could make text messaging faster and less cumbersome to use.

FACT: The decision to hire someone is usually made within the first thirty seconds of meeting the candidate. That doesn't give you a whole lot of time to impress your prospect with your intelligence, conversational aptitude, or winning ideas. So do yourself a favor and also show up well-groomed and looking the part. Leave the stilettos (or the dusty work boots) at home.

Good rule of thumb: wear an ensemble that is 25 percent more pulled-together than what you would wear if you were already working there.

82.

We are interested in generating "word-of-mouth" advertising for our client. What are the most important criteria for turning a product or service into a "word-of-mouth" success?

A. Well, Charlie, that's a very interesting question. As far as I can tell, there are three critical things that need to collide to spark positive "word of mouth." First, your product or service has to address a need that isn't being met in the marketplace. Second, you will need "messenger/influencers" to bring the word forward. Third, it often helps to have some "context" for masses of people to care and pay attention to your message.

Off the top of my head, I would say that when Snapple iced tea first came out, it achieved "word of mouth," even before there was any advertising for it. After years of having canned iced tea beverages that really didn't taste like brewed iced tea, consumers suddenly found Snapple on their shelves. What was great about the product was that it looked exactly like real iced tea. You could see it in those glass bottles, which, at the time, was a refreshing idea.

The "messengers" who carried the word forward were disgruntled canned iced tea drinkers who were also mavens of the marketplace. They knew this product was really different than anything out there. Finally, the "context" was that Snapple first appeared on the shelves during the hot summer months, when everyone is more likely to drink cool beverages.

Why This Technique Works

1. You answered a difficult question with "proof points" that you made up off the top of your head.

2. You showed that you can think on your feet even while you're sitting down.

EXTRA CREDIT

Review the *Wall Street Journal, Business Week,* and all relevant trade publications before your interviews. Most periodicals have online versions that are easy to skim if you're pressed for time. Then if you find yourself referring to an interesting case study, tell your interviewer where you read about it.

Questions That Have No Correct Answer (But Require Logic to Answer Them, Anyway)

It seems like a paradox. But there are a lot of questions that seem like they only have one correct answer, when, in fact, they have several. Unfortunately, this doesn't mean that these questions are easy to answer. In fact, they can be surprisingly harrowing, since they're asked purely so that the interviewer can assess your reasoning ability under pressure.

When given this type of conundrum, first, take a deep breath. Feel the tight knots ease from your stomach. Then let your mind uncover different facets of the question as you reason through it aloud. The question that follows has been making the rounds at certain financial firms.

83. How many cigars are smoked in a year?

A. There are 250 million people in the United States. Let's suppose, for the sake of argument, that roughly half of them are men. That would mean that there are 125 million men. Then again, studies show that women live longer than men, so let's round the number of men down to 120 million. Let's say that 30 percent of these men are between the ages of zero and twenty-one, leaving approximately 80 million men of smoking age. Of these 80 million men, we have to guesstimate on this, figure that 20 percent of them smoke. So roughly 16 million men smoke. Of those who smoke, let's guess that about 20 percent of them smoke cigars. That's 3,200,000 men who smoke cigars. How many times a week will a man have a cigar? I would venture to say 3 times a week, so 9,600,000 cigars are smoked a week, or 499,200,000 cigars a year.

EXTRA CREDIT Talk about female cigar smokers. Again, make certain assumptions about the number, and share them with your interviewer. You might mention that there are 130 million women, none of whom smoke cigars regularly. However, 1 percent of them will smoke a cigar a year at a party or after-hours club, so you can add 1.3 million more cigars to the total above.

How to Correctly Answer a Question That Has No Correct Answer

With all due respect to cigar aficionados, most people couldn't care less how many cigars are smoked in a year. (It's fairly likely that your interviewer doesn't even care all that much.)

Yet, there you are, sweating bullets as you struggle to calculate the "correct answer" to the cigar question. Why? What possible reason could your interviewer possibly have to ask you this silly, who-cares-about-the-answer question? Simple. He wants to see you demonstrate your facility with details.

When you are asked to solve a puzzle like this, it's critical to:

1. Make certain assumptions about the problem (and share them with your interviewer as you go along).

2. Throw in certain telltale details that will demonstrate that your answer is more thoughtful than other job seekers' answers.

For example, in the cigar question, the detail that "women live longer than men" is important. Subtracting the number of men who "haven't reached smoking age" from the general pool of men is another significant detail.

Never be afraid to cite those telling details that show you are a thinking person possessed with a great deal of common knowledge. You'll gain points for thoroughness. Okay, now that you're a whiz at answering this type of question, test your prowess on the question that follows.

84.

How many skis are rented each year?

A. There are 250 million people living in America. Let's suppose that the number of skiers is 15 percent of that, or 37,500,000. Of those, let's figure that 28,175,000 of them own skis, leaving the number who rent at: 9,325,000. Then, let's add the number of tourists who ski, say, 1 million. So the grand total of renters would be: 10,325,000.

Now, let's assume that the renters who live here take 3 trips a year, while the skiing tourists visit the U.S. once a year. The number of rentals for residents per season would be 3 times 9,325,000, or 27,975,000. While the number of rentals for tourists would be 1,000,000. Let's add those two numbers together to arrive at the total number of rentals each year, which is: 28,975,000.

EXTRA CREDIT Never attempt to tackle a brain tickler without a pen and paper, unless you do math in your head easily. Even then, it's a good idea to write down your calculations as you go, so that you can double check them easily. Be sure to bring a pad and pen with you just in case.

85.

There's an ad on the back of a phone kiosk on Third Avenue and 47th Street. Can you tell me how many people are exposed to it every day?

A. Well, let's see…8 million people live in New York City, and let's suppose that half a million of them work in Midtown. Midtown covers a fairly large geographic area, and people who work on the Avenue of the

Americas rarely walk all the way over to Third Avenue, even at lunch. So I am going to think of this in terms of subsets.

The first subset is the group of people who work within a five-block radius of Third Avenue and 47th Street. Let's say that's approximately 100,000 people.

The second subset is the group of people who take cabs by that location, plus the cab drivers themselves. There are 10,000 cabs in New York. Let's imagine that 1,000 of them will drive by the location twice a day, carrying two passengers each. Then again, only the passengers sitting by the windows facing the kiosk would probably notice the ad, so that's 2,000 taxi passengers who would see it, plus all 1,000 cab drivers. We're at 103,000 people so far.

If the ad were lit, of course, there might be an additional 1,000 passengers who would see the ad at night, bringing our total up to 104,000 people.

I believe that ads are more difficult to spot if one happens to be sitting on a bus. So let's add a fraction of the people who take the Third Avenue bus every day to our number—50 more people a day (bus passengers and bus drivers) would see the ad.

Another subset of people would be those living, but not working, within a five-block radius of the ad. I'm going to guess that's an additional 50,000 people. We're at 104,550.

Lastly, we should take tourists into account. Perhaps 1,000 tourists might stroll by that location on their way to another Midtown destination. Grand total: 105,550 people would see the ad every day, Monday through Friday.

On Saturdays and Sundays, however, Midtown is fairly empty. Busses and cabs are rarely full, since there isn't all that much to do in Midtown during the weekends. I think we can safely assume that the 50,000 people who live in the area would see the ad, plus perhaps 200 tourists, 10 people taking the Third Avenue bus, and 800 people taking cabs. So on the weekends, the total would drop to 51,010 people.

How to Be a Great Salesman (When the Product that You're Selling Is *You*)

Everyone has needs—including interviewers. So find out what your future employer is looking for in a candidate, and then demonstrate that you can fill the need. But don't be smarmy about it. Hold your interviewer's gaze without boring into her eyes. Listen closely to what your interviewer would like to see in a candidate, and then explain that you have the attributes she's seeking, using different language than hers. Back up with relevant case examples.

Ethical Questions with a Twist

In the past few years, several blue-chip accounting firms pursued unethical practices that were widely reported in every newspaper in the country. As a result, questions about ethics are on the rise at all kinds of different firms. When you are riddled with this type of question, you will need to demonstrate that you believe in ethical behavior and "best practices"—even when those around you do not.

86. When have you confronted unethical behavior and chosen not to say anything in order not to rock the boat?

A. One of the companies where I worked had signed contracts to use "union talent" to advertise their product. There was a union strike for a couple of weeks, and it came to my attention that someone on staff who wanted to do freelance voiceover work was actually recording her own voice on our company's test demo spots during the strike. One of the spots ended up testing very well in focus groups. To my astonishment, that woman's voice was later used, as recorded, on the on-air TV commercial!

Once the strike was over, I mentioned to several higher-ups that I thought it would be wise to re-record the voiceover using union talent, because if the union ever found out that a voiceover "scab" had been used, there would be hell to pay. My bosses sort of patted me on the head, and told me not to lose a lot of sleep over it. They didn't seem to think it was a big deal. And because I really wanted to keep my job, I let the matter drop.

Why This Technique Works

1. You're a rational pragmatist. You tried to do the right thing, and were prevented from doing so by your unethical bosses.

2. Wisely, you recognized that continuing to push them would jeopardize your job.

 **What if you knew that giving someone who worked for you the raise that she deserved would cut into your own raise, making it only mediocre?**

A. A lot of times, there is a pool of money set aside for raises, and one person's raise really does cut into someone else's—particularly these days when money is tight. On the other hand, I believe in rewarding people for a job well done. Because if we don't reward our best people, they will turn around and leave the company.

I would suggest that top management give "mediocre raises" to me and to my colleague immediately—with the promise that we'd both get small, additional raises in six months. I think that both of us would be delighted to know that our job performances merited more money (even if the company couldn't pay it right away). And a raise in the not-so-distant future would be a great morale-booster.

EXTRA

CREDIT

Discuss a time when giving a mediocre raise but a fantastic written review to one of your employees kept her morale up. Studies show that praise for a job well done is almost as effective as a huge raise.

88. What would you do if you really wanted to hire a woman under you, and you knew the perfect candidate, but your boss really wanted to hire a man for the job?

A. That's an excellent question, Sarah. In my last job, I faced this situation, but in reverse. I was told that I had hiring authority when I took the job, and that we needed to find an associate who would report to me. I actually knew a young man that I thought would be ideal. Meanwhile, my boss wished to hire a woman who had been recommended to her by the CFO of the company.

Figuring that the political odds were heavily stacked against my candidate, I went to my boss and asked her directly if we should just hire her candidate. "Why, what's your solution?" she asked me with surprise. I recommended that we perform an on-site "test," by hiring both candidates on a freelance basis for two weeks each. My candidate performed very well, hers did also, and both candidates were offered full-time jobs four weeks later.

Why This Technique Works

1. Your interviewer asked you a general question, but you immediately made it specific by referring to a situation that you faced on the job.

2. You've proven that political "hot potatoes" don't burn you.

The World's Best Time for an Interview

Studies show that people who interview in the morning are offered the job more often than those who take afternoon interviews. There might be several reasons for this. First thing in the morning, you are not competing with lunch for your interviewer's undivided attention. You are also less likely to encounter unwelcome interruptions, such as spontaneous meetings that could cut your interview short. Finally, your interviewer will be in less of a rush to clear the work off of her desk and get out of there than she might be during the afternoon.

The three best times for an interview are:

Tuesdays, 10–11 a.m.

Wednesdays, 10–11 a.m.

Thursdays, 10–11 a.m.

If you have a choice, always aim for these early-morning interview time slots. At certain financial companies, you may even want to request an earlier time for your interviews, say 9 a.m. In creative fields, you're probably safer taking a 10 a.m. meeting. It can be nerve-wracking to sit around endlessly, waiting for your interviewer to show up to work in the morning.

89.

If your boss told you that you needed to develop a PowerPoint presentation with ten to twenty slides in one week, and you felt strongly that the material only merited eight slides, how many slides would you create for your presentation, and why?

A. First, I would develop the presentation with the correct number of slides that would cover the content. In other words, eight slides. Then, I would look for ways to reformat the presentation. Air and bullets often aid legibility, so I would do my best to expand the presentation to twelve slides. If, after creating the twelve slides, I felt that the content on some of them seemed a little "light," I would go back and review the material thoroughly to be certain that I had tackled all of the compelling points.

If I thought that the topic had been totally "nailed" in those twelve slides, I would arrange a time to take my boss through a "practice run" of the PowerPoint presentation to see if he believed there were any areas that needed more coverage.

Why This Technique Works

1. You come off as both a go-getter who doesn't need a lot of supervision and a team player who can take direction (even when you disagree with it).

2. By giving your boss a sneak preview of the presentation, it gives her a chance to get behind it. On the great corporate ladder of life, you will go far.

90.

What if you were working with someone who managed to "take credit" for all of your great ideas. How would you handle it?

A. If the person were a colleague, I would first try to credit her publicly with the ideas that were hers. Sometimes, by being very generous with credit, it spurs the other person to "return the favor." If I still heard that she was taking credit for my ideas, I would try to work out an arrangement where we each agreed to present the ideas that were our own to our bosses. If that didn't work, I would try to openly discuss the situation with her. I would stress the fact that teamwork matters, and that positioning both of us as "good, strong idea people" to our superiors would help our team be taken more seriously.

However, if the person who was taking credit for my ideas happened to be my boss, I would tread cautiously. To some extent, I believe that my job is to make my superiors shine. If I were being rewarded for my ideas with raises and promotions, I would be happy. On the other hand, if a whole year went by, and I felt that I wasn't being rewarded financially for my ideas, I would ask my boss for a performance review, and behind closed doors in her office, broach the matter very delicately.

7 Classic Interview Don'ts

1. **Don't commandeer the interview by pummeling your interviewer with questions.** Resolve to listen astutely. When there is a break in the conversation, mention that you have some questions, and politely ask your interviewer if it would okay to bring them up.

2. **Don't grill your interviewer.** If he seems to be particularly sensitive about a topic that you raise, gracefully drop it, and move onto a question that covers more neutral ground.

3. **Don't take notes during the interview.** Some interviewing guides suggest it, but it's generally a bad idea. Information may surface in your meeting that your interviewer considers highly confidential. If you are sitting there taking notes, he may feel squeamish about discussing various aspects of the job that you need to know. Also, it's difficult to write and listen at the same time. So don't fritter away valuable "face time" by attempting to multitask.

4. **Don't feel overly embarrassed by occasional pauses in the conversation.** It's frequently better to allow your interviewer to break the silence, rather than rummaging through your head to "say anything" to overcome the awkwardness.

5. **Don't overstay your welcome.** The average interview lasts for forty-five minutes, but if an interviewer happens to be either very introverted or extremely busy (or both), he may wish your meeting to run considerably shorter. Even if you are chronically disappointed, don't "plant" yourself in your interviewer's office, refusing to budge, until he answers more of your questions!

6. **Don't stalk your interviewer.** If he signals that your meeting is over, (by standing up and shaking your hand, for example), politely inquire about your next steps and leave. What if you know for a fact that you are both headed in the same direction after your meeting? That's no reason to suggest "sharing a cab together," or dropping him off in your car! The bottom line: do not try to prolong the interview.

7. **Don't perform some practical joke on the interviewer to prove that you've got a sense of humor.** No jumping out of cakes. Use common sense when contacting your interviewer in your follow-up communications too. It's fine to be engaging; it's horrendous to be slapstick or tacky. When in doubt, pull yourself back.

"Pigeonhole Yourself" Questions

An interview lasts for approximately forty-five minutes. Since the time you spend with your interviewer is so short, sometimes he will ask you to help him make a snap judgment about you—by asking you to put yourself in a certain category. When you are asked to pigeonhole yourself, it generally makes sense to break out of the coop. So stretch the boundaries. Why settle for being one type over another? Demonstrate that you are *both* types. Position yourself as multidimensional and multitalented. With all of the rounds of layoffs that have been happening in company after company, fewer people are expected to do a lot more.

91.

Are you better at "managing up" or "managing down"?

A. If you aren't good at "managing up," you rarely get the opportunity to "manage down." Fortunately, I've always been quite good at self-management. I've never had a deadline that I didn't meet. Sometimes when I've needed various bosses of mine to come through with a particular piece of information to help me do my job, I've had to give them a reminder nudge. Even some of my most disorganized bosses have thanked me for my persistence and follow-through.

Once I was promoted into middle management, I learned how to manage down effectively. Now, I always call a big kick-off meeting to help team members understand the scope of the assignment. At this meeting, I set deadlines to help keep the momentum flowing. After that, I try to let my people manage their own time, because nobody likes a boss looking over his shoulder.

But if one of my employees has trouble completing his tasks, I will sit down with him and suggest a better working method. Sometimes, I've even volunteered to help out certain stressed-out employees, which always guarantees a great deal of cooperation from them on the next assignment.

EXTRA **CREDIT** **If you've had them, mention "360-degree" evaluations. In many companies, people are reviewed by their bosses, colleagues, and underlings simultaneously. If you've ever experienced this type of evaluation (and the results were positive), bring it up in your interview to show that you manage up, down, and even sideways effectively.**

92.

Are you a better visionary or implementer? Why?

OOPS! **TRICK QUESTION SIGHTING.**
See "The Trick with Trick Questions."

The Trick with Trick Questions

Great interviewees are able to recognize trick questions and handle them gracefully. No doubt about it, the "visionary-or-implementer" question is a classic trick question, because there is no perfect answer.

Most people are either visionaries or implementers, and recruiters know it. Visionaries make good leaders, but they need implementers under them or their visions don't get implemented. On the other hand, claiming that you are an "implementer" can make you sound like a busy worker-bee drone with no vision whatsoever!

When you are asked this type of question, the "trick," if you will, is to target your answer to the company where you are interviewing, by:

1. Finding out what the company is looking for, and

2. Modeling your response accordingly.

If you will be reporting to a visionary, you're an implementer (with some vision of your own). Conversely, if the company is filled with implementers, you are a visionary (that's relatively grounded). Study the two answers to this question that follows. There will be a pop quiz later (at your interview).

Visionary Answer: I am more of a "big-picture" person, but I do investigate the facts so that I can make my dreams happen. For example, I understand that your company has a product line of 300-thread cotton sheets in vibrant colors like pink, orange, and purple. I think that they're gorgeous, and actually, I own several sets. But I also believe that your organization may be missing a potential "gold mine" in the children's market. If we could push the entire line to children as well as to moms, I think that we would be able double your department's profits in the next three years.

Implementer Answer: As Ludwig Mies van der Rohe once said: "God is in the details." And boy, do I embrace those details! I keep meticulous lists of tasks and follow them, never letting a deadline with a buyer slip. I'm great at making inroads into trade shows where we could showcase your product. I happened to read several articles about how your CEO, Stephen Pauly, is trying to enter the children's linen market right now, and I'm very jazzed up about his efforts. I brought a list with me today of possible venues where we can show your colorful linens. Time permitting, I would love to share my findings with you.

EXTRA CREDIT Don't feel weird about using the word "we." Look for ways to weave it into your conversation. Start acting like a member of the team even before you're officially hired, and you will significantly improve your chances of being offered the job. We will prevail!

93. Would you rather get permission from your boss before undertaking a brand-new project, or be given enough rope to "hang yourself"?

A. During my first week on the job, I would ask my boss how she would prefer for me to handle projects. If she indicated that she really wanted a take-charge person under her, I would take the ropes. If, on the other hand, she told me that she wanted me to run my ideas by her first, I would happily comply. I think the real challenge is being able to adapt to your working environment, and I'm flexible and easygoing.

94. Have you ever been so firm that people would describe you as "stubborn" or "inflexible"?

A. When women are firm, they are sometimes pinned with these unattractive labels. I am not shy or mousy, so probably one or two people I've worked with might have thought that I was "inflexible" on a given assignment. But this adjective never came out about me on any kind of a performance review, and neither did the word "stubborn." I believe that, all in all, I've managed to be firm *and* flexible.

Inside Information

While recruiters can call anyone they please to check up on your past performance, they are not allowed to obtain copies of your past reviews at a company. So feel free to refer to glowing performance reviews (within reason, of course). If you have copies of one or two of them, pull them out when you are confronted with this type of question.

Questions That Send You to Confession (Or Oprah)

In this country, there's supposed to be a separation between Church and State. So why does interviewing for a job sometimes feel like you're going to confession? When you are asked questions about risks you've taken, mistakes you made on the job, and regrets that you have, always demonstrate what you learned from the experience. Remember this always: professionals rise above setbacks, and you are the consummate professional. You have no problem discussing a mistake that you made along the way, because the experience made you stronger, more capable, and even more employable.

95. What are the biggest risks you've taken in recent years? Which ones worked out the best, and which ones failed?

A. I used to work at a large, global PR firm where life was sleepy, but comfortable. It was a "white-shoe" organization; people left every night at 6 p.m. and our clients were big biotechnology companies that really trusted the top management of our firm. After a couple of years went by, I felt like I wasn't learning anything new, and I confess that I began to feel bored. I thought that if I took a job at a smaller PR firm, I would feel more challenged.

I joined a small PR boutique that had only been in business for five years. This turned out to be a colossal mistake. The top management was terribly unprofessional, plus they didn't have the contacts with newspapers, TV, and cable stations that we really needed to service our clients properly. I canvassed my own contacts, of course, but I was the only person in the entire firm who had any contacts! Promises were made to clients that couldn't be kept. It was a fiasco.

After six months, I called up the large, global PR firm and begged for my old job back. Fortunately, they hadn't replaced me. They slapped my wrist for being disloyal, but they happily rehired me. I've been working there ever since, grateful, but bored…which is why I'm meeting with you today.

The Fine Art of Interview Jujitsu

Questions about risks and mistakes need to be turned around as quickly as possible to show how you excelled in adverse conditions. Bring out the "silver lining" in all negative experiences. Also, respect your interviewer's reason for asking the question. Keep your answers related to business.

Many interviewees, fearing that their past business mistakes will be held against them, attempt to distract their interviewers by admitting to mistakes they've made in their personal lives. Do not fall into this trap. When you are asked about a risk or mistake that you made, the biggest mistake you can make in your interview is discussing some failed personal relationship that you had with a husband, wife, or significant other. As the saying goes, "don't mix business with pleasure." However, in certain situations, it's perfectly okay to discuss the love life (or lack thereof) of one of your colleagues. See the following Q&A.

96.

What if you knew that someone on staff who was very talented was looking for a job elsewhere? Let's say she had made you promise that you wouldn't tell anyone. As a top manager of this firm, what would you do?

A. When I was working at Bidden, Bowden & Atlas, I actually confronted this situation. A very dedicated coworker of mine, Paula Jeffries, and I became great friends. We would socialize after hours at this watering hole near the office. And Paula, who I felt was in line for a promotion and big raise, would tell me how miserable she was at the office. She was single, and honestly felt that the hours at BB&A were so excruciating that she couldn't find any time to date.

I was also up for a promotion, and knew that if I were given the new title, I would be managing Paula, so it was in my best interest to convince her to stay. I never betrayed Paula's confidence. Instead, I struck a deal with her.

"Look, Paula, if you and I are both promoted, you'll be reporting to me. And I really don't want you to leave. So this is what I can offer you. If you stay at BB&A, I promise that I will let you leave the office at a decent hour, say 6 p.m., two nights a week."

Paula agreed to my terms. We were both promoted; I gained her undying loyalty and she's still working for me. She hasn't met her ideal match yet, but two nights a week, she's at least out there meeting men.

EXTRA CREDIT

If you are ever asked to choose between a colleague and your company, you need to stay loyal to the company. But if you can handle the situation diplomatically, often the problem disappears and everyone wins.

97.

What are a couple of the most courageous actions or unpopular stands that you have ever taken?

A. I used to have a partner who would cut out every night at 5 p.m. to get home to his family, and a boss who wanted everyone to stay until 8 o'clock at night, whether or not their workloads merited it. When it came to my boss's attention that my partner was leaving so early, my boss used to draw me into his office after hours to complain about my partner. My boss would detect tiny mistakes in my partner's performance (which he blamed on my partner's work ethic) and berate him—behind his back.

The easiest thing for me would have been to simply listen to my boss's rants; he evidently liked the fact that I was a good "sounding board" for his fury. Instead, I insisted that he talk to my partner directly about the problems he was having with my partner's performance. I also persuaded my partner to go talk to our boss. They worked it out, and my partner ended up keeping his job.

Alt. A. I used to work for a boss who managed four offices in the United States, making his time ultra-limited. He was rarely in the home office, which is where I worked. During his absences, people would come and ask me how to reach him. Flooded with their emails and phone messages, he eventually called me one day, and begged me to review their work "unofficially." But there had been a long history in my office of people who would "act like the boss," sans any official title, only to be "beheaded" a few months later for overstepping their bounds. I told my supervisor that if he wanted me to be "acting boss" in his absence, he needed to let people know officially, and that giving me a new title wouldn't hurt either. He resisted for a while, but ultimately, he came around.

A Guide to Minefields in the Executive Suite

1. If your interviewer asks about an "unpopular stand" that you took, you need to describe an action that was unpopular with at least one person.

2. Do try to contain your examples to times when you only ruffled one or two people's feathers. You don't want to come off as a rabble-rouser. Avoid stories about how you "joined the Women's Group" at your firm to gripe about "how they never promote women from within," or railroaded some objectors on staff into giving money to the United Way (or another corporate "cause").

98.

Under what circumstances have you found it acceptable to break a confidence?

A. When the person doing the confiding has shared the fact that she was doing something unethical—and if I felt that I might be able to stop her behavior by telling someone else about it. I used to work at a company that wasn't doing all that well. A "rainmaker" was brought in to solve the problem. She would get the company involved in new business pitches that would take months, often relying on one particular outsider as a paid "new business consultant."

After a couple of months, this woman and her new business consultant would call large internal staff meetings to tell everyone what our "next steps" were. One day, I bumped into the CFO of the company and asked him whether we were being paid for any of these new business pitches. Sadly, he just shook his head and said no.

I finally approached the "rainmaker" after hours, and asked her point-blank about our prospects. "You have to keep the illusion of having a lot of balls in the air," she told me, "even if none of them ever turn into real business. This keeps people employed." I mulled over what she had confided, decided it was a recipe for disaster, and contacted the chairman of the company to discuss it. He fired the "rainmaker" and her new business consultant that afternoon. Naturally, I also worried about my own job. But I was spared.

99. What mistakes did you make during your last job? And what would you have done differently, if you could do it over?

A. My last job was at a very small company where people wore a lot of "hats." Everyone needed to do three jobs competently. When I first arrived, I was told to hire two specialists from big firms immediately—which I did. The problem was, that in both cases, these specialists did one thing superbly, and they weren't able to branch out and tackle some of the other assignments, because in their old firms, these tasks hadn't been part of their job descriptions. After a couple of weeks, I recognized my error, and had to fire both people—replacing them with two people from smaller companies. They both worked out very well.

As they say, "hindsight is 20/20." Had I been blessed with perfect foresight, I would not have bowed to the excruciating pressure to hire two people so quickly. I would have tested them out on a freelance basis for a couple of weeks, recognized that they couldn't perform all of the required tasks, and then ultimately hired the two people from smaller firms who were appropriate for this company.

Inside Information

If you made a mistake in your last job and are asked about it, own up to it. But strive to show: 1) how you corrected the problem, and 2) what you learned from the experience.

100. **Do you know who painted this work of art? It's an original Jasper Johns. I can see by your blank stare that you have no idea who that is. So tell me, why should I put you in my Private Client Services Group, where you would be servicing high-net-worth individuals?**

A. I'm sorry, David, if I appeared for a moment there to stop and stare at that gorgeous Jasper Johns. I confess that I was simply marveling at its beauty, texture, and form. The last time I saw one was at a traveling Jasper Johns exhibit two years ago. I vowed then and there that I would commit myself to servicing high-net-worth individuals, so that one day, hopefully in this lifetime, I would be able to afford a small Jasper Johns painting of my very own. Yes, I know that sounds ambitious, especially given what his paintings fetch at auction houses. But I figure that you're no stranger to ambition. You need people in this company who have big dreams and visions. I intend to be the most productive person in your entire department. Please tell me more about some of the investments that you've recommended to your high-net-worth clients.

Alt. A. You're absolutely right. I confess that I know absolutely nothing about Jasper Johns! I never took an art history class when I was at Harvard, and once I got to Columbia Business School, I was so wrapped up in my corporate finance major that I never made it to a museum. But you should feel confident that I will pick up the knowledge that I need to service your high-net-worth clients. I'm a quick study, and I recognize that being able to talk to clients about their interests is critical.

101. **Have you ever lost your cool? Please describe.**

A. I once helped a woman get a job at my company. I didn't really know her all that well. She and I had worked together for a nanosecond at a previous company many years before, but on separate teams and for separate bosses. I figured that since the previous company was a blue-chip organization, this woman was probably talented and extremely competent.

The moment that she arrived at my new company, however, she tried to sabotage my efforts. She reported to me, so her actions were potentially quite destructive. Every time that I would bring a new deal to the table, she would go on and on about why it was "a terrible idea" to pursue. Eventually, I called her into my office, closed the door, and said: "I am supposed to be your leader, and by flouting my authority publicly, you are hurting both of our chances for survival at this company. I feel like I got you this job, and the way you have chosen to repay me proves that I made a serious error in judgment. If you don't stop sabotaging me in meetings, I will be forced to fire you. So if you have a problem with my deals, I strongly suggest that you come talk to me first. You have two weeks to turn the situation around."

Even though I was quite angry with her, I delivered this "bitter pill" calmly. She took my threat seriously, and, fortunately, I never had to follow through on it. She was eventually transferred to a different department, though, because others on my team didn't like her attitude either. But we have long since patched up the "bad blood" between us. And we're both still working at the company.

Why This Technique Works

1. You admitted that you were angered by someone's behavior, but in fact you didn't lose your temper. You showed steely resolve under pressure, and you were not afraid to solve the problem, permanently, if necessary.

2. You repaired the "broken fence" with her, even though others in your department didn't like being around her either.

102.

What have been the most difficult criticisms you have ever faced?

A. I think that the most difficult criticism is something that you can't do anything about. For example, if someone told me that I was "too hard on my people," I would loosen up. If I ever heard that I was bad at delegating, I would take a class in management and delegate more. But I was once told that I was "too passionate," but not to change it, because my passion evidently helped me get my work done. I thought about the comment a lot, and decided that my supervisor was probably right. I'm still just as passionate, but I've learned how to rein it in over the years, simply by expressing it less.

Why This Technique Works

1. Asked about a criticism that you received, you cited your "passion," which most people would consider a positive trait.

2. The fact that you learned how to moderate the way that you express your zeal shows a maturity and self-knowledge interviewers can't help but admire.

103.

Let's discuss a time when you missed a significant deadline.

A. I would absolutely love to, but honestly, it's never happened. Some- times, for whatever reason, clients have imposed an absolutely brutal deadline to show them the first round of work. And I have always respected their wishes. "Give me the freedom of a tight deadline," as one of my former bosses used to say.

That's a Wrap

1. Pop essay questions don't have a "right" answer versus a "wrong" one, but being thorough adds major points to your interview score (while being superficial subtracts them).
2. Logic questions become easier to tackle once you break them down into smaller subsets of problems requiring simple math skills. Just don't forget to let your interviewer in on the assumptions that you are using to solve the problem.
3. Ethical questions are more common now than ever, due to the discovery of unethical practices at many blue-chip firms. Your interviewer is trying to figure out if you have integrity. Prove that you do, even if everyone that you ever worked with seems to have forgotten the meaning of the word.
4. If an interviewer asks whether you are more X or Y, and both seem like valuable corporate assets, pick one, but demonstrate that you also possess the other quality in spades.
5. "Confess" to certain errors that you made if you have to, but never admit to technical incompetence. You meet deadlines, you're super-organized, you have interpersonal "people skills" galore. Any problems that you encountered on the job were a result of confusing or unethical management practices that existed before you joined the company and were beyond your control.

CHAPTER 5

How to Ace the Personality Test

References, once the bastion of the interviewing process, are nearing extinction as million-dollar lawsuits filed by employees given bad marks from their former employers are becoming more commonplace. Companies are counseled by their in-house lawyers to simply confirm or deny that a particular person was employed for a certain period of time without going into the details. As a result, personality testing is being adopted by more and more companies to help them get to know the people under consideration a little better.

In theory, a personality test simply measures someone's strengths. Are you a leader or a manager? Are you a type A personality or a type B?

The problem is: at companies that use personality testing, records are kept of which types of employees tend to succeed or fail. So in the hiring process, executives are looking to fill slots with only one "type" of employee —the type who succeeds.

There are five types of oral personality exams you may encounter:

1. *Questions about How You Filled Out the Written Personality Test (Or Would, If There Were One).*

2. *Questions That Get You to Reveal Your Personality (When You Don't Realize It's Being Tested).*

3. *Questions That Test Your Political Prowess.*

4. *Questions That Ask You to Take Off Your "Work Mask."*

5. *Questions Freud Would Approve Of.*

If you are not psychologically inclined, get online, go to Ask Jeeves, and look up "personality testing." You will find a number of articles about it, plus some personality tests that you can download for a small fee.

Questions about How You Filled Out the Written Personality Test (Or Would, If There Were One)

Most interviewers will tell you that it's "just a formality." But if the written personality test really were just a formality, you'd be offered the job without any strings attached. Then the company would have you take the personality test once you were already on staff. When filling out the personality test, you want to come across as dependable, emotionally stable, agreeable, and industrious. Additionally, there are certain qualities that are considered important to have in different fields. For a sales job, being extroverted is generally considered a vital trait. For a job in the arts, creativity is considered desirable. What happens if you fill out the personality test in a different way than the company expects? See the following Q&A.

104. At our company, we're looking for wolves, not sheep. We need leaders, not managers. One telltale sign of a leader is having a headstrong, type A personality. But on your personality test, I noticed that you're really more of a type B personality.

A. True leadership requires the ability to motivate all different kinds of people: type A personalities, type B personalities, managers, and dreamers. It would be my job to give lazy employees the kick in the pants they need to succeed, and to rein in some of the "wolves" so that they can become more organized and productive. Since type A personalities are generally more headstrong and opinionated than type B personalities, they are really far better off having someone who has the emotional intelligence and psychological distance to deal with their outbursts, as well as their flashes of inspiration.

Alt A. I successfully led forty people in my last job, and frankly, they were all different types of people. I have the grace under pressure to motivate, cajole, encourage, and inspire any kind of employee in your organization. Being a leader involves people skills, and this is my true area of expertise.

EXTRA CREDIT

Don't let psychobabble unnerve you. Counter all hypothetical theories (type A personalities are stronger leaders than type B personalities) with something tangible: proof that you're the man for the job (even if you happen to be a woman).

Testing, 1-2-3

Recent studies estimate that 34 percent of resumes and 73 percent of job applications contain information that is either false or, at the very least, embellished. Hence, the rise of personality testing at all kinds of different companies, including commercial banks, investment banking firms, insurance corporations, retail, computer, and trucking companies.

There are numerous personality tests that corporations might use. Some tests are industry specific. Others are really aptitude tests. Still others are designed as disaster checks, which attempt to help recruiters weed out potential "problem employees" with drug addictions or serious psychological disorders.

Why leave your score on a personality test to chance? Try to find out if the company conducts personality tests before your interview. Ask your contacts. If you know someone at the company, urge him or her to tell you what qualities the company is looking for in its employees. Then answer the personality test appropriately.

105.

Here's a test for you. As you will see, there is a blank piece of paper with a line on it. Please fill in the one word that best describes you.

A. Perspective. (I stay calm under pressure.)

Alt. A. Flexibility. (I work well with others.)

Alt. A. Leadership. (I motivate people effortlessly.)

Alt. A. Persistence (I prevail in spite of obstacles.)

EXTRA CREDIT With this kind of test, don't be too cute with your answer. Avoid cliched metaphors, such as "captain," "cheerleader," or "right-hand man." Find words that are serious and business related.

106.
Do you consider yourself a leader? Why or why not?

A. Oh, yes, absolutely. I have all of the leadership qualities. I'm extroverted, but I also happen to be a terrific listener. I consider myself a "big-idea" person, but I can also be hard-nosed and practical when necessary. I was promoted to senior vice president five years ago, and turned a division that was limping along aimlessly into a profitable contender. I helped our team generate $20 million of new business revenues, and even more significantly, retain $80 million of current business.

Alt. A. I don't think that you can be considered a leader until you've actually led a team at a company. Leaders are made, not born. But I am a leader in waiting. In college, I was on the student council. I had gained the "freshman fifteen" (pounds), and I really felt that all of the fried food in the school cafeteria was partly to blame. So I led the drive to get more nutritionally balanced foods on the menu. This involved collecting petitions from the student body and discussing the situation with several members of the administration. Until I become a leader at your company, I'm determined to learn the ropes from the recognized leaders in your department.

107.

How would you describe your working style?

A. Well, I took the Myers-Briggs Type Indicator personality test, and apparently, I am an "INTJ," in other words: introverted, intuitive, thinking, and judging. This makes me a "logical visionary." I know how to plan strategically, but I also keep my eye on the future. I set broad, long-term objectives, and have the stamina to see them through. I accomplish tasks and meet deadlines religiously. According to Myers-Briggs, my skills make me the ideal researcher for you to have on staff.

EXTRA CREDIT If you are right out of college and are looking for your first job, you may well be asked to describe your personality. When you answer the question, using "objective" Myers-Briggs criteria, it has a certain ring of authority. So download the test from the Internet, figure out your strengths, and sell them as if your future happiness depended on it.

Questions That Ask You to Reveal Your Personality (When You Don't Realize It's Being Tested)

If you don't know why a certain question is being asked, it's often because it's designed to be an on-the-spot personality test. How well do you deal with surprises? Often, this is the very thing the interviewer is trying to assess! In these situations, remaining calm scores major points. So does having a can-do attitude. Above all, have confidence that your interviewer will respond favorably to your personality, and generally, he will.

108. I understand that you're an international marketer. RR&G does not need international marketers, and we have no plans to expand, given our strong business in the U.S. I think that you are probably wasting your time even interviewing here.

A. I have developed contacts throughout Europe and also in Latin America. In the last five years, while I was working in the Madrid office of BL&S, I was the single largest producer of new leads, and 50 percent of them generated live, active deals, which actually closed. Your chairman, Strom McPherson, asked his assistant, Cleo Summers, to arrange these interviews for me in New York today. So all I can say is that there may be plans on the horizon for RR&G to expand its scope. A European or Latin American operation wouldn't necessarily have to compete with your U.S. operation. I certainly have a team of people whom I could bring over to RR&G to develop your portfolios abroad.

EXTRA ✔ **CREDIT**

At some companies, interviewers try to trip up candidates by asking them to meet with an in-house psychologist who asks questions designed to anger the interviewees. Apparently, the technique works, and a lot of job applicants storm out of the room! The most important thing to remember when you are asked a question that seems obnoxious or rude is simply not to get upset about it. Recognize that this is a pop personality quiz, and ace it. Smile, look your interviewer in the eye, and state your qualifications with poise.

It's All about the Bottom Line

Hiring mistakes cost companies thousands of dollars each quarter. And in the aggregate, hiring mistakes cost businesses hundreds of thousands of dollars every year. Many hiring managers hope that by adding a written personality test component to the behavioral interview, it will raise their chances of accurately predicting performance. Realize that if you were sitting in the HR manager's chair, and had one or two hiring mistakes in your dossier, you might become a fierce advocate for personality testing in your firm, too. So always be a good sport about taking any personality test that you're asked to fill out.

109. I am looking for an assistant who can handle boredom well. I'm not going to be around most of the time, so I don't really need someone who's chomping at the bit to move up in the organization. You would basically be "on call" for me. I might only need you for half an hour during a given day, but when I need you, I need you.

A. I'm a self-starter with a keen interest in business, but I am also excellent at keeping myself entertained. I will arrive at 8:30 in the morning and deal with all of your correspondence and scheduling requirements. And when I have downtime, I will use it to study for my finals—I've been getting my MBA at night at Baruch College. You will always be able to reach me, because I'll be sitting right here at this desk, "on call" for you.

110.

How many hours a week do you usually work, and why?

A. Honestly, I work pretty long hours most of the time. I would say that I put in a good ten to twenty hours of overtime a week, if you look at a typical work week as forty hours. With the extra time, I try to think of ways to "add value" to each assignment, both my own and the firm's. When our clients read our reports, I want them to think that no one else could have possibly written them, except for our company. In a way, each report that we create is also an "advertisement" for our firm. So we have to make absolutely certain that it's brilliant.

EXTRA CREDIT Bring one of the reports with you and show it to your interviewer, as long as you're not breaking client confidentiality. Alternatively, offer to take one of the company's old reports and rewrite it to show the "value" that you would add to it.

Why the Worst Insult You Can Get from a Date Is the Biggest Compliment You Can Get from an Interviewer

If a date ever tells you that you have a great personality, it's probably "code" for the fact that you don't measure up to his physical type in some way (you're a breathtaking brunette, say, instead of a blonde bombshell). However, if an interviewer thinks that you have a great personality, you are three-fourths of the way towards landing the job.

111.

Does a company need B players? Or is it better off only having A players on staff, and why?

A. I've actually thought about this a lot, Morris, and I believe that a company really needs to have both A and B players. When you're pitching new business, you want the A players on the front line. They're the people who have the star power. Clients have often heard of the A players. These people have fantastic reputations, and there's a certain celebrity status to having them run the meetings and make the pitches. But behind the A players, you also need a team of B players who can hammer out the details of the projects and stick with them on a day-to-day basis. Having too many A players on a team leads to ego clashes and a disorganized, anarchical way of doing business. On the other hand, having too many B players leads to work that is humdrum, and lacks the spark of creativity. So the perfect blend, in my opinion, is to have teams comprised of one or two A players and four or five B players to see the assignments through.

Are You Executive Material?

There are thousands of articles about dressing for success. And indeed, this is important on a job interview. But being mentally prepared for success is even more critical. Demonstrate that you're "executive material" by being a cut above your competitors when it comes to finessing your answers to difficult questions. Balance smart management ideas (such as having fewer meetings) with diplomacy, tact, and a genuine appreciation for your former employers.

Inside Information

A players can be either type A personalities or type B. So can B players. If you're going to walk the walk, you need to talk the talk. Know your lingo.

112.

Tell me about the last time you made a major change. Why did you do it? How did it work out?

A. I used to feel shy in front of large groups of people, and public speaking was totally terrifying for me. I would actually have a small anxiety attack right before I would begin talking. And my nervousness was very obvious to people in the audience. For years I wanted to fix the problem, but classes are expensive, and so I kept putting off taking one of them. Then one day, several of my close friends asked me what I wanted for my birthday. So I asked them to pitch in on a public speaking course at the Dale Carnegie Institute. It was phenomenal, and by the end of the seminar, I felt a lot more comfortable giving speeches. Since then, I've joined Toastmasters, where I get all the practice that I need. And now that I've overcome my fear, I actually look forward to giving these talks.

Why This Technique Works

1. You took the steps you needed to become a charismatic speaker. Not only does this make you a more skilled employee, but it also saves the company money on any training that they would need to give you.

2. Since you were willing to invest in yourself, you come across as a valuable person to have on staff.

How to Erase a Mistake from the Past
1. Confess to the mistake.
2. Show how you fixed it to turn the situation around.

113. What were the least enjoyable aspects of your last job?

A. I really loved my last job, and basically only have positive things to say about the experience. If I could have changed one thing, though, I think I would have had shorter group meetings. There was one boss on staff who really liked to mull over everyone's projects for hours and hours and hours. While he did so, twenty people would be forced to sit in the room, listening to the minutiae of everyone else's assignments.

I think that group meetings are great for morale, and it is kind of interesting to hear what everyone is working on. But had I been running the show, I would have made the group meeting a forum where members of the team gave a five-minute top line of where they were at on their projects. Then I would have had my staff make individual appointments with me to comb through the details of each assignment.

Questions That Test Your Political Prowess

Every company has its fair (or unfair) share of internal politics. Whether you're a "people person" or a loner, your ability to map out the political landscape of a company, complete with its peaks, troughs, and hidden minefields, is as important to your success as any task-related talents that you possess. Did you take a bullet or successfully dodge one? Can you wrestle a room filled with piranhas? See the Q&A's that follow.

114.

Please give an example of the most difficult political situation that you've dealt with on a job.

A. I was hired by a woman who, unbeknownst to me at the time, was on her way out. She had irked several of the top managers in the company, and asked me to be her "fall guy" on a number of assignments. I always completed my projects on time and to her satisfaction. But when the day would come around to deliver the work to others in the company, my boss would pull me into her office, close the door, and command me to hold the work back—for several more days. Of course, the managers would then call me to ask where the work was. Eventually, I just learned to drop the assignment off with my boss on the day that it was really due. And then, when the managers would ring me up, I would recommend that they simply follow up with her. This kept me out of hot water with my boss and with them.

Why This Technique Works

1. Your boss was on a crash collision course with the other managers in the firm. You smartly recognized that this was "her problem," and it didn't need to become yours.

2. You stayed focused on the work. Even in a political tempest, you can be relied upon to come through.

115.
How aware are you of internal politics that may affect your performance?

A. Let's put it this way: I'm sensitive to internal politics, and respect authority figures. But I also do my best to never become embroiled in office politics. At my level, I consider this to be a wise course of action. I like people, and can pretty much work with anyone. So I concentrate on doing my job, listening to directions, surpassing expectations, and leaving the internal political battles to the politicians.

Why This Technique Works

1. You know enough about office politics to stay out of them, which happens to be an extremely politic move.

2. Hence, there's nothing distracting you from doing a superb job.

116.
Tell me about a "bad call" you made in dealing with people.

A. To get a group's consensus can be somewhat challenging at times. I think it's critical to let everyone in the group take ownership of the project and get their buy in, or else you will find little support for your work. It took me awhile to recognize this truth about human behavior. In the job that I had four years ago, I made the mistake of thinking that, after the initial meeting, the direction was set and I could go off by myself and just complete my tasks. It turned out that one of the people on the review board was furious that I didn't call more meetings just to let everyone know about my progress. However, once I discovered that she felt this way, I met with her privately, told her where I was on the project, listened to her suggestions, and dramatically retooled the plan. She gave it her support, and it ended up getting approved.

117.

Tell me about a time when you tried to help someone else change. What strategy did you use? How did it turn out?

A. There was a man that I used to work with in the past who was hired in a leadership position at my new company. Before he started, he was counseled by several people in the firm to be "very tough on the staff." The pervasive feeling was that many of the staff members had become complacent and needed to be "whipped into shape"—and it was his job to do it.

I thought that he might have misinterpreted the directive somewhat, however, because after a couple of months, everyone was gossiping about how mean-spirited he seemed. One day he took me out to lunch and asked me how I thought he was doing. "Well, Kurt, I think that you've certainly shaken things up around here, which I know was what you were told to do," I said. "But personally, I would take it down a notch. Everyone now knows that you can be relentless. I think I would try softening it with a little empathy." He disagreed with my assessment, and continued to "ride hard" on the employees. A few months later, he ended up losing his job.

The Situational Interview: A Cross Between Acting Class and Reality

You arrive at your interview dressed to the nines and thoroughly prepared to face any curveball that can be thrown at you. You've studied the company thoroughly. You've gotten the lowdown from friends of yours who work there. You're ready for any type of interview—traditional, behavioral, even a logic brain tease. But instead, your interviewer asks you to pick up the phone and handle an irate customer who's screaming about an account discrepancy.

While you attempt to talk the customer down off the ledge, your interviewer watches your reactions like a hawk. Are you sweating or taking in the situation serenely? How are you processing the information? Are you making the customer a promise that you can't keep, or is your commitment to follow through realistic?

In general, when you are confronted with the situational interview, it's best to acknowledge "the company's error" with clients. Remain courteous. Try to be genuinely helpful. And above all, don't get miffed. This type of interview is testing your mettle under fire. So strive to be as relaxed and cooperative as possible.

Questions That Ask You to Take Off Your "Work Mask"

Some interviewers really want to know what you're like outside of a work context. Why? The plain fact is, you will spend more time at the office than you will with your spouse or significant other. By probing about what you're really like, your interviewer is trying to figure out if his staff will enjoy being around you for eight, nine, or even ten hours a day. When you are asked to reveal the "real you," the most important thing is to come off as likeable.

118.

How would you describe your sense of humor?

A. Well, I'm definitely not a stand-up comedian, but I do have a wry, witty side—which I've found to be very helpful when clients are acting ultra-demanding. Last year, all of our secretaries fell ill on the same day. One of our clients was very unhappy about it, because she thought that her clerical changes to a document weren't going to get made. I offered to "demote myself" for the day and make the changes myself. The client got a real kick out of my offer, and kept calling me up throughout the afternoon to find out how I was enjoying my "new career."

Why This Technique Works

1. It's hard to convince someone that you have a sense of humor via clear, rational arguments. Still, you pointed to a time when your wit actually helped to defuse two problems: the lack of manpower at your company and your client's mounting frustration.

2. Your client thought it was humorous that you were willing to be a secretary for a day. On a scale of 1 to 10, give yourself 11 brownie points.

119.

Do you have any commitments outside the office that might whisk you away when I need you the most?

A. My most important commitment will be to do a superb job for you. And I will happily let my other commitments slide whenever I still have work to get off my desk. But to answer your question, I am involved in my neighborhood community watch, which I enjoy because it keeps the area safe. It also gives me the chance to meet my neighbors. As you know, this isn't always easy to do in a big city like ours.

Why This Technique Works

1. Most managers prefer an employee who "has a life," as long as his life outside of the office doesn't make him unavailable for overtime on the nights that he really needs to stick around.

2. You were asked about multiple commitments, yet you wisely chose to discuss just one.

120a.

Please tell me about a time when you were in a new situation and were unsure of yourself.

A. Would you like me to describe a work situation or a personal one?

120b.

Let's start with a work situation.

A. I used to work for a professional fundraising firm. We would be hired to raise money for different charities and schools throughout the United States. I had a fantastic track record with fundraising for schools; in fact, my numbers were better than everyone else's. Then one day I was asked to raise money for a religious organization in New Mexico. I was a bit concerned that the tactics I had refined wouldn't work as well when it came to raising money for a religious entity. I worried that I might come off as too aggressive, or alternatively, too secular. However, these worries turned out to be unfounded. I just tackled the assignment with my normal enthusiasm, and generated $1.3 million of capital campaign contributions.

Why This Technique Works

1. Your interviewer's question wasn't clear. You asked him if he was inquiring about your work history or your personal life. Clarifying a question is often a good idea.

2. Your work story was interesting and had a positive outcome. Your personal story was the type that you should reveal (if asked), because it leads to your strengths: persistence and not panicking under pressure.

121. Okay, now tell me about a time when you were in a personal situation that made you feel insecure.

A. I was swimming in the ocean one day, and had gone pretty far away from the shore. Suddenly, I found myself in sort of a whirlpool, which I could not swim my way out of. I actually wondered if I might drown, which is scary because I'm a strong swimmer. Just as I was beginning to panic, however, I remembered that a friend of mine had always told me to, "swim parallel to the shore whenever you feel like you're being pulled out to sea." I followed his advice, and got back safely.

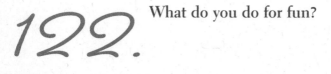

What do you do for fun?

A. I go swing dancing. There are a lot of terrific swing clubs where you can learn new steps and find other people who enjoy the genre.

Alt. A. I go to art film festivals. I particularly enjoy the ones where you have a chance to hear the director speak about his process.

EXTRA CREDIT   You can say that you do anything for fun, but make sure that it 1) sounds like it really is fun, and 2) is a more unusual hobby than tennis, golf, or lifting weights at the gym.

Questions Freud Would Approve Of

Tell your superego, ego, and id to be on the alert. Some of these questions are straight out of the psychoanalyst's lexicon. Nevertheless, they're being asked in the executive suite with increasing frequency. The good news is, the same answers that would have impressed Freud also will persuade nine out of ten interviewers to think very seriously about hiring you.

Another Way of Piercing the Corporate Veil: Background Checks

In an effort to prevent hiring mistakes, a lot of companies contract with outside firms to conduct background checks on the applicants being considered. Here are some of the things that these employment-screening services may investigate about you.

1. Employment verification

2. Education verification

3. Criminal records

4. Social security trace

5. Basic references

6. Comprehensive references

7. Credit history

8. Motor vehicles record

If you are concerned about what an extensive background check on you might reveal, the best thing to do is to hire a firm to conduct a background check on you *before* your interview. Find out what facts the firm will uncover, and, if necessary, counter them in your interview.

123.

What do you daydream about?

A. I dream about making a difference. I want others to take some of the ideas that we've discussed in my career consulting practice and use them to better their own careers. I'm happiest when a client of mine calls to tell me that I really helped him succeed in some way that he never thought was possible.

EXTRA CREDIT

Avoid the classic flub to the daydream question: "I don't daydream about anything...daydreaming isn't productive."
FACT: Professional athletes fantasize about their own success constantly. And studies show that daydreaming about your success can help it become a reality. So don't automatically dismiss the "What do you daydream about?" question. Tell your interviewer that you fantasize often about your career aspirations, and let her in on what your dreams are.

124.

If you could be doing anything you wanted to be doing right now, what would it be?

A. Celebrating with my friends after getting this job offer. I would make a reservation at a posh restaurant, and treat my four closest buddies to a tremendous feast. Let's talk more about my next steps, so that, hopefully, I can make that reservation next week.

125.

What are some of your pet peeves?

A. False deadlines. I know that a lot of people in our field can sometimes be irresponsible about delivery dates, which is probably why the false deadline was invented. Yet I find it somewhat unfair to jump through hoops on a project, only to discover that the real deadline isn't until three days later. But don't worry. If your managers ever give me false deadlines, I know that I will be able to deal with them, because I've had to so many times before. Of course, if you give me the real deadline, I promise that I'll come through for you.

Why This Technique Works

1. Your interviewer asked you an open-ended question that could have easily derailed you from the main task, which is winning this job.

2. Instead of getting sidetracked, you politely steered the conversation back on track.

126.

Given a completely blank slate, what would you do to fulfill our company's vision?

A. First, I would invite the top managers and salespeople in the company to a two-day retreat. The purpose of the retreat would be to arrive at a mission statement for the company, and boil it down to two or three sentences. I would distribute this document to every single person on staff. A couple of weeks later, I would invite certain top performers from each department

How to Polish Your Personality Skills for Any Job

Whether you are asked to fill out a written personality test, answer oral questions about your personality, or handle a situational interview that puts your interpersonal skills on trial, you should anticipate that your personality will be tested. Here's an exercise that will help you rise above your competitors.

Pick five adjectives that you believe capture your ideal "work persona." You might start with two adjectives that you would use to describe yourself to a close friend or a date, for example:

1. Intelligent

2. Perceptive

Then, fill out your list with three other adjectives that you feel will help you do a great job in your line of work, such as:

3. Industrious

4. Empathetic

5. Creative

Answer any personality tests that you are given in way that proves you possess your five ideal traits. If you choose five traits that really describe you, and these traits are in heavy demand for the job that you're seeking, chances are excellent that your interviewer will think that you're the perfect person for the job.

to another two-day retreat. The purpose would be for them to each critique how well their own department was living up to the mission, and to identify action steps and improvements that could be made in the departments that were falling short. I would give each of these departments two months to make these corrections. After that, I would organize a task force to redo the company's website, posting the mission there as our message to the outside world of what we stand for. The whole point would be to communicate our mission statement to every single employee on staff, so that they could have it on the top of their minds throughout the day.

EXTRA CREDIT

Your answer was appropriate, if, in fact, the company actually believes in corporate mission statements. Research the organization to find out if they do. If it turns out that they are jaded on the whole "mission statement" idea, don't pull a Jerry McGuire on them. Instead, tell them that you would sit down with several of the top managers to identify the issues that are holding back the company. Is there a problem department? Are the ten-year-old computers always crashing? Is there an unreliable vendor the company uses? Once you've discovered the problems that are riddling the company, you would then outline a method to fix them within a reasonable time frame.

127.

You really don't have to be smart to do this job.

A. Well, I am smart, and therefore, will take the job to a whole different level. I am sure that you're right in a way...I mean how brilliant do you

Avoid Subtracting Points from Your Personality during Interviews

1. **Be the best-rested interviewee.** Fact: people are more articulate, happier, and look healthier after a good night's sleep. Arrive feeling well rested and sharp, and determined to make a superb first impression.

2. **Be a gracious "guest."** If your interviewer is late to your appointment, shrug it off with good humor. If the phone rings constantly and he keeps picking it up, smile graciously, and don't let it rattle you. If people unceremoniously barge in and interrupt the meeting, laugh it off. Whatever you do, don't keep glancing nervously at your watch. Interviewers easily detect signs of irritation and boredom, so don't get irritated or bored!

3. **Give it your personal best.** You know that you're the best candidate for that particular job. Prove it to your interviewer by strenuously avoiding canned answers and lame, generic, forgot-to-do-your-homework questions.

4. **Recognize that every interviewer has her own style (and it may not conform to yours).** Is your interviewer asking you too many questions? Not enough questions? Questions that are weird and out there? Don't try to dominate the interview. Meld your style to your interviewer's style.

5. **Embrace the middle.** Are you in a creative field where the daily dress code is "anything goes"? Dress more conservatively than you would if you were already working there. Are you in a conservative business where people wear three-piece suits to the office? Wear the uniform, but choose one item, perhaps a tie or a belt, that expresses your personality. Don't show up in clothing that makes you look invisible, but also take care not to look too funky for the job in question.

6. **Empathize, don't criticize.** Everyone hates to be criticized. So, if you're asked your opinion about a mediocre piece of work that the company created, or even how you like the new orange and purple lobby, tone down your criticism. If you can't bring yourself to say that you like it, tell your interviewer that it's thought-provoking.

7. **Be there.** Resolve to be fully present and pay close attention to what your interviewer is saying. You really never get a second chance to make a first impression, so do your best to make a positive, indelible impression the first time around.

have to be to run Xerox copies, set up conference room times, and coordinate people's hectic schedules? Still, I would have the satisfaction that comes from doing a job really well. I think that the people around here would be delighted to have a bright, enterprising young person on staff who would give it her all, instead of someone who was just going through the motions.

 How are you different from other candidates applying for this job?

A. There is no one in the world who wants this job as much as I do. I have been following your company for the past ten years in the trades, and have applied here three times. During the past two years, I have kept in touch with you and Sheila Kelsey religiously. But even though I feel like I'm pretty familiar with your corporate culture and your company's initiatives, I still have a couple of questions that I'd love to ask you. How is the XYZ launch going, and is there anything I can do to make it more successful?

EXTRA CREDIT Do not allow anyone to chip away at your self-esteem, or put you in a position where you feel like you need to defend your best attributes. Remind yourself that you are smart, capable, competent, and a great "catch" for any company. These qualities will make you a better, more talented employee at any rung of the corporate ladder.

That's a Wrap

1. Even if your interviewer tries to downplay its significance, remember that the written personality test is not just a formality. To practice for it, download some personality tests from the Internet, including the "MBTI" test from Myers-Briggs.

2. Personality tests are frequently oral. And there are plenty of them popping up in the executive suite. Sometimes, an in-house psychologist will deliberately try to unnerve candidates. Other times, applicants might be mercilessly tossed into a simulated pressure-cooker situation. For example, they might be asked to field a phone call from an irate client. When you find yourself in these trying situations, remember that your ability to handle stress is the key thing that's being tested. The easiest way to pass the "stress test"? Don't become unraveled.

3. Are you a diplomat or a political lightweight? If you are asked how you deal with internal politics, it's often best to take a nonpolitical stance. If that's woefully inaccurate, try to demonstrate how you rose to the occasion and gracefully dodged a bullet.

4. Matchmaking is part of the interviewer's job. If you are asked to take off your "work mask" and reveal the real you, don't hold back. Especially in companies where overtime is a way of life, interviewers often want to try to figure out how the rest of the staff will feel about spending their days and nights with you.

5. Everyone's an amateur shrink, interviewers included. So don't be psychology-phobic. If you are asked a psychological question, answer it with verve and gusto, and relate your response to business.

CHAPTER 6

None of Your Business (Or, Are You Really Allowed to Ask Me That?)

I f you have to ask if they're allowed to ask, they probably aren't. In the United States, it is illegal for an interviewer to ask an applicant's age, weight, religion, political views, ethnicity, sexual preference, financial status, or marital status (although if you wear a wedding ring, it's normally a good indication). Interviewers are also not allowed to inquire if you have kids, drink liquor, vote, or do charity work.

But just because they're not supposed to ask you certain questions doesn't always prevent them from doing so. (And if they do, saying "Hey, are you allowed to ask me that?" probably isn't going to earn you major brownie points.) Remember that you can always pass on the job later if you decide that the company seems too unprofessional for you.

There are five types of "none-of-your-business" questions:

1. *Questions about Your Marital/Significant Other Status.*
2. *Questions about Your Beliefs.*
3. *Questions about the Kids.*
4. *Questions about Your Ability to Deal with People Who Are Not Exactly Like You.*
5. *Sneaky Questions about Your Financial Lifestyle.*

Here's how to contend with those awkward, gee-I-thought-you-couldn't-ask-me-that questions. (Hint: having a sense of humor about your answer will take you a lot further than acting flabbergasted that your interviewer is breaking the law.)

Questions about Your Marital/Significant Other Status

At first glance, these questions seem harmless enough. After all, if you were at a cocktail party and met someone new, within five minutes that person might turn to you and nonchalantly ask if you were married. And probably, you wouldn't think twice about telling him.

In a job interview, however, this question is far from casual. Your interviewer may even have a secret agenda for asking it. For example, if you're a woman and the interviewer finds out that you're married, he might assume that he won't have to pay you quite as much as a single woman with your exact capabilities. One good tactic is to answer this question briefly, and then speedily move on to other questions that will identify whether you are a suitable match for the company.

129a.
Are you married?

A. Yes.

Alt. A. No.

129b.
Are you divorced?

A. Yes, and loving it.

Alt. A. No.

129c.
Do you have a girlfriend (or boyfriend)?

A. There are a lot of people whom I hang out with in my spare time. But there's no special person who will distract me from giving you my all. At this stage in my career, my job is my "first love." Can you tell me more about how your team is structured? Phoebe Jenners told me that there might be the perfect spot here for someone at my level.

129d.

Are you married? To a man, that is.

A. I have a partner whom I have been living with for several years.

Alt. A. No, I'm not.

EXTRA CREDIT

Queer Eye for the Straight Guy **is a runaway hit show, and everyone raves about it. Nevertheless, there is a lot of latent prejudice that's still in the closet at some firms. Unless you are 100 percent certain that the man who is asking you this question is also gay, keep your answer short and to the point. Legally, you are not obligated to answer this question. So why reveal more about your living arrangements than you have to?**

Questions about Your Beliefs

If you are applying for a job at a religious foundation, a question about your beliefs may not strike you as terribly out of line. But if you're looking for a position in a secular organization, there is no reason on earth (or in heaven) that you should have to discuss your views on religion, politics, or any other taboo topic. Still, screaming about your "legal rights" probably won't be conducive to landing a job. So, you have two choices. You can either distract your interviewer with charm (see the answer that follows), or try to figure out the real reason that he's asking you the question (assuming there is one), and assuage his concerns.

130.
Are you Protestant or Jewish?

A. Did you ever see that old *Mary Tyler Moore* episode? The one where Lou Grant asks Mary if she's Protestant? It was pretty funny. She asks Lou if he's allowed to ask her that, and so he immediately moves on to the next question. He asks her: "Are you single?" She answers: "Protestant."

Why This Technique Works

1. You've gently reminded your interviewer that questions about religion were frowned upon even way back when *The Mary Tyler Moore Show* first hit the airwaves.

2. But you've done so with humor, charm, and interviewing savvy. You go, girl. (Or boy.)

131.
Is it important to you to take off the Jewish holidays?

A. There are only three high holy days a year, and I've analyzed this at length—one of them almost always falls over a weekend. I promise you that I will get all of my work done in advance, so that on the two days that I need to take off, you won't even notice that I'm not here.

Alt A. It's not quite as important to me as it is to my Jewish mother. And I would never hear the end of it if I decided not to take them off. I already know that your company doesn't give them as paid holidays, but that's all right with me. I'll just use my three personal days, and the great thing is, I'll be the only employee here, I bet, who won't mind working on both Christmas Day and Easter.

132.

Are you a republican or a democrat, and why?

A. I read that your CEO helped mastermind our local republican's bid for City Council. I am a registered republican, and am pleased to report that I voted republican in the last election for that very city councilman.

Alt. A. I take each election on a case-by-case basis, and really think a lot about what each candidate has to offer. I'm a registered independent, and just wish that independents were allowed to vote in primaries in our state. Why do you ask? Does the chairman of this company take an active interest in local politics?

Alt. A. I am a registered democrat, but I don't always vote for the democratic ticket. In the past few elections, I was what you would call a "swing voter." I tend to study what each contender is promising, decide if he can deliver, and make my decision twenty-four hours before election day. I am curious about why you are asking me the question. Is there a political aspect to working at this firm? I read a lot about your company in the trades, and don't recall seeing anything alluding to lobbying efforts. Please tell me more, I'm totally fascinated.

An Open Mind Opens Doors

Chances are, you were taught to "never talk about politics at the dinner table." So it can feel bizarre to discuss them at the conference room table, especially if you don't happen to be towing the firm's "party line." But with the tact of a politician, you can usually overcome the awkwardness by simply professing to have an "open mind." The great thing about demonstrating that you're open-minded is that it usually encourages your interviewer to be equally open-minded about hiring you, whether you belong to the Republican, Democratic, Independent, or Green Party.

133.
What's your opinion about gay marriage?

A. Generally, I'm supportive of people being allowed to pursue their own lifestyles without a great deal of interference. I've been reading quite a lot about some of the gay marriages that have been taking place in this town, and realize that it might be a lightning-rod issue for some people. But I've always had a "live-and-let-live" attitude, and I've also been privileged to work with some gay couples rather closely in my practice.

Alt. A. I can work with anyone, as long as they're professional. I've managed a number of gay men over the years, and occasionally would be invited to meet their "spouses" over a quick drink after hours.

EXTRA CREDIT It's a fact. To work well with others, you need to be able to get along with them. So always strive to be open, friendly, and tolerant.

Questions about the Kids

In social situations, questions about the kids are the norm. Perhaps you live in the suburbs, belong to the PTA, and have a couple of children. Why wouldn't you talk about your kids? Married parents do it. Divorced parents do it. Every parent does it. But in a business environment, questions about the kids are almost always asked as a way to ferret out how "available" you will be to work overtime. Your answers need to be well crafted—long enough to cover the topic and appease your interviewer's concerns, but pithy and pointed enough to gently steer the conversation back to why you are the ideal candidate for the job at hand.

The One Time When Honesty Is Not Your Best Policy

Even if you are planning on having more kids, it might be a good idea to claim otherwise. Some employers still have painfully outdated notions about having women in the workplace. Think of it as a built-in genetic resistance to deserving members of the fairer sex. Tell one of these "good ol' boys" that you're planning on having more kids, and it's like rubbing salt in an old wound. Then, while you're waxing prolific on why you're the perfect candidate for the job, the only thing on his mind will be the six weeks of paid maternity leave that you might take three years down the road. Don't go there.

134. Do you have kids?

A. I tend to think of the projects that I'm working on as my children, so yes, at the moment, I have at least twelve. By the way, what are some of the projects that you have going on here? Perhaps you could tell me about some of the things that your wonderful team has been working on.

EXTRA CREDIT

You can always refer to your pet as a "kid" (e.g., "I have one beautiful child...would you like to see her picture?"—then pull out a photo of your gorgeous Siamese cat).

135.
Are you planning on having more children?

A. Nope. Two is more than enough!

Alt. A. I'd love to tell you the answer, but my husband and I haven't even found a minute to discuss it. So, at this rate, probably not!

136.
Who takes care of your kids during the day?

A. Sometimes my mother watches them, and when she's unavailable, there's a very reliable babysitter. I also drop off my kids once a week at the day-care center in my area. My kids are very well taken care of, which frees me up to concentrate on my work. Incidentally, I've been following your competitors with interest, and have a lot of questions to ask you and insights to share with you today.

EXTRA CREDIT Build on your momentum. Launch right into your list of questions, and start getting your interviewer back on track.

Make the First Two Minutes Count

Most interviewers make their hiring decisions in less than two minutes. They spend the other forty-three minutes of the interview rationalizing their initial decision. So the key thing is to say nothing during the meeting that will make your interviewer revise his first impression of you (assuming it was positive). This is the real reason that you don't need to "sweat the details" over some question that should never have been asked in the first place. Just say something that's polite, ingratiating, or even clever. And your interviewer's initial reaction to you will be positively confirmed.

137. I know that you're a single mom with two kids. What time would you need to leave here at night, because we tend to work pretty late?

A. There is no set time. I am determined to stay as late as it takes to get the work off my desk. At this point, my kids are old enough to take care of themselves, and they have adjusted nicely to the "latchkey" lifestyle. My job is to make absolutely certain that, when the time comes around, I can afford to send them to college. So don't worry about my feeling "distracted" by the kids. I promise that I will be yours, every night, night after night, for as long as you need me to stick around. Can you tell me more about some of the projects that you have on your plate right now?

4 Surefire Ways to Handle the Prickliest, Most Personal Questions

Like prickly pears, personal questions need to be handled delicately. Depending on your unique style, you can address them in the following ways:

1. Politely state that you don't think the question is job related.

2. Just answer the personal question honestly, because you don't have a huge problem with it. But keep your reply brief.

3. Answer the question noncommittally, and try to redirect your interviewer back to asking you business questions.

4. Answer the question with some flair, so that hopefully your interviewer will realize that he had no business asking it. This technique may encourage him to redirect the conversation on his own initiative.

With some practice, you will be able to figure out which method will work best for both you and your interviewer.

138. **Are you planning on getting pregnant in the next two years?**

A. No. My "biological clock" hasn't even begun to tick! But speaking of clocks, I know that you had an interest in keeping our meeting to exactly forty-five minutes. Can you tell me more about how your company has started to target teenagers? I read several articles about your efforts in the *Wall Street Journal,* and would love to hear more about the inroads you've been making in this tough-to-crack market.

Alt. A. No, no, no. Next question?

The Gifted Conversationalist

In some ways, an interview is just a lively discussion. You and your interviewer will exchange facts, share ideas, and hopefully come to a meeting of the minds. Some of the time you will be listening. Some of the time you will be talking. And some of the time you and your interviewer will pause, simply to absorb and focus on what the other person has said. Here are five rules that will help make your conversations with interviewers more engaging and productive.

1. **Recognize that your interviewer is in the driver's seat, but that sometimes you have to take the wheel.** Generally, your interviewer will steer the conversation by asking you the majority of the questions. Still, if these questions are either illegal or uncomfortable for you to answer, it's your mission to gently navigate back to questions that will help you demonstrate your job suitability.

2. **Know your "material" well enough to be spontaneous.** Brush up on the company's mission, your past work history, and your strengths so thoroughly that you can improvise on the spot. The most successful interviews are those where you leave feeling like you conveyed everything that you had planned, but also had a surprisingly interesting conversation about something that you never anticipated.

3. **Look for commonalities.** Is there an intriguing piece of art hanging on your interviewer's wall? Inquire about it (if you know something about art). Or perhaps there's a book lying around her office that you've read. If so, mention it.

    Don't pepper her with questions that are off the beaten track. But if some artifact in her office coordinates with an interest of yours, bring up the topic. (If she doesn't respond, drop it, and concentrate on proving that you are smart, reliable, and above all, talented at solving problems.)

4. **Show appreciation.** Did your interviewer make a funny joke? Laugh heartily. Did she identify an area of the company that might be open to a person of your skills? Thank her profusely.

5. **Get your chitchat down pat.** At the beginning of an interview, and frequently at the end as well, there may be several minutes of chit-chat. When you arrive, your interviewer may say something to break the ice, such as "I'm happy that you found the place." Smile, and toss a little chitchat right back at him. "Yes, your directions were absolutely perfect. You have no idea how unusual that is. Thank you." This will put him at ease, which will make for a more pleasant interview. At the end of your meeting, there may also be some idle banter. Always be polite, but make certain that this closing chitchat doesn't distract your interviewer from your next steps.

139. Do you trust your nanny to take care of the kids after dark?

A. Oh, yes, of course. I wouldn't let anyone into my home that I didn't trust around the kids, day or night. Let me try to take a small leap here, Stewart, and answer the question that I think you're really asking. My childcare needs are completely covered, and I promise that I will be free to focus on the work that you give me, without constant phone calls home to check up on the kids.

140.

How do you and your ex-husband work out seeing the kids? What's your arrangement?

A. They live with me, but my husband gets to see them whenever he wishes. In a way, this is the ideal arrangement, because it also means that they can stay with him anytime that I need to stay late at the office. So you shouldn't think twice about giving me substantial assignments that I can really sink my teeth into. The truth is, I've got much more time available since the divorce than I ever had before. But in my life anyway, my job has always come first.

Help Your Interviewer Become Better at His Job

Hopefully, you will never be asked even one of the questions in this chapter. They are all illegal, but research shows that they continue to surface anyway. If your interviewer asks you something that is patently none of his business, recognize that it's not necessarily because he is trying to trip you up. He might just be overly curious and a bit naïve. When you accept people's essential humanity, it really helps them like you more. So instead of feeling defensive about answering a certain question, resolve to help your interviewer become a better interviewer by gingerly leading him to the correct interviewing path.

Questions about Your Ability to Deal with People Who Are Not Exactly Like You

By law, companies are not allowed to discriminate based on gender, creed, nationality, or color. (See chapter 3.) The anti-discrimination laws have helped many companies become more racially diverse, and today's corporations are no longer the all-white-male bastions that they once were. When an interviewer inquires about your ability to deal with people who are not exactly like you, he's really asking if *you're* prejudiced. The answer is a resounding no. And if you can prove that you enjoy working with anyone of *any* nationality or background, this issue will disappear.

141. How do you feel about people from minority groups?

A. I feel great about working with all different kinds of people. I grew up in a mixed area in a small city, and I consider myself privileged to have lots of friends of all different nationalities.

Alt. A. I live in Queens, where, at last count, there were over two hundred and fifty different nationalities of people cohabiting in just a few square miles. In the great melting pot that is America, Queens is one of the most racially diverse areas in the entire country. I am completely, 1000 percent, comfortable working with anyone, male or female, of any nationality.

142.

What is your feeling about homosexuals in business?

A. Well, as a woman, I confess that I love working with gay men. They've always been very supportive of my career ambitions. There's no wall whatsoever between us. I've considered myself very lucky, in fact, that several of my ex-teammates happened to be gay.

EXTRA CREDIT Mention a lesbian boss or colleague with whom you worked in the past. The gist of your answer should be that the woman's reputation for being a lesbian had no impact on your working relationship with her.

143.

Have you ever been in the military?

A. No. But it's funny…a lot of people have asked me that, maybe because of my crew cut. The truth is: I've always worked in the civilian world. I brought my resume with me to discuss today. (Pull it out.) As you can see, I have a lot of experience in firms that are very similar to this one.

Sneaky Questions about Your Financial Lifestyle

In the United States, there is a bias against hiring people who "really don't need the job." And unfortunately, this bias sometimes hurts women in two-income households. By law, people in equal positions are supposed to earn the same salaries. But the fact remains that today women are still earning

70 cents to the dollar as men for similar jobs. This salary discrepancy is well documented, which is why, if you are a married woman, some interviewers may automatically assume that your husband is the "primary breadwinner," and that your salary is incidental. Yes, this is frequently untrue, not to mention totally unfair. Still, in the interviewing game, perception often becomes reality. So why give anyone the perception that you don't need the money?

144. Do you intend to send your kids to private school?

A. I doubt it. The Westchester public school system is great, and my kids have acclimated to it nicely.

Alt. A. They're in private school. Believe me, I would love to send them to public school, but as you know, the public schools around here can be dangerous. So, until I find a good public school that's safe, private school it is.

Inside Information

You always want to come off as someone who needs the job. This is easy to do if your kids are in public school. However, if your kids are in private school, it makes sense to position the reason as "needs-based." If the public schools in your area are dangerous, sending your kids to private school becomes a necessity rather than a luxury.

FACT: Most people in the executive suite frown on those who are "to the manor born." So if you do happen to come from a long line of bluebloods, never mention it. Or your interviewer will cross you off "the short list" faster than you can say: "Hey, wait a minute! I'm not really an aristocrat."

145.

Who chauffeurs the kids to soccer practice?

A. There's an army of people who take care of the kids on a daily basis. The neighbors and babysitters show up with a military precision that's admirable. Everything works like clockwork so that I can be completely available for my work.

146.

Does your spouse work? What does he do?

A. Yes, he works. Fortunately for both of us, he's in a completely different field from ours. So there is no intra-marriage rivalry between us. And it's kind of nice after a long day at the office to get home and hear about someone else's job. But let's get back to talking about the position that's open here. Do you have any questions for me about my past experience? Is there anything more that I can tell you to demonstrate that I am your ideal candidate?

EXTRA CREDIT

If your husband works in job that's considered lucrative, this question can be an especially trying. Resist the urge to tell an interviewer that your husband is an "investment banker," "real estate developer," or "venture capitalist," even if he doesn't happen to be a wealthy one.

147.

Who's the primary breadwinner in your house-hold? '

A. We both do our best to pitch in equally.

Why This Technique Works

1. You've answered the question without giving up any additional information that could make your interviewer think that you don't need the job.

2. Your answer is so short and noncommittal that it should encourage your interviewer to move on to more appropriate questions.

148.

When your husband lost his job, how did that affect things on the home front?

A. Well, it was a little weird, because he was suddenly home for the entire day, and probably felt bored. The minute I would walk in the door, he would start asking me all kinds of questions about my sales calls... something that he had never done before! But I appreciated having him around, and his "sabbatical" turned out to be a good thing. He had the opportunity to find himself and discovered that he really wanted to get back to teaching English, while I kept plugging away at my job.

149.
Brenda told me that you and Stanford got divorced last year. Is that why you're looking for a job now?

A. No, Paul. The divorce was in the works for a long time, and went surprisingly smoothly. But I never was what you'd call a "Stepford wife." I believe that it's important for women to continue to work, no matter what their husbands are doing. And the fact that I now live alone will make me work even harder than I ever did in the past, if that's even possible. I brought some case studies to show you today. Would this be a good time to share them with you?

EXTRA CREDIT

Have a dress rehearsal with yourself. If you have case studies, make sure that you have thoroughly practiced your presentation a couple of times before you walk into your very first interview.

150.
You live in a one-bedroom apartment. How much does it cost?

A. It's a rental, and fortunately, I started living there a long time ago, so it's actually pretty affordable.

The most important thing to remember is that your interviewer will have no way of actually knowing if the number that you reveal is accurate. You must appear to need the job, so even if you are paying 50 percent of your after-tax salary towards your rent (not uncommon in Manhattan) you may want to fib just a little bit, scaling the number back to what you were paying three years ago. See the answer that follows:

EXTRA **CREDIT** **Your answer is appropriate if you are applying for a job anywhere in the United States, except Manhattan. But unfortunately, for whatever reason, in Manhattan people gossip endlessly about the actual price of their apartments. For out-of-towners, this may seem jarring at first. Still, when in New York, do as the New Yorkers do...**

Alt. A. (for Manhattanites only). It's a rental, and I have been paying a whopping $2,000 a month for the privilege of living in a miniscule, quote unquote "one bedroom" that's really a glorified studio apartment. It's a walk-up, and I live on the fifth floor. So the good news is: I save a lot of money by not going to a gym, because I get tons of exercise each day running up and down the stairs.

151. How old are you?

A. You know, I never tell anyone my age. But if you really want to find out, just take another peek at my resume, and skip down to the year that I graduated from college. I hope that the fact that I'm a tiny bit older than the last person who held this position won't impact your hiring decision. Because in those X years, I really got a tremendous amount of experience under my belt. I'm a lot more mature about deadlines, servicing clients, and dealing with pressure than anyone could be who's right out of school. But at the same time, I'm enthusiastic and very "young" at heart.

Alt. A. Old enough to have the experience and "street smarts" to do the job that is required, but young enough to learn everything you have to teach me, and to enjoy working for you for years to come.

Inside Information

Just because a potential employer asks you something doesn't mean you have to answer the question. But be playful and light about it so that you don't offend the interviewer or come off as a hotheaded troublemaker.

152. Are you sensitive about your weight?

A. Nope. I come from a long line of size-16 women; so actually, I'm considered "the thin one" in my family. I also grew up in a small town, where almost no one was a standard size 8. I think everyone had to carry an extra thirty pounds on them just to survive those frigid Minnesota winters. I hope that my weight won't weigh on your mind too much when it comes to considering me for this position.

Alt. A. Wow! I don't want to "get heavy" with you, but that's the first time I've ever been asked that on a job interview! Hopefully, my weight won't prevent you from seriously considering me for this job.

How to Address Particularly Insensitive Questions

You may not have a problem answering the real question that your interviewer is asking. And if you don't, there's no reason to be coy and cute with your reply. Just answer the question directly. But if you really don't wish to answer a question—either because it's illegal or because you feel that your answer may hurt your chances of being offered the job—it's perfectly acceptable to politely remind your interviewer that, in your opinion, your answer should not be used as a criterion for making the decision.

153. Did you come from a poor background? And how will you feel about working closely with several people who are listed on the *Forbes* 400?

A. Yes, I grew up in rural Arkansas, where my parents struggled to make ends meet. But I have never had a problem working with people who are from the privileged upper classes. In my last job at a magazine, many of my colleagues came from unbelievably wealthy backgrounds, and their parents continued to "support" them by buying gorgeous designer clothing for them that they could have never afforded on their meager "associate editor" salaries. Fortunately, I have never been jealous of people who are richer than me. In fact, their lifestyles intrigue me. Who are some of the people that I would be working with here?

Alt. A. Would you mind terribly if we circled back to that question after we've talked some more about my qualifications for the job? I've had a tremendous amount of experience in dealing with people from privileged backgrounds, as you'll see when I tell you about my last three positions.

When All Else Fails:
The Hail Mary Move of the Executive Suite

Let's suppose that this is the job of your dreams. You've studied the company religiously. You walk into your interview, and after a few short minutes, realize that you and your interviewer are not hitting it off. Perhaps she asked you a blatantly insensitive question and you felt antagonized by it. Or maybe she threw a couple of illegal questions at you, and you became unraveled by them. What do you do if you still want the job?

You pull the Hail Mary move. Wait! Do you mean, like they do in football? Yes, and just like in football, a certain percentage of the time, the Hail Mary move actually works.

The Hail Mary move of the executive suite is when you stop the interview, acknowledge that it isn't going as smoothly as you had hoped, and ask the interviewer to start over again. Here's how to accomplish this miraculous feat:

1. Wait until you are absolutely certain that you need to pull the move. This is important, because the first few minutes of an interview are frequently awkward. Try to gently redirect the conversation, using humor, playfulness, or a brilliant segue. However, if you tried (and failed) a couple of times to steer the conversation back on track, realize that you are going to need to do something dramatic to have a shot at the job.

2. Make a "time out" signal to your interviewer. (Put your right hand up vertically in front of your nose and "cross it" with your left hand to form a "T.")

This gesture will probably cause your interviewer to stop talking, mid-sentence, in surprise.

3. Say something along these lines: "Lucy, as you know, I really want to work at your company. At the same time, I do not feel like this interview is going as well as I had hoped. I have so many strengths that I believe would make me the perfect candidate for this position. And yet, I also feel as if I've haven't had the chance to discuss them. Would it be okay with you if we took a little time out right now, for me to tell you why I believe that I belong here?" Chances are, she will say "okay," and then you should pitch your selling points as if you never had to call the time out. If she won't let you redirect the conversation, politely ask her if you might reschedule your interview with her for another day so that you can have a second chance to "put your best foot forward."

4. While it might be tempting, never ask your interviewer if there is someone else at the company with whom you could meet.

5. In any follow up communications with your interviewer, just act as if the Hail Mary move never happened, and continue to "sell" your interviewer on your strengths.

That's a Wrap

1. If you are asked about your marital status, answer the question honestly, but succinctly. Recognize that your response could hurt you from a financial standpoint. If you are a married woman, the less you say about your husband's earning potential, the better.

2. Is an interviewer curious about your religious or political beliefs? A particularly charming answer might help to distract him. Alternatively, you can try to figure out if there is a legitimate reason why your interviewer needs this information, and then try to answer his real question.

3. Any questions about kids, plans to have more children, or childcare arrangements are generally asked to weed out candidates whom interviewers feel are "overcommitted" on the home front. Gently disabuse your interviewer of this notion.

4. There are plenty of laws prohibiting employers from discriminatory hiring practices. So don't be surprised if someone obliquely asks you if you're prejudiced. It's not enough to simply claim that you're not. Prove that you're not—by referring to specific examples from either your work or personal background.

5. People don't like to hire people who don't need jobs to survive. So take care to always come across as someone who could use the salary. In the executive suite, nothing is a bigger turnoff than trust-fund babies and spoiled rich kids. If you are a married woman, some interviewers may conclude that you really don't need the job. Take great pains to convince them otherwise.

CHAPTER 7

Good Cop/Bad Cop Routines in the Interviewing Game

Over the past several years, large numbers of middle managers have been cut in company after company. This sometimes leads to an "hourglass" situation: a lot of people at the bottom, a lot of people at the top, and very few managing anything—or anyone—in between. As a result, many times, one middle manager will have two bosses to whom he reports—both of them at the exact same level. In these situations, it is fairly commonplace for one of the bosses to adopt the role of "good cop" while the other boss acts as "bad cop" in the organization. The good cop delivers good news, morale-boosting pats on the back, and juicy, plum assignments to the staff, while the bad cop has more of a financial role, holding back on raises and promotions for all but the most deserving.

Interviewing at companies that are structured in this way poses a special challenge, because more often than not, the good cop and bad cop interview candidates together. Both cops will be in the room asking you questions at the same time, which can be off-putting.

There are five types of "Good Cop/Bad Cop" questions:

1. *Your Philosophy 101 Questions.*
2. *"Defend Your Job Performance" Questions.*
3. *"Do You Have the Right Stuff?" Questions.*
4. *Mirror, Mirror on the Wall (aka Self-Assessment Questions).*
5. *Why Us, Why Now?*

When you are being interviewed by two people at once, the most important thing to remember is to do your best to give both of your interviewers "equal time." Even if one of them appears to be "the real boss," it's imperative that you also engage the other interviewer in conversation.

Your Philosophy 101 Questions

If one interviewer, alone in a room, ever asked you to describe your work philosophy, the question would be considered a "softball." What makes this type of question significantly harder in the presence of two interviewers, is the speed with which the bad cop can take *any* answer that you give and turn it around, adding a negative spin to it. The only thing to do is to get into the game. "Spin his spin" into a reply that makes both interviewers admire your finesse.

154a.

Good Cop Q: Where do you see yourself in five years?

A. Working for both you and Peter at this excellent organization, but promoted to VP level. I look forward to having two bosses with two very different management techniques, and know that it will enable me to learn twice as much twice as fast.

154b.

Bad Cop Q: What if you work here for five years and don't get promoted? Many of our employees aren't. Won't you find it frustrating?

A. Well, I consider myself ambitious, Peter, but I'm also practical. As long as I am continuing to learn and grow within my position, I'll be a happy camper. Different companies promote people at different rates, and I'm pretty confident that working for you and Peggy will keep me motivated and mentally stimulated for several years to come.

155a.

Good Cop Q: How would you describe your work philosophy?

A. I consider myself an "architect of the future." As the leader on the ZZT business, I reengineered our company from scratch. I created teams of people that exactly mirrored the way that ZZT was structured. There was a key contact person on each team who coordinated with their opposite number at ZZT.

Every Tuesday, I would meet individually with each contact person, get a status update, and zero in on the projects that needed my guidance. A few days later, I would circle back to the person in charge to give him strategic direction. The process worked brilliantly, and ZZT rewarded our company with so much new business, that I was forced to hire additional teams to service it.

1556.

Bad Cop Q: But we're not looking for leaders, because May and I will be leading the troops. We really need someone to manage the process.

A. Well, several years of being in a leadership position have also strengthened my management skills. I'm a quick study and understand corporate directives. With you and May at the helm, I will be able to concentrate on nailing the details of any project that you give me. I work well with others, and know that for your team structure to succeed, we will all have to pull together seamlessly. Can you tell me more about the way that you've structured the SJN business? I've been following it in the trades, and am very excited about your team's progress so far.

Why This Technique Works

1. At your last company, you were a manager who was promoted to a leadership position, but for this job, you'd have to be a manager again.

2. By describing how you rolled up your shirtsleeves and helped your managers do the heavy lifting, it's obvious that, even as a leader, you had a "hands-on" management style.

The 3 Rules of Playing Good Cop/Bad Cop

1. The Good Cop and Bad Cop may seem like they're polar opposites, but always remember that they're on the same team. It's your job to prove that you can get along with *both* cops.

2. When you're meeting with two interviewers at the same time, you're twice as likely to have your interview in a sterile conference room rather than in one of their own offices. The good news is: because both bosses are hanging out together in a place where important meetings are held, phone call interruptions are relatively rare. Take advantage of their undivided attention to present your case with maximum impact.

3. If the two cops appear to be exchanging glances with each other, or even speaking to each other in code, just pretend that you're unaware of it. They've probably been working together for years and, like an old married couple, have simply developed their own shorthand communication.

156a.

Good Cop Q: Did you ever have to conform to a policy with which you did not agree?

A. Yes. There was a "problem employee" who thought he was doing a great job simply because he would come in three weekends out of four to clear the work off his desk. He would also complain about all of the "unpaid overtime" he was putting in. My bosses and I, however, were gravely concerned that he needed so much time to complete his tasks. Honestly, work was slow, things were light, and we weren't terribly busy. We were worried that when September rolled around, our busiest season by far, this employee would not be able to complete his projects.

I really wanted to call him in before his review, discuss the situation, and figure out why he was taking forever to complete his assignments. Was he just slow? Or was he a diehard workaholic who always had to appear busy? My bosses urged me to wait until the formal review period. Naturally, I respected their wishes. The guy ended up getting a terrible evaluation and was canned on the spot, with no warning.

156b.
Bad Cop Q: By acquiescing to your bosses' demands, do you feel like you took the easy way out?

A. Not at all, Ross. I called a meeting with both of my bosses, and expressed my feelings. They explained that the company had to protect itself from lawsuits, and that I should just follow "the company way." I decided that they probably had a valid point, and so I simply did what I was told.

Why This Technique Works

1. You were a great employee who wanted to help a struggling colleague perform better.

2. When you were prohibited from following your heart, you used your head and listened to reason.

157a.
Good Cop Q: If you could do it all over, what would you do differently?

A. I would get my MBA immediately, right after college. I know that it's politically incorrect to admit it these days, but an MBA puts you on a whole different career track from day one. You get paid more money, you get into better "tracking" programs, you advance more quickly up the corporate ladder, and you're given meatier, more interesting projects from the get-go.

1576.

Bad Cop Q: So, does that depress you…that you can't start over again?

A. Oh, no, I didn't mean to imply that! I'm very happy with where I am. I started my career at the best management consulting firm in the world. They had an awesome training program, and helped me get my MBA. It *is* true that I've had to work a lot harder over the years, just to stay even with those guys who got their MBAs right out of college. Still, I kept my nose to the grindstone and prevailed.

But as a Harvard alum, I do a little recruiting for the undergraduate school. And whenever I meet with these bright, enterprising students, I always advise them to graduate from Harvard, and then go directly to business school. After all, if they get their MBAs immediately, they'll have faster, smoother, easier career rides. Can you tell me a little more about the opportunities at your firm for someone at my level?

Why This Technique Works

1. You had to work harder to prove yourself because you didn't get your MBA right out of school.

2. You're smart, civic-minded, and executive suite–bound.

158a.

Good Cop Q: Are you more comfortable dealing with concrete, tangible issues or more abstract, conceptual issues?

A. Well, a concrete, tangible issue has a set of boundaries. There's a defined measuring stick, and therefore, a benchmark that you can leap over. A good example is the time when I was asked to help our diamond store client increase retail sales by 25 percent. That seemed like a reasonable goal, but through in-store promotions, sponsorships, and urban guerrilla marketing drives for "Self-Esteem Day"—a holiday that I actually invented to get women to buy diamonds for themselves—I was able to help our client improve sales by 30 percent.

158b.

Bad Cop Q: So does that mean that you're bad at dealing with abstract, conceptual issues?

A. No. But by their nature, they're just more open-ended, so it's a bit tricky to talk about hard results. One of the stores that I used to consult for sold fashionable dresses in plus-16 sizes. For a long time, they had no real competition. There were other stores that sold women's clothing in these sizes, but their merchandise was more mass market and a lot less stylish. Then one day a rival store, selling plus-16 sizes in fashion-forward cuts, opened around the corner.

Overnight, my client's brand had to be totally repositioned. After a lot of brainstorming, we decided to start a "Femme-Plus" club. It wasn't just a club "on paper"—giving rewards for buying the clothing. It was an actual, physical club where shoppers could meet, bond, drink coffee, catch up on their email, even drop off their kids at the daycare center. The Femme Plus clubs generated a lot of positive word-of-mouth for the stores.

159a.

Good Cop Q: How do you measure success?

A. I used to measure my success purely in terms of profit and loss. On the great balance sheet of life, I looked first at the money that I made personally, and then at the money that I saved for my clients. But September 11th was a real wake up call for me. I decided that it was also imperative to love what I do. We live in a new era where we can't be 100 percent certain what tomorrow will bring. So these days, I spend a lot more time trying to have some fun on the job and bringing a spirit of playfulness into the office.

159b.

Bad Cop Q: But your current job hasn't exactly lived up to that standard, has it?

A. No, it hasn't, Pedro, in spite of my best efforts! That's why I'm applying for a job at your company.

Where to Sit to Stand Out

Ideally, you should sit across the table from both of your interviewers, so that you can address them either one at a time, or together, without awkwardly moving your head back and forth. This is easiest to achieve if your interviewers are sitting next to each other, on the same side of the table.

If they happen to be sitting at the end of the table facing each other, always try to sit in between them, at either the head of the table, or the foot. It will feel a lot more comfortable than sitting at the opposite end of the table, or next to just one of them.

Inside Information

If you can talk about hard results, do. If you can't, talk about soft, touchy-feely results, like generating "positive word-of-mouth." Talking about past results often results in new job offers.

"Defend Your Job Performance" Questions

The road to the executive suite is paved with questions about your job performance. But having two people simultaneously asking you questions about it can give you a whopping case of performance anxiety. Need a way to get your confidence up? Identify one of your proudest achievements *before* you walk into your interview. And then, resolve to weave it into the conversation, no matter what you're asked. See the answer that follows.

160a.

Good Cop Q: Can you describe your decision-making approach?

A. I like to build a consensus. When I solicit people's opinions, it helps to foster a sense of team unity and spirit. For example, when I was promoted to manager of the Research Department, there was zero sense of morale among team members. Everyone was working in a bubble on their own separate assignments. And people from different departments would always comment on how difficult it was to get anyone from Research to help them.

Meanwhile, the Research Department had almost a "back office" attitude about the work. Everyone would punch in at nine and out at six, like clockwork. Phones would ring off the hook. One time, I secretly timed how long it took someone in our department to pick up the line... five minutes! I walked around and asked the people in my department to submit ideas to me about how we could improve our morale.

We implemented a series of measures that the staff suggested. One of their requests was more training. So, we taught the team to ask a lot more questions up front about their individual research assignments. This helped to engage them more in the process. Another idea was instituting a team "coffee klatsch" on Friday mornings, where we would each report on our own assignments. A third suggestion was giving a token $200 gift certificate to the "Best Researcher of the Month." All of these ideas were small, and patently obvious, in a way. But collectively, they helped pull our department out of a serious morale quagmire.

1606. Bad Cop Q: Can you describe a time when this consensus-building method of yours failed?

A. Well, after a while, our team felt so empowered, that a group of my employees wanted to challenge the way that upper management determined bonuses! My team actually had a very clever idea for how to restructure the bonus pool, and I dutifully "ran it up the flagpole." But management informed me that, while they respected how far my department had come, they weren't about to change their tried and true Company Bonus Plan. I went back and told my team members about the decision, explaining it as: "Unfortunately, this isn't a democracy. But the good news is: we're all down for raises."

Why This Technique Works

1. You're a leader. You know how to empower people to get work accomplished.

2. You're also a team player. You know how to keep morale up, even though top management isn't always open to your team's ideas.

Good Cop/Bad Cop Etiquette

If either cop offers you a cup of coffee or something else to drink, take a lesson from your favorite cop TV show, and wait until *after* the interrogation. Concentrate on answering their questions and getting a call back interview, instead of worrying about whether they have light cream in the company mini fridge.

161a.

Good Cop Q: Please give me an example of when you were highly assertive, and the outcome was favorable.

A. I used to work in a hierarchical firm with a company flow chart that looked like a family tree. There were scores of underlings slaving away at the bottom, a smaller group of middle managers overseeing them, and a miniscule group at the top who would supervise the middle managers. Then one day, a huge chunk of business left the company, and 30 percent of the staff was cut, from all levels of the organization.

I was "kicked upstairs" into top management. There were four other people at the top whose jobs had also been spared. To their astonishment, I told them that we had to change the way that we did business. I said that we were still acting like a huge company, which we weren't any longer. And that if we didn't find a smarter way to get things done, our company would soon become as extinct as the Brontosaurus. I advocated empowering everyone on staff to make decisions for themselves.

Change is never easy, But over a few very vocal objections and a lot of hemming and hawing, I lead the reorganization. Two years later, our company picked up $20 million of new revenues in the first quarter.

161b.

Bad Cop Q: What about a time when being assertive lead to an unfavorable outcome?

A. I felt that one of the four top executives did very little work for the immense salary that he was being paid. I chose not to say anything about it until the CEO solicited my opinion about the guy. Then, in strong, assertive language, I suggested that there was a talented woman on staff who could fill his shoes at half of his salary. The CEO heard me out, but ultimately decided that the top manager should stay.

Fortunately, our CEO did not expect everyone to agree with him all of the time. He gave me a huge bonus that year and told me that he really liked me because I "kept him honest."

EXTRA CREDIT

If someone asks you to describe an "unfavorable outcome" try to discuss a situation that did not impact you unfavorably. Do yourself a favor, and never "unsell" yourself in an interview.

162a.

Good Cop Q: Can you tell me when you anticipated a problem, and developed preventative measures?

A. I was brought in from the outside to oversee a staff of twenty. After a few weeks, it became evident that there was an entrenched "old guard" at the company, and that several of the members were seething with resentment that they hadn't been promoted to my position. I felt that if I didn't do something to contain their antagonism, I might lose my job.

I called a general staff meeting where I announced that I would be taking a "diagnostic" of the company, and urged every single person to arrange an appointment to see me privately. When members of the old guard would stop by my office, I found out that they felt betrayed by years of promises from the company that hadn't been fulfilled.

I worked out goals and action plans with six people, promising that if they stepped up to the plate, I would help them make the case for their long-overdue raises. They followed through, and so did I. These men liked the fact that I was willing to stand up for them, and I managed to turn these would-be enemies into allies.

1626. Bad Cop Q: Can you tell me when you failed to see a problem that was right under your nose?

A. At my last company, there were weekly memos about keeping our clients' confidentiality. "Don't talk to anyone about new business in the elevators," these memos warned. "Don't talk to anyone about your clients in a restaurant." I felt that these constant reminders were somewhat remedial. After all, any executive worth her salt should know that you can't talk about company business in a public place! After I had received a ton of these memos, I finally asked my boss about them. "There's a leak," she told me. "Somehow, our biggest competitor is getting the inside track on our new business initiatives. They're continually scooping the business right out from under us."

It turned out that one of my closest colleagues was dating someone who worked at the rival company. It took me months to put it together, because she seemed so above-board. But one night, when I was out to dinner with her and her boyfriend, I actually heard her tell him about a new, highly confidential project!

I reported her lapse to my boss, begging her to keep everything I said confidential. My amazing boss respected my wishes and managed to plug the leak without firing the woman, or telling her what I had said.

Why This Technique Works

1. In the first example, you single-handedly stopped an interoffice revolution by negotiating raises for an angry, disheartened, vengeful mob.

2. In the second example, you not only found the leak, you exposed it, helped plug it up, and negotiated your own protection from any reprisals.

How to Nail the Two-on-One

The two-on-one interview is designed to jolt you. It's always harder to connect with two total strangers than just one. Nevertheless, with some practice, you can become a master. Here are three ways to nail the two-on-one:

1. If one interviewer asks you most of the questions, make a special point of asking the other interviewer at least three questions of your own.

2. Refuse to get bruised. This situation is supposed to be awkward, bizarre, and off-putting. So put on some mental armor (or a structured business jacket at the very least) and go with the conversational flow.

3. Write both interviewers two completely different thank-you notes. For example, if one of your interviewers strikes you as having a sense of humor, be sure to send him a more humorous follow up than the note that you send to the other interviewer. While you want to come across as somewhat consistent, also remember that, "consistency is the hobgoblin of little minds." So bring out different selling points about you. Above all, have fun. Where? On an interview? Surely, you jest.

163a.

Good Cop Q: Tell me about the best boss you've ever had.

A. My best boss was approximately twenty years older than me, and believed in my potential to develop into as strong a writer as he was. He trained me in tiny "baby steps." The first assignment that he gave me was writing one whole paragraph. And the funny thing was, he gave me a week to do it!

"This is excellent," he said, "now, take a stab at writing six paragraphs." I would always beg him to give me bigger assignments, but he said, "not until you're ready." Then one day, the master finally thought that I was. He gave me a huge assignment. I "passed with flying colors"; he was ecstatically happy and he continued to give me larger and larger projects.

163b.

Bad Cop Q: Okay, now tell me about the worst boss you've ever had.

A. You've heard of *Invasion of the Body Snatchers*. This was like *Invasion of the Credit Snatcher*. Whenever I would come up with something interesting, it was never credited as an original thought. Instead, my boss would always claim that he had had the idea first. I didn't say anything about it for months, because my boss did seem genuinely pleased that I was on staff.

Then, one day, in a very large internal meeting, my boss actually took total credit for an idea of mine that he had never seen before. I approached him afterwards, and brought up the topic, gingerly.

"I'm sorry," he said, "I didn't mean to imply that it *wasn't* your idea. I just *also* thought of it myself six months ago. I was sure that I had mentioned it to you, but I guess I never did. As they say, 'great minds think alike.'"

In our field, narcissism runs rampant; and as narcissists go, the guy was actually pretty fair and broad-minded. So I learned not to let his credit-snatching tendencies get in the way of our relationship.

Why This Technique Works

1. Your first boss taught you how to be a great writer.

2. Your second boss, probably jealous of your ideas, took total credit for them. You were brave enough to bring up the problem with him, but smart enough to drop it.

164a.

Good Cop Q: Did you ever make a mistake that cost your company money?

A. I suppose that asking for name-brand vodka at the Christmas party, instead of the generic swill that they normally serve, doesn't count, right? No, really honestly, I'm delighted to report that I never made a mistake that cost my company money.

164b.

Bad Cop Q: That doesn't sound half bad. I could get into name-brand vodka. So what *is* the worst mistake that you ever made?

A. In my first job, I went for the salary, rather than the prestige of the company. I started at a "bucket shop" instead of at a name-brand investment bank. I never realized how important the training programs were at the big shops, until it was too late. As a result, I eventually had to take corrective measures, and it took me a long time to get my career back on track. However, my last job was at a very prestigious firm, where, thankfully, I finally picked up the training that I needed.

A Sense of Humor Can Be a Serious Asset

It may sound a little like a lyric from a certain movie musical, but just a teaspoon of humor can really help the interview go down in the most delightful way. And the great thing about being interviewed by two people at once is that one good joke generally gets *two* big laughs. (So you're being highly efficient.)

"Do You Have the Right Stuff?" Questions

The Good Cop and Bad Cop spend a lot time around each other at the workplace. Sometimes, just like "real" cops in a police force, they may take a donut break together. Or they may stroll down to the water cooler together. Or they might hang out at the company gym for an hour or two during a slow week. Occasionally, amidst their travels around the office, one cop may turn to his partner buddy and say: "Boy, you and I couldn't be more opposite. And we're both doing pretty well at this firm. What do you suppose is the one quality it takes to really succeed at this company?" When both cops seem intent on figuring out if you have this one special trait, realize that, in their estimation, it's the secret elixir for success, and the one critical ingredient you need for them to both unanimously want to hire you.

165a.

Good Cop Q: How creative are you?

A. I consider myself extremely creative in terms of solving problems. A couple of years ago, I used to work for a telephone sales company. Once I was promoted to management, I started reviewing the numbers, and noticed that pretty much 10 percent of the time, the person was able to close the sale on the phone, no matter which product or service they happened to be "selling." Clearly, the sales solicitations that we were creating weren't compelling enough. And they were only designed to sell the product if the customer stayed on the phone!

I challenged myself to find a way to intrigue customers the second they picked up the phone, so that they would stay on the line—instead of just hanging up. I worked with a team of people to create what we called "promise language." One of our most successful promotions started with a promise that the customer would hear in the first three seconds of the call. "Good morning, Mrs. Starkey. I promise that I can save you $25 on your long distance service, and just for listening to me today, I would like to reward you with a free iced coffee at a Starbucks in your neighborhood. Do you like iced coffee, or might I tempt you with a large cup of black tea instead?" On that promotion, sales jumped 30 percent.

165b.

Bad Cop Q: Well, that's pretty good, but it sounds like what you really have is "business acumen." Is that the same thing as "creativity"?

A. Perhaps we should call it something else entirely, like "the ability to startle and amaze people." In our business, we need to always search for ways to shake people out of their reality, just for a moment. Let's face it.

Everyone is super-busy. They've got better things to do than listen to our sales spiels and solicitations. I know what it takes to make people stop and pay attention to what our clients have to offer.

EXTRA CREDIT

Fresh, innovative language impresses interviewers. Try to think of new ways to describe your skills, and pull out your vocabulary toolbox whenever anyone tries to put you in a semantic stranglehold.

166a. Good Cop Q: How are your fact-finding skills?

A. I'm extremely diligent about uncovering the facts, even when they don't conform to what our clients wish to hear. In our field, we have to be honest with ourselves, or else our business will die on the vine. When I used to work at the oldies radio station, the station manager assumed that our listeners, all forty-plus, enjoyed listening to all music from the 1970s. Even heavy metal bands, he figured, brought our listening audience back to "the best years of their lives," high school and college. There was a particular DJ who was a huge Led Zeppelin fan. He used to play a lot of '70s metal during afternoon drive time—even though we knew for a fact that our audience hated the newer heavy metal bands that were coming up at the time, like Nirvana.

I recommended surveying our listeners to find out how they felt about heavy metal. Our station manager sort of ignored me, until the Arbitron ratings came out and our numbers were way down. Then, overnight, surveys were developed that asked our listeners to list their two hundred most favorite oldies. And guess what? Heavy metal bands didn't even make it to the very bottom of their lists!

I suggested doing even more research.. For the next three weeks, every person who called in was asked his opinion about '70s heavy metal. Perhaps one person in forty said they could tolerate it. The rest of them hated it passionately, and always had! We promptly removed all heavy metal from our programming mix, and, miraculously, our numbers shot back up again. Facts reveal all.

1666.

Bad Cop Q: But what if the station manager had refused to listen to the facts?

A. Station managers know that ratings are their bread and butter. It may have taken a while to convince my station manager to look into the heavy metal issue, but the second that our ratings dropped, he was eager to investigate the facts, and make the necessary changes.

Why This Technique Works

1. You realize that soliciting feedback is an important component of success. And if the feedback happens to be negative, you don't mind making adjustments.

2. You've proven that you have one of the most important skills that interviewers look for: perseverance.

167a.

Good Cop Q: Please describe a complex situation in which you had to learn a lot quickly. How did you go about learning?

A. One of our subsidiaries wanted to do a special promotion for Black History Month, but there was no time to test it through focus group research. I decided that it was important to conduct our own research on the promotion to figure out whether or not we had a home run. So, I stood on different street corners for two weeks, and asked total strangers their opinions about it!

What I learned from this was:

1. Always wear sneakers.
2. We were almost there—but not quite.

We made some changes to the promotion, and then had an outstanding success on our hands.

167b.

Bad Cop Q: So, if we find ourselves in that situation—we need focus group research, but there's no time to do it—we'll just come to you, and you'll stand on a corner, asking people questions?

A. I'll be delighted to conduct a focus group for you any time you need one, Victor, but next time around, I'm going to try to do it through a message board or blog!

Why This Technique Works

1. Persistence is the ability to get things done in spite of all obstacles. You refused to let the fact that there was "no time to do it right" hold you back.

2. You had the confidence to respond to the bad cop's query with some humor and flair.

168a.

Good Cop Q: Did you ever have to make a split-second decision on the job?

A. On the recommendation of our ad agency, we were using "bad boy" Matt Eagleton in a national advertising campaign that cost our company $700,000. Matt was in all of our TV spots, print ads, and even on the radio. Then, one day, Matt was at the center of a huge public scandal, and he really got a great deal of negative publicity.

Our company had always been very conservative, and there were a lot of people in positions of power who wanted to pull Matt off the air immediately. While I identified with them, and was actually quite shocked over Matt's behavior, the truth was: we had no back-up plan. Pulling him off the air would have creamed our sales for the entire year. I made the split-second decision to ride it out with Matt, although I agonized about it for weeks afterwards. I argued for this decision with management based on the idea that Matt's time in the spotlight—bad or good—would ultimately mean free publicity for us.

168b.

Bad Cop Q: And then, let me guess: they said, "No, we have to pull Matt off the air."

A. No, actually, top management listened to me. The scandal blew over, and our sales actually increased by 20 percent last year. Now, they're insisting on using Matt again!

Why This Technique Works

1. You made a ballsy decision in an instant. And you had the courage to stick with it.

2. You were also lucky (because your judgment turned out to be correct).

The Top 5 Things Anyone Ever Said about Perseverance

1. "If you only knock long enough at the gate, you are sure to wake up somebody." —Henry Wadsworth Longfellow

2. "The difference between perseverance and obstinacy is: the one often comes from a strong will, and the other from a strong won't." —Henry Ward Beecher

3. "I have not failed. I've just found 10,000 ways that won't work." —Thomas Edison

4. "When you come to the end of your rope, tie a knot and hang on." —Franklin D. Roosevelt

5. "It's not that I'm so smart, it's just that I stay with the problem longer." —Albert Einstein

Mirror, Mirror on the Wall (aka Self-Assessment Questions)

Self-assessment questions have always been staples in the interviewer's arsenal. However, they tend to crop up even more frequently when two people are doing the asking. It's almost as if, since they're both scrutinizing you so closely, they want you to join in on the fun and scrutinize yourself! When you are confronted with this type of question, the most important thing to remember is to use hard, specific proof to defend your assessments. Even if the questions are vague and hypothetical, your answers need to be concrete and detailed.

169a. **Good Cop Q: What is your personality style? Do you tend to be more logical or emotional?**

A. I tend to be more emotional, in that I have a strong gut instinct that I've learned to trust because it tends to be spot on. But in our field, logic rules. You certainly can't tell clients: "Well, we should just do it this way because I have a strong hunch about it." So, I go with my hunch, but always do tons of research to make sure that it's accurate. If it is, then I have *two* reasons to pursue it. If research proves that my hunch is wrong, then I follow what the research says. My emotions are tempered with research.

169b. **Bad Cop Q: Okay, but what if your clients are ranting and raving? Don't you find that being emotional when they're emotional can turn them off?**

A. Strong outbursts of emotion actually tend to calm me down. I think the best thing you can do with a ranting client is to hear the person out. I've seen a lot of people get in trouble with clients by offering to fix the problem on the spot. A saner method is to really listen to what the client is screaming about. Was she promised something that wasn't delivered on time? Did the company make a mistake? Is there a billing discrepancy? Was the work sub par? I feel that an effective, calming strategy is to let the client diagnose the problem, and then promise to get back to her with a solution within twenty-four hours. At least, that's always worked for me on the BBR, FFO, and CTP accounts.

170a.

Good Cop Q: How would your friends describe you?

A. I'm pretty certain that most of them would call me outgoing and gregarious. I tend to be camp counselor of the group, and arrange activities and play dates for us. For example, last year, I organized a four-day biking tour of Vancouver for five of my closest friends. It was a great bonding experience, and we're determined to do it again over the summer.

170b.

Bad Cop Q: What sort of first impression do you think you make?

A. I think that most people who meet me quickly realize that I'm pretty outgoing. I make friends easily, and I'm not exactly shy. I also happen to think that being extroverted is practically a pre-requisite for doing well in our business. I've always found it beneficial in terms of bringing in new clients, and putting current clients at ease. So far, you both feel pretty comfortable with me, right?

Why This Technique Works

1. You come off as strong and sure of yourself, which gives you double bonus points in a two-on-one interview.

2. You half-jokingly asked your interviewers if they agreed with your self-assessment. That wasn't just playful repartee; it's the type of interviewing strategy that earns appreciative chuckles (and jobs).

171a.

Good Cop Q: Jackie, what characteristics do you admire in others?

A. I think that the most important criterion for success in any field is having a take-charge, get-things-done mentality. It's simply amazing what human beings can accomplish when they put their minds to it. I've always worked approximately fifty-five hours a week, and, due to my dogged persistence; I have been fairly successful. But I know several people in our field who also work slaves' hours, and then somehow, on top of that, manage to publish books about our business. I've always admired those people who sacrifice weekends to commit their ideas to print.

171b.

Bad Cop Q: What flaws in your own personality have prevented you from doing the same thing?

A. I don't think I would characterize it as a "flaw," but I do like to achieve a certain balance in my life. Let's be honest: all work and no play makes anyone a dull employee. So during my free time, I play coed touch football, work out at the gym, and, believe it or not, read fiction. It always surprises me that people in our industry almost never find the time to read anything other than business books and the *Wall Street Journal*. I'm happy that I manage to find about five hours a week to read new works of serious fiction, rather than just reading blurbs about them in the *New York Times Book Review*.

EXTRA CREDIT

Tell your interviewers some fact about you that makes you different than all of the other candidates. It's a superb way of distinguishing yourself from the pack. But make sure that you also come across as someone who is dedicated to your career and available to work on weekends.

Why Us, Why Now?

Asking candidates why they want to work at a company is standard interview fare. But what often makes this type of question more challenging in a two-on-one interview is the fact that both interviewers may take the opportunity to see how well you deal with mind games. Typically, the good cop will throw you a question. You toss back a sincere answer, which suddenly boomerangs back at you in an unpredictable way, via the bad cop. When you find yourself in the middle of a mind game, force yourself to get into the "sport" of it, and you will perform considerably better.

172a.

Good Cop Q: Please describe your ideal work group.

A. I think that a scenario where everyone is working on their own projects is conducive to the most collegial atmosphere. The best situation is where you can walk around the halls, knock on people's doors, pick their brains for help on your own project, and help them out with their assignments. An ideal work group fosters teamwork instead of unbridled competition.

172b.

Bad Cop Q: I hope you don't expect that you're going to find that here!

A. Well, according to every article that I've ever read about your firm, it *is* like that here. Is that true, or is that just "positive propaganda"? And even if it is propaganda, I still want to work here! But in all seriousness, how do things really work inside the hallowed halls of MPC Partners?

EXTRA CREDIT

Your answers were perfect, if, indeed, the Bad Cop was only playing with you. If you are asked to "describe your ideal work environment," make certain that your answer closely conforms to the corporate culture of the company where you are interviewing.

173a.

Good Cop Q: What interests you most about this position?

A. I like the fact that your firm has a tremendous reputation. And because it's large, there will be ample opportunities for me to grow on a variety of different businesses, which makes it the perfect training ground for me. This is my dream job. And I think it's no secret that I've had visions of working here since before I went to college.

173b.

Bad Cop Q: What interests you least about it?

A. Well, the two of you are now managing fifty people, and I'm a little worried that I might get lost in the shuffle. I know that I may have to work extra diligently given the intense internal competition, but I'm willing to do that for this tremendous opportunity. What are my next steps?

Why This Technique Works

1. Your passion comes through loud and clear. No harm in telling a company that they are your very first choice.

2. You're a go-getter. And your drive to succeed will distinguish you from the horde of interviewees pounding on the door of the executive suite.

Games Interviewers Play

Board games are divided into games of skill and games of chance. By contrast, The Interviewing Game is almost always a game of skill. In "Good Cop/Bad Cop," the fact that your interviewers are each playing a different role means that you have to be particularly agile. You always have to be prepared to turn your answers around 180 degrees if necessary, and in front of both people. Here are some other hiring games that you may encounter in the executive suite:

1. **Future Tense.** "We're thinking of...expanding/moving to the West Coast/starting a new department." The object of Future Tense is to play along for several months before asking if this future plan is ever going to materialize. Strategy: Just try to hang in there. Don't show your impatience. Resolve to stick it out for as long as it takes.

2. **Musical Chairs.** "We're going to reorganize. As part of this reorganization..." The object of this game is to speculate with your interviewer on how the new department will work, months before your interviewer actually knows if it will. Strategy: Be a font of ideas, and add two months to whatever timetable your interviewer predicts. (Continue to call your headhunter about other jobs while you wait.)

3. **What If?** "We might be open to hiring...but aren't sure about the level of the person that we need." Board games have pieces. So do boardroom games. Let's say that your piece is an "orange." The object of this game is to compare yourself to every "apple" that also answered your headhunter's phone call. There are many players in this game, and there will only be one clear winner. Strategy: Position yourself as the best value out there. You have many skills for your ultra-reasonable salary base. Good luck.

174a.

Good Cop Q: It looks like you've been promoted fairly quickly, especially considering what a short time you've spent in the field.

A. Yes, it's been a combination of being in the right place at the right time, and demonstrating that I can handle responsibility well. I think that colleagues of mine know that when they give me a project, it's in good hands.

174b.

Bad Cop Q: Will you be out to take my job?

A. Maybe in about twenty years, Pete, but by then, I suspect that you'll be running the entire company, and will need a good, loyal lieutenant to help you manage this department! Can you outline for me your needs for right now?

EXTRA CREDIT

A lot of interviewers are paranoid. And sometimes, the task of hiring new talent can make this trait surface even more than usual. Do your utmost to convince a paranoid interviewer that he has nothing to fear from you. You will be loyal to him forever, and make him look good to his higher ups. His job will be more secure if he hires you.

The Lowest Common Denominator

You need to pay equal attention to both of your interviewers, but you also need to come off in your best possible light. If one of your interviewers strikes you as significantly sharper than the other one, gear your responses to that person's IQ level. Dumbing yourself down is rarely smart.

**175a.** Good Cop Q: What will you do when I give you one set of directives, you follow them, and then, Stan over here, changes everything I suggested?

A. I know that I will have truly mastered the material. Revising my reports several times will help me understand the projects even better. Naturally, I'm going to do my best to do them right for you the first time. But I will also be truly grateful for any insights that you and Stan can add to my own. We're a team, and I believe that one should always be open to having one's work touched by genius.

175b. Bad Cop Q: Fair enough. But let's say that Lisa changes it back again.

A. Oh, I'm quite certain that will never happen…

That's a Wrap

1. With two cops in the room hammering questions at you about your work philosophy, be prepared to turn your answer around, upside down, and even inside out if necessary. The key things to remember: "go with the flow," have fun, and don't get flustered.

2. Anticipate that you will be asked to defend your job performance. The presence of a bad cop in the room may make this question considerably more difficult than normal. But sometimes, you can sweeten the sting with a sense of humor. You'll get twice as many laughs, which equals double bonus points in any round of the interviewing process.

3. If the good cop and bad cop ask you about one special skill, they consider this trait to be the key ingredient that you will need to succeed at their company. Prove to them that you have "the right stuff," and they will do right by you by offering you a job.

4. If you are asked to assess your personality, interpersonal skills, or innate talents, use hard proof from your work history to back up your assertions. Turn intangible questions into tangible answers. Hypothetical answers are antithetical to your mission—which is persuading these two important people to hire you.

5. What if you are asked to describe your ideal working environment? Make sure that it mirrors the corporate culture of the company exactly. If the good cop and bad cop seem to be playing mind games with each other, simply ignore them. Chances are, they do it all the time. Heck, it's kind of amusing, and it makes the day go by faster. But if you're the one with whom they are playing mind games, just do your best to not get psyched out. Part of their game is to rate how well you play the game. So play it to win.

CHAPTER 8

Questions from Another Galaxy, Far, Far Away

There you are, having the greatest interview of your life when suddenly, WHAM!—your interviewer socks you with a bizarre question. Of course you didn't see it coming. No one could have (at least none of us who reside on this planet).

Similar in nature to the Impossible Question, but even more random, is the Crazy Question. The question that makes you pause and wonder if you actually heard it correctly. The what-in-the-world-does-that-have-to-do-with-getting-this-job question? Often, nothing whatsoever. And when it doesn't, you should just take a deep breath, and answer the question with flair. But sometimes, when a weird question from a very remote planet comes hurtling towards you, there is a way that you can bring it down-to-earth.

There are five types of questions from another galaxy:

1. *Questions That Are Dimly Job Related (Very Dimly).*
2. *Questions about Life-Changing Events.*
3. *Questions about Your Core Values.*
4. *Questions That Ask You to Predict the Future.*
5. *Questions That You'd Ask a Friend in a Bar.*

To repeat: when you are confronted with a question from the ozone, you have two choices. You can either try to relate your answer to the job for which you are applying (although it may be a streeeetch), or recognize that, to some extent, *any* answer will suffice as long as it's interesting. Practice on the Q&A's that follow, and remember this: you are not your Interviewer's "keeper." All you can do is the best job possible with the material that you're given.

Questions That Are Dimly Job Related (Very Dimly)

Let's be honest. Not every interviewer out there is gifted at asking questions. The person might be very good at his primary job, but interviewing candidates is a special skill. HR managers get tons of interviewing practice, but many other managers interview candidates rarely, and occasionally, their unease shows.

If you are asked a question that's dimly job related, all you can do is try to make your answer as job-focused as possible. Imagine that the question is like a distant star, and that you're observing it through a telescope. Then, try to bring the star into focus with your handy telescopic lens. You may succeed, and you may not. (But even if you fail to give your interviewer an answer that grounds him, you could still land the job if your interviewer likes you well enough. Stranger things have happened.)

176. How on earth do you know Jennifer? I used to date her.

A. My executive recruiter hooked me up with her, so I've only met her once. I hope the fact that you and Jennifer have broken up won't hurt my chances of getting this job.

Why This Technique Works

1. There is no "triangle" between you, Jennifer, and your interviewer, except possibly, in his own mind. Intelligently, you did not allow a question about your relationship with Jennifer to set your interview off course.

2. By referencing your recruiter, you've gently reminded your interviewer that you're here to talk about business.

177. Are you a heavy or a medium-weight writer/ salesperson/manager?

A. I'm a really great _____. And I'm figuring that the last thing you need around here is a lightweight.

When an interviewer asks a vague question about your level, it's usually a guarded attempt to figure out your salary requirements. And if your salary is too high for the job, he will automatically eliminate you from the process. Instead of answering his real query, charm him with a little lighthearted humor. The time to discuss your salary is at the end of the interviewing process, never at the beginning.

178. What have you heard about me?

A. Only good things! I know that you used to work at the parent company, and that you had a team under you that brought in millions of dollars of new business, injecting new lifeblood into the firm. I also read that approximately four years ago, you became a partner and opened this subsidiary office. My friend, Stacy Johnson, told me that this division first turned a profit two years ago, which has got to be some sort of a milestone in our business. What else do you feel that I should know about you as a potential boss? For example, what are you looking for in an employee?

Tact Is Golden

If you haven't "heard anything" about your interviewer, never pretend that you have. Instead, bring out the business facts that you do know about his company, then ask him how long he's worked there, and if he enjoys it. What if you have heard something negative about your interviewer? Don't mention it. As Samuel Butler once said: "It is tact that is golden, not silence."

179.

Can you tell me about your childhood?

A. Certainly, Lucy. I grew up in the outskirts of Chicago, where I attended a pretty good public school. I loved to ice-skate, and, for a long time, had dreams of becoming a professional skater. However, when I turned eighteen, I had to decide whether I wanted to pursue professional ice-skating or go to college. I was accepted at Ohio State University, and during my freshman year, dropped ice-skating to pursue a new passion: modern dance.

I've always loved sports, and understand how important they are to developing a healthy sense of self-esteem. I believe that my lifelong commitment to athletics, plus the fact that I got my MBA in marketing, make me the perfect person for this job.

Why This Technique Works

1. Asked about your childhood, you gave your interviewer the edited version, rather than your whole life story chapter by chapter.

2. You brought up a personal enthusiasm to demonstrate why you are ideally suited to the job.

180.

What's your passion?

A. I've always had a great "eye" for design. As a teenager, I used to do hundreds of "home-ec" projects like painting, wallpapering, and sanding. When I went to college, I ended up majoring in psychology, but I minored in art. I created sculptures and immense, floor-to-ceiling murals, and, sometimes, I even mixed mediums. For example, for a performance art piece, I once mixed beautiful African poetry and synthesized jazz rhythms with documentary footage of Houston's urban sprawl.

I started as a secretary in a decorator's showroom. My boss would sit down with me each morning and give me a daily "to do" list. As I would check off each task from the list, I couldn't help doodling all over the piece of paper.

One day, a very famous graphic artist strolled into the showroom and noticed my doodles. He advised me to go into textile design; as a matter of fact, he was adamant about it. And I actually listened to him. I enrolled in a local art school, where I took night classes towards a second degree in textile design. I brought my portfolio of designs with me today for you to review. (Then, pull out your portfolio.)

EXTRA CREDIT

Why try to fit a square peg into a round hole? Make sure that your passion and the primary skill that you need for the job are one and the same.

181.

If you were to give a speech to a group of executives, what topic would you select, and why?

A. I would give a speech about overcoming obstacles. It was certainly difficult for me to break into our closed "auction house" world without an art history background or an uncle in the field. But I kept banging on the proverbial door, and miraculously, it eventually opened. I feel like everyone in our business has probably encountered some setbacks along the way, and I think that a speech describing how to rise above them would probably motivate a lot of people.

182. What would you change about yourself?

A. I think that, sometimes, our lead times are a lot longer than one can possibly predict. To deal with them, patience really is a virtue, and so I have been trying to practice it. It's ludicrous to expect instantaneous results, no matter how good a concept you might have.

When I was toiling away at my first record company, I really thought that we should be trying to court some of the new hip-hop bands that were coming up. A lot of the people at the company disagreed with me, but one of my mentors there actually thought it would be a great way to attract a younger clientele. He helped me push through some of our very first recording contracts. It was rough going there for me for a while, because once everyone jumped on the hip-hop "bandwagon," we all expected immediate results. Instead, it took almost three years, but we did eventually get the sales figures that we had hoped for. A new hip-hop spinoff label was created, and I was ultimately promoted to help manage it.

EXTRA CREDIT

A twist on "What's your biggest weakness?" is the question that asks what you would change about yourself. However, since this question is phrased in relatively mild language, it's smart to pick a small, mild, (practically insignificant) weakness that leads to one of your strengths.

Why Interviewers Sometimes Ask Questions That Are Light Years Away from the Job

Some interviewers are space cadets. Some interviewers are mavericks. And some interviewers don't take the task of reviewing job candidates all that seriously. They may know that you're going to be meeting with three or four other people, quite possibly higher up on the company "totem pole," and may not feel as if their own opinion of you, one way or the other, will carry all that much weight.

Hence, instead of asking you questions that probe for your skills, they toss you a question that they hope will reveal your personality. For this reason, it's usually a good idea to make your answer snappy and engaging.

There is another reason why an interviewer might ask you questions that are only very distantly related to the job—and it's particularly irritating. If there already is a candidate whom he has met and liked (and whom the other people on the team are in the process of interviewing), your interviewer may be regarding you as his "backup plan." Ouch!

If you suspect that this is the reason why your interviewer keeps asking you questions that are far off the beaten path, it's perfectly okay for you to inquire about it. In fact, it may be your best job salvaging strategy. Say something to your interviewer in this vein: "Gee, Mario, I'm having such a wonderful time talking to you, and in a way, some of the things that we've been discussing are ideas that I've tossed around with some of my closest friends on the planet. But I am wondering about the position. Is it still open, or have you found someone else to fill it already?"

While any query about your competition is a brash move, it may jolt your interviewer just enough to share where his company is in the hiring process. He may even confide something about your fiercest competitor. Then, armed with *that* information, you can devise an intelligent job landing strategy.

Questions about Life-Changing Events

If you've been following the advice in this book, you've spent one full week preparing for your job interview. But you can't automatically assume that your interviewer has spent even one hour thinking about your meeting. There's a good chance that hiring you (or anyone else) is just not his top priority. As a matter of fact, you can't even assume that the job is his primary concern. It could be, of course, but it's equally conceivable that something from his personal life is top of mind.

If your interviewer is experiencing some life change—marriage, divorce, mid-life crisis, problem with his girlfriend, or a recent illness in his family—he might very well ask you a question about some life-changing event that you've experienced. Don't worry too much about trying to connect your answer to the job that you're going after, because it may sound "forced." Just be certain that your answer is thorough, engaging, and shows you to be the compassionate soul that you are.

183. Where were you on September 11, 2001?

A. I was standing on Sixth Avenue and 44th Street when the first plane hit. I saw it with my own eyes, but it took a couple of minutes for it to register. Like many other New Yorkers, I automatically assumed that it was an "accident," and not part of a vicious terrorist plot.

I tried to run to my office on 48th Street, but during the next few minutes, the streets filled up with people, all screaming and crying, and it was pretty difficult to move. I called my wife at home, told her to stay put in our apartment, and turn on CNN. I was able to break away from the crowd eventually and stopped in a small electronics store on Fifth Avenue, where I watched CNN for about half an hour. I then made my way back to our apartment, where my wife and I basically camped out by the television for the next four days.

While September 11th was by far the worst thing that I have ever experienced, it did reconfirm something to me. I absolutely love working in corporate finance. This is the one thing that I wish to be doing with my life, and I now feel grateful every single day that I have another day to devote to the career of my choice.

If you live in New York City or Washington, D.C., don't be afraid to answer the question literally. Your interviewer wants to hear where you were when the devastation struck. Did you see the airplanes hit the buildings in real time, or watch it later on TV? If you live in a different part of the country, the interviewer is really asking how the tragedy affected you (and possibly your family as well).

Can you tell me about a lesson that you learned in your personal life?

A. When I was growing up, my mother always wanted me to spend more time with my grandmother. But of course, that would have cut into soccer practice, flute lessons, and my other studies. Then, one day, my grandmother fell ill. Fortunately, it was just a scare, and it gave me the "heads up" I needed to realize that my grandmother wouldn't be around forever. After that, I spent every single Saturday afternoon with her until the day that she died, some five years later.

185.

Have you ever been in love, and how did you know?

A. Actually, the definition of "love" is changing. There is a new school of thought that says that, rather than being a feeling, love is a chemical drive. When the body emits massive quantities of a hormone called "dopamine," for some reason, the brain interprets this as "being in love." So, honestly, I can't say whether or not I've ever been in love with anyone by this definition. But this I know for a fact: I sure would love to be offered this job.

Why This Technique Works

1. Questions about your love life (or lack thereof) have no place in the executive suite.

2. You quickly turned the question around and helped to steer the interviewer back on track.

Two Heads Are Better Than One

If a headhunter is representing you at a company where an interviewer has asked you a series of off-the-wall questions, definitely call your recruiter, and pick his brain about it. He may be able to unravel the mystery behind your bizarre meeting. But be sure to approach your headhunter diplomatically. Remember that he will get a commission for placing you at this company. So never sound off the heavy "alarm bells" when you call. Simply tell your headhunter that you really want the job, and that you're "double checking" with him, to find out whether your interviewer feels that he learned enough about you to be able to make an informed decision.

Questions about Your Core Values

If you happen to be single and are ever set up on a blind date, he or she might ask you some of the questions that follow. In the task of finding the right mate, it's fairly typical to ask your potential love interest all sorts of questions that attempt to unveil core values. Wouldn't we all love to know what makes someone else really tick?

On a job interview, part of what makes these questions more frustrating is the imposed time limit on your meeting. While your interviewer is busy trying to get to know the real you, you're sitting there, wondering if he's ever going to ask you anything that will help you prove why you deserve this job. What's the best thing to do under these circumstances? Relax. Relinquish the desire to control the interview. Remember that good chemistry is a vital ingredient to landing any job, and resolve to make your interviewer like you.

186. Who are your heroes?

Woman's A: I always admired Edith Wharton for the three-dimensional female characters that she created in her books *The Age Of Innocence* and *The House Of Mirth*. I know that some critics may consider her a "feminist," but really, she was just writing about some of the problems that women back then used to encounter. *The Age Of Innocence* won a Pulitzer Prize, so it was also acknowledged as a literary masterpiece.

Man's A: I always thought that Albert Einstein was particularly noble. Not only did he discover the theory of relativity, he also had to overcome a series of setbacks such as dyslexia. His teachers thought that he was "mentally slow." It's sort of ironic that someone who had to face down several personal demons turned out to be the genius of our time.

EXTRA CREDIT The "heroes" question is similar to the Pop Essay question, in that it doesn't matter which heroes you choose, as long as you know enough about them to defend your answer. (Also: if you happen to be a man who prefers the woman's answer or a woman who prefers the man's answer, feel free to use it.) One caveat: It may be smart to avoid controversial heroes and heroines who have been in the news due to scandals.

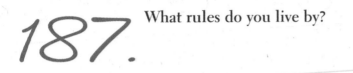

187. What rules do you live by?

A. Well, on the job, I think there are basically two rules.

1. Have fun and prosper.

2. Help our clients have fun and prosper. Speaking of clients, I *know* that yours are prospering. Are they also having some fun, I hope?

Why This Technique Works

1. You gave the perfect answer to a generic, "out there" question. And you even managed to make it business-related.

2. You smoothly segued to the type of conversation that you and your interviewer should be having.

The Other Reason Interviewers Sometimes Ask Questions That Have Nothing to Do with the Job: There Is No Job

You've studied long and hard for your appointment, and walk into your interviewer's office, more prepared than you've ever been for anything in your life. But somehow, unbeknownst to you, the "job specs" have changed. A position that was open merely a week ago is now in the process of being "downgraded" to freelance or to a salary level that's a lot lower than yours.

Instead of telling you the truth (and trying to figure out if you're still interested), your interviewer decides to ask you a series of bizarre questions that have nothing to do with the job, because, as far as he knows, there may be no job.

What do you do in this scenario? Take a deep breath, and force yourself to have a meeting that's as genial as possible. What else *can* you do?

 **Is it more important to be lucky or skillful?**

A. I think that it's more important to be lucky, although being very skilled can help to create more opportunities. I used to work fourteen hours a day for a very talented boss in the MIS department of a *Fortune* 500 company. The man, Rod Berensen, really took the time to teach me how he would diagnose computer problems. He also let me "fill in" for him occasionally, and we both discovered that I had a genuine knack for solving computer glitches. When Rod decided to get married, his fiancée was suddenly transferred to Hong Kong, and Rod decided to move with her. I was immediately promoted to Rod's position.

Certainly, Rod's confidence in me inspired the decision makers at our firm to trust that I could do the job. But clearly, I also happened to be in the right place at the right time.

Alt. A. I believe that if you are truly talented, you will eventually get the "lucky break" that you need to succeed. You can't predict the future. You can only position yourself to be ready to take your shot when it happens. I used to slave away at a telephone sales company, trying to sell telephone service add-ons to a bunch of bored housewives. I finally got out of there and started as a secretary at an in-house promotion agency. One day, someone asked me to type up a telephone conversation that had been recorded on a CD. I couldn't hear all of the words, so I sent the CD to an outside clerical service for them to type it up. They couldn't make out the words either, and promptly returned the CD to me.

Eventually, I approached our creative director and asked him about the contents of the taped conversation, so that I could type up the report. He explained that it was a discussion between him and one of his financial service clients about a telephone sales solicitation that needed to be written. I told him all about my background in telephone sales, and he asked me to take a crack at writing the script.

I did a tremendous amount of homework on the financial services company, found out what they were offering, and then drafted an intriguing way to sell it to customers over the phone. The telephone sales script ended up making our client 2.5 million dollars, and I was promoted to junior copywriter.

EXTRA CREDIT

"Which came first, the chicken or the egg?" The chicken! The egg! "Which is more important, luck or skill?" Luck! Skill! Like the "chicken or egg" puzzle, both sides of the "luck or skill" riddle have their true believers. And ironically, those who have been luckiest in their careers generally attribute the reason to skill, while those who are the most talented generally attribute their rapid career rise to luck. It doesn't matter whether you happen to believe more in luck or in skill, as long as your answer makes a nod to the other critical ingredient to success.

189.

What would you do if Peter Gallant walked into your office and started to flirt with you? How would you handle it?

A. I don't think that I give out "flirtatious" vibes, so I seriously doubt that he would. But if he did, I would probably tell him that I was happy that he hired me, that I had already studied up on his clients' issues, and that I would be working gangbusters to solve the attrition problem on the DLP account.

Why This Technique Works

1. Peter Gallant obviously has a flirtatious reputation. There's nothing that you can do about that, except keep your conversations with him strictly focused on business.

2. You've subtly let your interviewer know that you don't flirt on the job, you wise, wise woman.

190.

What, in your opinion, is the value of a college education?

A. I think that a college education fosters a lifelong love of learning, which is very beneficial in our field. To be good at our business, we really have to understand how other businesses work—the products they manufacture, who their customers are, what their margins look like, and how to evaluate profitability. I have found that having a great deal of curiosity helps enormously. I'm anxious to learn every facet of the businesses in which we invest, and I really believe that this makes me a better analyst.

Why This Technique Works

1. It's common knowledge that most colleges don't teach any practical skills that readily translate into business skills. But you've argued that your education gave you something that's priceless: the ability to continue to learn.

2. Curiosity is a skill which is always in heavy demand and sometimes in remarkably short supply.

Inside Information

Here are three critical areas to avoid discussing with your interviewer, no matter what.

1. Any plans to get married (unless you're a man and you're getting married next month).

2. Any plans to have children (unless you're a woman and you're already "showing").

3. Any plans to retire.

Questions That Ask You to Predict the Future

Being able to accurately predict the future of a business often separates the rising stars from the average performers. But questions where you are asked to gaze into a crystal ball, and predict where you, personally, might be ten or twenty years from now generally will *not* help you make the case for why you deserve the job today. Most questions that ask you to look this far into the future are really superfluous tangents. But with some verve, you can quickly turn them around to demonstrate why you are the most qualified, deserving candidate right now.

191. When do you think you'll peak in your career?

A. I come from a long line of healthy, hardy, mentally active types, and so I confess that I never even think about "peaking" in my career. That having been said, I do think it's important to have some self-knowledge, and to recognize when one is past one's prime. The last thing I would ever want is to become some old, doddering chairman emeritus whom nobody on staff paid any attention to! But as I have just started to hit my stride, fortunately, that problem is several decades away for me.

192. What will you do when you retire?

A. It's so many years from now, that I can't begin to possibly imagine! Right now, I'm very excited about the developments that have been going on in our field. The Internet has completely changed the way that we do business, opening up hundreds of new markets that have never been tapped before. Can you tell me more about some of the initiatives that your group has been spearheading?

193. What do you really want to do in life (when you grow up)?

A. Quite honestly, Spencer, I'm pretty much doing it right now. I always wanted to work for a real estate developer. I find that nothing is more exciting than tearing down an old, decrepit building and replacing it with a new, beautiful condo. It's like the mythical Phoenix rising from the ashes. In our business, I feel like we make money and help people by improving their neighborhoods with gorgeous new buildings and parks. And with any luck, you'll end up offering me this job today, so that I will not only be working for a real estate developer, but one whom I've always admired.

Why This Technique Works

1. You are not waiting for your life to happen. You're all grown up with someplace to go: the job of your dreams.

2. You have charisma, and it will whisk you right up the corporate ladder of life.

Don't Go Back to the Future

Your interviewer may ask where you see yourself at some point after you are no longer working in the field, but there is no benefit to telling him. Resolve to stay in the present, where you can make the case for why you deserve to be offered the job in the very near future.

194.

Do you plan to start your own business some day?

A. I think that it's highly doubtful. I took a stab at it once when I was first out of college, and frankly, wasn't all that crazy about being an entrepreneur. So I got it out of my system a long time ago. I really want to come on board at your company. I have tons of ideas about how we can galvanize your company's efforts in the southern market. I read in the trade journals that this was perhaps the one area where sales could be improved. Why, in your estimation, is this market so hard to reach?

Why This Technique Works

1. Nobody wants to hire an employee who has dreams of starting his own business because it could lead to a serious conflict of interest down the road.

2. You answered the question effortlessly, and then gave your interviewer a great reason to hire you, namely, your dogged enthusiasm.

195.

What specific goals, other than those related to your occupation, have you established for yourself for the next ten years?

A. I know that this might sound like a relatively small dream, but I would love to eventually own an apartment with a large, eat-in kitchen. Right now, I live in a small studio rental with a tiny kitchenette. Meanwhile, I'm an amateur "three star chef" on the weekends: I enjoy whipping up gourmet, three-course dinners for my closest friends on Saturday nights. In the kitchen of my dreams, there will be plenty of room for all of my pots and cutlery, and enough counter space to create a magnificent duck l'orange.

Why This Technique Works

1. Almost everyone can identify with the need for more space; having a "real home" is part of the American dream.

2. With your allusion to duck l'orange, you've whisked your interviewer's mind pleasantly far away from today's "gray meat" special in the company cafeteria.

196. What will you do if you don't get this job?

A. I tend to think positively rather than negatively, so honestly, I can't imagine what I will do if I don't end up getting this job, because I've dreamt about working here for years. So let's talk some more about why I feel like I'm the perfect candidate. (Then sock him with your savviest, smartest "sound bite" to convince him that you were born to do this job.)

Why This Technique Works

1. By asking you this question, your interviewer may be hinting that he's already found a candidate whom he considers to be better suited for the position.

2. But your earnest response will make him at least pause—to reconsider you with an open mind.

Questions That You'd Ask a Friend in a Bar

No doubt about it, there is a social aspect to most jobs. You work with the people all day long. You're also there night after night. At the end of a few short months, everyone in your office will probably come to know your entire wardrobe by heart. And contrary to popular belief, familiarity breeds camaraderie. But when you find yourself answering questions in an interview that sound exactly like questions that you might ask a close buddy of yours over a round of beers, it can feel off-putting and weird. If you possibly can, try to connect your answers to your task—which is landing the job. And with pluck, perseverance, and practice, you should be able to!

Above all, try to have fun. Interviewers tend to remember candidates who dive right in with gusto over those who hold back. Remember always: she who hesitates is lost, whereas she who doesn't, manages to snag the jobs and opportunities of a lifetime. Give yourself permission to get into the spirit of the interview.

Inside Information

Apparently, the "What type of animal would you be?" question is making the rounds at many different firms these days. Maybe it's not from a galaxy so very far away?

197. If you were an animal, what type of animal would you be?

A. I would be a lion cub. Raised by a lioness, I would quickly master the laws of the jungle: how to hunt for food, protect my cub mates from enemies, warn my den mother when danger was near, and rise to a position of power.

Classic Flub Answers to the "What Type of Animal Would You Be?" Question

1. I would be a lion. (Sounds like you're already in a position of power and don't need the job.)

2. I would be a tiger. (Sounds like you're vicious. Or, depending on the breed of tiger, already extinct.)

3. I would be a kitten. (Sounds too sexy, like you're mixing your personal life with business.)

4. I would be a werewolf. (Sounds like "Werewolves of London," which is both too retro and too Goth.)

198.   What's your favorite song?

A. I've always liked John Mellencamp's song "Small Town." I was also born in a small town, and hearing his rocking ballad always makes me feel like I've come a very long way in my career in just a few short years.

Alt. A. I'm a closet Frank Sinatra buff. In my generation, liking Frank Sinatra wasn't exactly considered cool. Still, I find the lyrics to his songs, and especially his phrasing, absolutely phenomenal. One time, when I was in Rome on vacation, I heard Frank Sinatra's song "New York, New York" blasting in this tiny Italian disco, and I have to confess, I practically burst into tears. I felt so homesick that I just wanted to get back to the States, even though I've never lived anywhere near Manhattan.

If you're ever asked about your musical taste, it means that your interviewer is seriously into music. So look for clues about his preferred genre. Are there any CDs lying around his office? Is there a poster of a heavy metal band on his wall? Does he have an earring in his lip? Figure out what kind of music your interviewer follows, and then, answer the question accordingly. If there are no telltale signs to guide you, choosing a song from one of the recognized masters of any musical medium will generally pull you through.

199. If you were on a desert island and you could bring three people, living or dead, who would they be?

A. Hmmm…excellent question, Carl. I think I'd probably bring Dorothy Parker, because she always came up with these wonderful witticisms. I suspect that she'd be a tremendous conversationalist, and would prevent me from getting totally bored. I think I'd also bring Bill Gates along, and beg him to privately tutor me on knowledge management, digital technology, value networks, and inventory management. After all, with all that time to kill on the island, I might as well learn something valuable. I would also certainly bring my aerobics instructor, who happens to be a great hunter and fisherman. This way, I'd pretty much guarantee that I'd be able to survive until I could signal a rescue plane and get back to civilization, where I would tell all my friends about the experience!

Why This Technique Works

1. Your answer was both engaging and practical, mirroring what your interviewer will take away about you.

2. You sound like a Renaissance Woman—fun, but with serious business skills—and the type of person who belongs on staff.

It's Your Job to Infotain

Think of it as a cross between information and entertainment. It's "infotainment"—the perfect blend of information about your skills and work experience, combined with the entertainment value that you bring to your interviews.

In this chapter, we have covered questions that will naturally lead to answers that are more entertaining than skills-based. By asking you questions such as these, your interviewer may be signaling that he wants to be entertained. And it's your task to fulfill this directive. However, you also need to remember that your interviewer *must* come away with *some* information about you that will help him "sell you in" to others in his organization that may not be as entertainment-inclined.

Did your interviewer ask you one or two questions from another galaxy? By all means, go with the flow, and entertain him. But if you feel like your entire meeting with him has been more like a stand-up comedy routine than a sit-down interview, gently redirect the conversation.

Here are three conversational segues that will help you push the pro-verbial interview "pendulum" back to a more typical interview, the kind where you get the chance to discuss your real qualifications.

1. "Gosh, we could talk about this for hours, but I know that your time is valuable. I've been so keen to meet with you, Harry, and I'm delighted that I finally got this golden opportunity. But I would hate to let it pass without discussing my credentials for this job. Along with having five solid years of experience under my belt, I also have..."

2. "Okay, now that you know absolutely every single thing about my personal values, I have a question for you. What, in your opinion, makes an ideal employee?"

3. "Gee, if you hire me, we can have conversations like this all the time over lunch. I brought you an extra copy of my resume today so that we could discuss my suitability for the position. Take a look, and please feel free to ask me any question you want..." (Then, pull it out.)

200.

Which is more important to you, money or job satisfaction?

A. Job satisfaction, definitely. I find it difficult to get inspired by the number of zeroes in a passbook savings account. But I also believe that if you "follow your heart" when choosing a career, you're far more likely to end up truly loving what you do, and that the money will eventually follow.

EXTRA CREDIT Studies show that most people feel like it's far more important to be satisfied at a job than to become rich from it. So always try to talk about your career in terms of "love," rather than "money."

That's a Wrap

1. If you are asked a question that's dimly job related, do your best to focus your response to make it more relevant to the job. But if, try as you might, you can't figure out a way do it gracefully, don't fret. Instead, simply concentrate on making your interviewer respond positively to your personal charm.

2. When your interviewer asks about a life-changing event, don't attempt to tie your answer to the job at hand, unless it comes naturally. Recognize that your interviewer may be going through some wacky life change of his own, and is probably more interested in finding out if you are a "kindred spirit" rather than the world's most talented executive.

3. Does an interviewer want to uncover your core values? Stop watching the clock and worrying about when the "real" interrogation will begin. Recognize that with today's incredibly shrinking job pool, not all open positions always stay on the market. But if your interviewer likes you well enough, he might be able to help you out anyway. For example, he may know of an open job at another company, or in an entirely different department of his firm.

4. Don't allow your interviewer to gaze into the "crystal ball" of your future, unless the exercise helps you make the case, in the here and now, for why you deserve the job. To land a job in the near future, keep your answers firmly focused on the present.

5. If a question strikes you as something that you might ask a friend of yours in a bar, go with your instinct, and make your response as engaging and entertaining as possible. Part of your challenge is to be the "most memorable job candidate," so make certain that your interviewer will remember you vividly when you follow up with him.

CHAPTER 9
So You Were Fired

While most people have been fired at least once in their careers (and many employees several times), let's face it: being fired is not a stellar asset to have on your resume. For this reason, it really pays to ask yourself one question before you immediately update your resume with your last place of employment—namely, do you have to include it?

If you worked at a company for six months or less, you may be far better off leaving it off your resume. Fibbing by omission is not the same thing as lying outright, and you might find it beneficial to fudge the facts a bit, rather than having to deal with the pernicious "Why were you fired?" question during an interview.

On the other hand, if you worked at a company for over a year, you will need to include it on your resume. Every job teaches us something—even if it's only why we should never take the same type of job again! When questions about why you were fired are being fired at you, try to focus on what you learned from your last job and bring it out in your interview.

There are five types of "so-you-were-fired" questions:

1. *Why Were You Fired?*
2. *Why Did You Quit?*
3. *Did You See the Ax Coming?*
4. *What Really Happened?*
5. *Are You a Big Risk?*

Here's how to answer these questions with dignity, and then move the conversation from why you were fired to why you should be hired.

Why Were You Fired?

You've finally recovered from being fired. For the first time, you feel like maybe it really *is* the "best thing that ever happened to you." You're free at last. You feel strong, confident, and optimistic about the future, that is until some interviewer slams you with the "Why were you fired?" question. Then, suddenly, in less than a nanosecond, you feel the sting and the shame of it all over again. Of all the questions in the interviewer's arsenal, this one is particularly barbed.

So how do you protect yourself from experiencing these painful aftershocks? First, anticipate the question, and have a strategy for dealing with it. Then, carefully plot out your answer in advance and rehearse it multiple times. Take care not to gloss over your answer, because the worst thing you can do is to reveal that being fired has somehow put you off your game. You're the consummate professional, and professionals learn to brush off being fired with aplomb.

201.

Why were you fired? What happened? Talk to me.

A. During the four years that I worked at the company, they had massive layoffs three separate times. Each time, the company blamed the financials. Certain projections were unrealistic. And there were also heavy business losses. They tried to contain the damage by first laying off "back office" employees. But almost immediately afterwards, their day-to-day operations deteriorated. Bills weren't sent to the clients on time—causing late payments, and damaging their bottom line even more. During the second round of layoffs, they cut 25 percent of their middle managers, a huge and terrible bloodletting. And as you know, middle managers are frequently the people who really get the work done. Then, clients started complaining that some of the people who were let go shouldn't have been, and eventually, some of those clients started pulling out of the company themselves.

It was a completely terrifying time for all of us, but I have to confess that when I made it through the second round of layoffs unscathed, I really thought that my job was secure. This turned out not to be the case. But even though working for a "sinking ship" is never fun, I really learned a lot from the experience. I had a wonderful mentor who, sadly, was laid off in round one. He taught me how to develop strategic plans, organize press events, and foster strong customer relationships.

Why This Technique Works

1. Your prospect asked why you were fired, but you have successfully positioned your leaving the company as a layoff.

2. You don't sound angry. In fact, you say that you learned a lot.

EXTRA

CREDIT

If you really were fired, and not just let go as part of a general downsizing, tread carefully. It will be easy for your prospect to check out the facts. So study the answer that follows.

202.

My good buddy, Nathaniel Burns, told me you were fired from your last job. He seemed to think that you had trouble dealing with some of the people on staff. Can you elaborate?

A. I was indeed fired from my job, and as the saying goes, sometimes these things are really "blessings in disguise." But I didn't have trouble dealing with anyone on the staff. In fact, it was sort of the opposite situation. My direct boss, Sheila Waterson, was away three weeks out of four, handling business in L.A. Staff members would find it difficult to reach Sheila at critical moments, and unfortunately, they started reporting to me about some of the organizational problems they were facing. These people were scared of Sheila since she has quite a temper, and so they "hid" behind me, asking me to confront Sheila about the various issues that they had. By getting rid of me first, Sheila was simply "shooting the messenger." But since I left the company, sadly, many of these other people also lost their jobs.

I would like to say for the record that Sheila is one of the most talented executives I've ever had the privilege of working for. I learned a tremendous amount from her, and genuinely respect her problem-solving abilities. But it's difficult to be in two places at once, and the company probably could have benefited by having a second "boss" around who was at Sheila's level—someone empowered to make executive decisions in her absence, and not simply report staff members' problems to her.

Why This Technique Works

1. You successfully made your ex-boss sound like a tyrant (by saying everyone was scared of her), but when it was your turn to say something nasty about her, you turned around and complimented her instead.

2. You sound like a fearless warrior; your ex-boss sounds like she pointed the trigger at the wrong person. Excellent.

 I was kind of surprised when I got your call, Katherine. Didn't you have a 3-year contract with BBK? How could they fire you?

A. Well, as you know, Marlene, contracts are fairly easy for companies to wiggle out of when they want to. When the new CEO came in, he was determined to make some swift changes. So I was taken off several of my accounts, and instead put in the risky area of "new business development." Unfortunately, the CEO wouldn't let me run with my ideas. He had canned the person who had been in charge of the department and was trying to replace him. As a result, I was told to "wait until the new guy arrived," but that never happened.

While I was "waiting for Godot" to appear, my numbers slipped. The company offered to buy me out of my contract, and I blissfully accepted. However, I have several ex-clients who love me, so if you hire me, I'm fairly certain that I can convince several of them to switch over to your firm.

Why This Technique Works

1. You used intriguing language, describing a "waiting for Godot" scenario that many executives have experienced firsthand.

2. You gave your interviewer a compelling reason to hire you: the new business you will bring to the firm.

Top 3 Tips for Being Invincible

1. **Have a battle plan.** If you were ever fired or laid off, chances are you will be asked about it. All great generals plan their moves in advance. So do master chess players and smart interviewees.

2. **Know your audience.** Target your answers to the place where you are interviewing. Moving from a large company to a small one? Decide what you will bring to the company, and don't be afraid to "sell it" on your interview. Transitioning from a small company to a big one? Custom-tailor your answer accordingly.

3. **Watch your language.** Always use language (both verbal and body) that demonstrates that you really deserve the job.

204.

I understand that you worked for the mercurial Stephen Bane. At the same time, I see from your resume that your stint with him didn't last very long. What was it like to work for him, and what were the circumstances that lead to your leaving?

A. One thing that you never hear about Stephen Bane is what a fantastic teacher he is. I considered it an honor and a privilege to work for him, even if he was prone to the occasional outburst. I learned so much from him along the way that I will be forever grateful. What people never realize is that Stephen is even tougher on himself than he is on his staff. He taught me a few cardinal rules that I will carry forward with me. For example, he told me that I should never start a project until I have all of the facts. In our field, the deadlines are severe and so a lot of people panic. They'll begin working on an assignment before they've marshaled all of the facts. This leads to work that is shoddy and poorly organized. With Stephen leading the way, I learned to gather the information first. As a result, you'll find my work thorough, logical, linear, and well reasoned.

Why This Technique Works

1. Asked why you left, you didn't answer the question, but instead focused on what you learned from your ex-boss.

2. If Stephen ends up giving you a mediocre reference, it will be discounted, due to his irascible reputation. And if he ends up giving you a fantastic reference, you'll be hired on the spot.

EXTRA CREDIT While it's never a good idea to bad-mouth your ex-bosses, take care to keep your praise to sentiments that are believable. You want to prove that you hold no grudges, yes, but go easy on the bs.

Why Did You Quit?

People react differently to adversity, and financial constraints often influence their reactions. When executives perceive that they are being mistreated at a company, some simply resign, figuring that it looks better to get out before they are booted out. Other executives slug it out, and try to turn the situation around. If they fail, then they may walk as well. Still other executives hang on until the bitter end, feeling that they may as well receive their severance packages and unemployment money. Often, when an interviewer asks why you quit, it's because he wants to assess how well you cope with frustration. But sometimes he may ask because he's trying to ascertain if you really quit, or if, in fact, you were fired.

205.

Were you fired from your last job or did you quit?

A. Honestly, it was more like a no-fault divorce, a process of "mutual disengagement." I was very unhappy when, after years of building up a healthy client base, a new partner came into the firm who forced everyone in my division to devote 50 percent of their time to making "cold calls." As you know, cold calls are not nearly as productive as canvassing current clients for more business. I started looking for a new job and my superiors found out about it. They told me that if I didn't stop looking, they were going to can me. I told them not to bother, and I walked.

I will say this: they were extremely upset to see me go. I've always been considered an efficient and hard worker. And had I stuck it out, I would have been up for a promotion in a year. I do have some excellent references from the firm, and brought them with me today to share with you.

EXTRA CREDIT

Dazzle your interviewer with a deal sheet that details your superior track record during the years when you were allowed to pursue business your way.

206.

In this terrible economy, why did you quit your job?

A. I believe that "cream always rises." Even in a soft economy, the most talented individuals always manage to snag jobs. Meanwhile, I found my last job to be disheartening. I was at the top tier of middle management in a small subsidiary of a major *Fortune* 500 company. The parent company treated our shop like an unwanted stepchild. As a result, they never took our suggestions seriously, ignoring us for weeks on end, even during emergencies. My bosses were put between a rock and a hard place, and so was I. We weren't able to move the business forward!

I got along famously with my superiors, but at the end of the day, I felt like instead of growing on the job, I was simply "treading water." I decided that my energy would be better used elsewhere.

Were You Fired, Laid Off, Or Let Go? The Language of Leaving

The way that you position your departure is vital. Being fired means that you, alone, were canned. Generally speaking, that means it was either due to your performance or your personality. Between the two, it's usually better to attribute the reason to your personality, since that's considered more of a subjective area than your performance.

On the other hand, if a new boss came into the organization and changed the criteria for performance, mentioning it can sometimes be your best strategy (because almost everyone on the planet can sympathize with this trying situation).

"Being laid off" implies that a huge troop of people from your company received pink slips during the same week. If this is what happened, make certain that your interviewer knows it, because it carries far less of a stigma than being fired.

Being "let go" is deliberately vague. Sometimes employers, wishing to spare the feelings of those they have to fire, try to numb the pain by using the phrase "let go." A boss may say something like: "Due to the fact that we lost two clients, I have no choice but to let you go."

If you're not sure whether you were fired or laid off, it's best to bring up the topic with your former employer *before* you leave the company. While the truth sometimes hurts, knowing it will at least help you craft your responses to interviewers' questions more honestly and intelligently.

While quitting a company is usually better than being fired, you never want to be seen as a "quitter." Reveal that you stuck it out for as long as possible. You tried really hard to work it out. But eventually you reached your wit's end, and had no choice but to leave.

207.

Why are you leaving your present job?

A. I work in a fairly entrepreneurial unit of my company. There are a lot of smart engineers, but not enough businesspeople to make the good, tough business decisions. The company is very process-oriented and there is little attention paid to marketing. As a result, I have found it to be very frustrating trying to get my ideas through. Instead of banging my head against the wall every day, which kind of gives me a headache, I figure that I should find a company where there's a more even distribution of people with different talents, and pitch my ideas to them. I read that there are many more businesspeople than engineers at this company. Can you tell me more?

Why This Technique Works

1. You're an engineer and the company needs engineers.

2. You've engineered a response that tells your interviewer why it would be a very good idea for the company to hire you.

208.

Why are you leaving your company? And are you sure that joining ours is the most logical move for you?

A. I've been working in a mid-sized firm for several years now that's been experiencing a "mid-life crisis." If the company were large, it would be able to attract big, blue-chip clients. If the company were small, it would be able to bring in smaller, entrepreneurial clients with an interest in shaking up the status quo. But because the company is mid-sized, it has lost its bearings. It doesn't know what it stands for anymore. It's also had trouble positioning itself in the marketplace. I've done what I can to help the situation, of course, but I feel that all things considered, I'm probably better off using my talent and drive to help a small company like yours attract ambitious clients so that it will grow.

EXTRA CREDIT

It's a lot more compelling to say that a company is having a "mid-life crisis," than to imply that "they have no idea what they're doing."

209.

It sounds like you quit your last job in frustration. What happens if you get frustrated here? Will you just quit in a huff?

A. No, that was a one-time event, and something that I never care to repeat. My company was always asking me to do the firing. After three years, I just couldn't stand it anymore. I had no hiring authority, just firing authority! When cuts needed to be made, my bosses would approach me and say: "You have to let this person go." A lot of times, I privately disagreed with them about who should be cut. But I would be forced to call in that employee anyway, and tell her the sad news. People were leaving my office in tears on a semi-constant basis. Eventually, I decided that I had had enough, and just turned in my resignation. My bosses begged me to stay, but they refused to take responsibility for their own actions and fire the employees themselves. I have dreams of working at a company like yours where my job will involve hiring people instead of always firing them.

Make sure that your prospective employer understands that you have no problem firing poor performers. Your issue was that you had no input into the decisions.

Did You See the Ax Coming?

Did you have a "heads up," and what did you do to try to save your job? Think of it as a critical survival skill in the corporate jungle. Sometimes having a "sixth sense" about the ax can prevent it from falling. Example: A new boss comes into the firm. After two weeks, you notice a horde of interviewees strolling into his office. From casual banter that you overhear, it seems obvious that he's intent on hiring an army of people from his last firm. Yet, you know that there is technically a "hiring freeze." Do you:

A. Keep your head down and meticulously finish your projects?
B. Call your headhunter?
C. Arrange a meeting with your new boss to emphasize why he should keep you?
D. All of the above?

When an interviewer is interested in learning whether you saw the ax coming, he's trying to assess your political prowess.

210.

I know that you were pretty happy at your last company for a while. When did things turn ugly, and what did you try to do about them?

A. Yes, I was blissfully happy there for about three years. I was promoted and given raises regularly. And I had a terrific team of people that I was managing very nicely. Then, the company decided to move my boss to Ann Arbor, Michigan, and they brought in a new boss from the Washington, D.C., office. Quite honestly, I think that my new boss felt threatened by the network of alliances that I had built in the organization. I heard through the grapevine that he was saying terrible things about me behind my back. He told upper management that I had "poor presentation skills." Of course, since these people were all based in Washington, they had no way of knowing that this rumor was false.

I called a meeting with my new boss and asked him to stop spreading these vicious lies. I also gave him the names of certain clients to call, if he needed proof of my competence.

In retrospect, I think that a better tactic would have been for me to have invited my boss to more client meetings. Then he could have seen for himself how happy my clients were with my performance. I guess I thought that years of great performance reviews would save me. I brought copies of them with me today, plus two letters from my clients to show you. (Then, pull them out!)

Why This Technique Works

1. You've proven that a new, chronically insecure boss was out to get you from day one.

2. Your performance reviews and letters from clients demonstrate that you were cut unfairly.

211.

If you knew that things at your company were rocky, why didn't you get out of the company sooner?

A. Honestly, I was working so hard to keep my job while everyone around me was being cut that I didn't have any time left over to look for another job. With all of the mergers that have been happening in our field, layoffs are a way of life. Yet, so far, I've been pretty fortunate. I'm also happy that I tried to save my job, even when all hell broke loose. At least I gave it my best shot!

212.

Were you there the day LBN folded? How did they tell people, and what was it like?

A. Yes, I was there the day LBN fell to pieces. It was a travesty. For months, rumors had been flying that LBN was going to be purchased by our biggest rival. Of course, everyone was quite upset about it because we all feared for our jobs. In a merger, you never know if your own job will be spared.

Still, my attitude was to keep my head down and just do the work. I was determined to stay out of the political fray. In fact, when allies of mine would march into my office and shut the door to bemoan our fates, I would always advise them to keep the door open and get back to work. Many of them would just nod and go gossip with someone else on staff. During the next few months, every single one of them was cut. I kept expecting that someone would call me in and let me go, but it didn't happen.

Then, one day, the last fifty people on staff were called in to a conference room. "The merger with SSP didn't pan out," we were told. "As a result,

LBN will be closing its doors in three months. Please feel free to use our office resources to help yourselves find jobs. We'll be circling back to each of you to discuss your severance packages." We were all in collective shock for about a week or two afterwards. But I used the next couple of months to get my resume together and start making the rounds with recruiters.

Why This Technique Works

1. You lost your job, but you didn't lose your head. In fact, you tried to advise your work allies how to keep their jobs.

2. You used emotional language to describe your circumstances, and, as a result, come off as a compassionate manager who should be rewarded with another job, pronto.

Inside Information

Always try to use words that distinguish you from others who were laid off. By explaining that in the second round of layoffs, they had to "cut the meat," your situation becomes much more sympathetic.

213.

You say you were laid off in a general downsizing. How many other people lost their jobs on the same day?

A. I don't know the exact number, but roughly 20 percent of the staff. And this was in the second round of layoffs. In the first round, 15 percent of the staff was cut. The company's numbers were weak for years, but to their credit, they really tried not to make any cuts for a long time.

I was told that in the first layoff they cut all the fat, and in the second layoff they had to cut the meat. I've been talking to a couple of companies, and I'm pretty close to an offer at one of them. But I'd much rather work for your firm, because I've always respected the work that you do. And I think that I'd fit in well with your energetic, vibrant corporate culture.

Why This Technique Works

1. You answered the question, then followed up with proof of your desirability: there's another company who's courting you right now.

2. You flattered your interviewer by revealing that you'd much rather work at his company. There may well be two job offers in your immediate future.

In the Numbers Game, Size Matters

Your interviewer asks you how many people were laid off from your last company. If the company was large, tell him the actual number (e.g., "fifty people"). If you worked at a small company, it's often better to talk in terms of percentages (e.g., "20 percent") because it sounds like more people were affected.

---

214. Who was the "ax man" during the time that you worked at your last company. What was your relationship with him like?

A. The "ax man" was named Norman Feinstein. But please don't tell him that I called him an "ax man!" Norman was a fantastic guy, and I always had a great relationship with him. He was forced to be the "bad cop" of the company, and I've never held the fact that he had to lay me off against him. They had to get rid of people to preserve their bottom line. Would you like Norman's phone number? He'd be the first person to say that my being laid off was purely a business decision based on numbers, and had nothing to do with my performance.

Traditional Interviews vs. Behavioral Interviews vs. Quiz Interviews

There are three types of interviews: the traditional interview, the behavioral interview, and the quiz interview that's chock-full of brain teasers and logic-based questions. In a traditional interview, the questioner asks a series of hypothetical questions. But just because the questions are hypothetical doesn't mean that your answers should be. Always refer to actual events that happened to you on the job. Back up your statements with hard numbers and results.

In a behavioral interview, the interviewer is trying to learn how you handled a particular situation in the past, so that he can extrapolate from that case example how viable a candidate you are. All questions about why you left a particular firm are, by their nature, "behavioral."

With rare exception, the best thing to do is to treat *both* traditional and behavioral interviews as "behavioral." Wherever possible, tell your interviewer what you learned from the experience, and what you can bring to the new company as a result.

In a quiz interview involving logic problems and brain teases, the interviewer wants to assess how well you think on your feet. You are more likely to encounter this type of interview at financial, engineering, and technology firms. To learn more about logic/brain teases, see chapter 4.

What Really Happened?

After you've been in a certain field for a number of years, you develop a reputation. And your reputation follows you from company to company. So don't be surprised if your interviewer has heard of you, even if you've never heard of him. He may know all sorts of details about your former company as well. When there are layoffs, the word spreads even faster than an office rumor. As a general rule, you should anticipate that if you are looking for a new job in your field, your interviewer might have some knowledge about the circumstances that led to your leaving your last job. When he asks, "What really happened?" he's simply trying to flesh out his own previous knowledge of the events.

215.

When your department was dismantled, did you try to transfer to another department in the company? What happened?

A. Yes. The company offered to place me, and because the economy was very soft, I decided to take them up on their offer. As you know, I had been in the mortgage-backed securities division. But the only department that needed additional people was the research department. Suddenly, I was expected to be a Research Analyst. I went into it very gung-ho. After all, most of the other guys in my department were just handed their severance packages. And I felt incredibly lucky to have survived the bloodletting. But after six months of working as a Research Analyst, I've decided that research isn't really what I want to do. I'm still working there, but I want to find a company that will let me pursue the specialty that I really love. My friend, Mac Clearwater, told me that your firm has openings in my area of expertise. And I'm keen to explore them with you today.

Why This Technique Works

1. Your company didn't want to lose you, so they made you a generous offer instead. You tried it, and have decided that you're not a research maestro. No worries, you still come off as a very valuable employee to have on staff.

2. By referring to the person who recommended you for the job, you helped steer your interviewer back to the real purpose of the meeting—which is figuring out if you will be a good "fit" with his company.

216. Do you attribute your leaving XYZ to a clash with your supervisors about your personality, general working style, or philosophy?

A. Personality. My philosophy is to adopt the company's philosophy, and I always try extremely hard to embrace it as my own. My general working style is flexible and easygoing, and to my knowledge, nobody ever had a problem with it. Two of my bosses totally loved me, and I have referral letters from them today to show you. My other boss, however, used to drag me into his office and chastise me for "not giving our clients enough of a workout" when it came to collecting bills from them. This confused me, since there was someone on staff whose job it was to do just that.

I tried to discuss the situation with all four people—my three bosses (both separately and together) and the "workout guy." But it was never adequately resolved. My boss really felt that shakedowns were part of my job description. I felt just as strongly that our clients would have preferred to discuss their billing issues with the "workout guy." What started as a simple disagreement about my duties blossomed into a clash of wills.

EXTRA CREDIT Ask your interviewer if giving "workouts" will be part of your job description at this company. If not, your answer is perfect. If they are, rethink your answer to show how you would have handled your boss's criticism differently, and what you learned from the experience.

217.

How did the company's merger impact your stay there? Is that why you left?

A. When the company first merged, we were told that no one would lose their jobs, and that our profit sharing of 15 percent would remain intact. After six months, they called us in for another meeting and told us that our profit sharing would be cut to 3 percent, but that no one would lose their jobs. Another two months slipped by uneventfully. Then the layoffs began. Every Friday, they would call a couple of people in and "behead" them. It was torturous. After approximately four months of this, I couldn't take the anxiety of wondering if I would be the next person to be cut. I kept asking them and I couldn't get a straight answer. Eventually, in order to protect myself, I decided to walk.

EXTRA CREDIT Your company betrayed you twice, and so you had no choice but to leave them. Tell your interviewer that you are a loyal employee, and that you appreciate loyalty in others. Back up with a compelling example.

218.

I read in the trades that you resigned from your last company. But I never believe anything that I read in those rags. What really happened?

A. Oh, I really resigned from my last company. As you know, the French conglomerate bought us out. They brought in teams of new people who imported a completely different corporate culture to the company. They assumed that we knew how the French company operated, but we didn't. We requested training; they kept saying, "Demain! Demain!" (tomorrow, tomorrow), but "demain" never happened. Eventually, I just turned in my resignation letter. Even then, it took them five weeks to respond!

Card Your Interviewer

The best way to get an interview at a company is to keep in touch with the interviewer while you are working happily somewhere else. So visit your local card shop every so often. There are 250 national holidays a year. Send Valentine's Day cards, holiday greeting cards, and other gentle reminders to people in the position to hire you...*before* you're in the position of looking for a job.

The Discreet Charm of the Interviewee

When you are confronted with a particularly tough question about why you left your last company, it never hurts to answer the query with a little charm. Here are seven ways to improve your job-attracting potential and become a Job Magnet.

1. **Go light.** Be playful about your answers without being frivolous. Emotional intelligence is a balance between answering your interviewer's questions honestly, and having some distance to shrug off a bad situation with humor. Think about the way you might answer the same question if a friend of yours asked it. Then weave some of that banter into your responses.

2. **Resolve to befriend your interviewer.** Look him straight in the eye and smile frequently while you answer his questions. Strive always to come across as likeable.

3. **Keep your interviewer on track.** Answer his questions thoroughly and forthrightly, but don't be shy about asking some questions of your own, especially questions that lead to your strengths.

4. **Shine.** This is your moment to impress, so seize it. Create a private mantra that works for you, and repeat it to yourself before you walk in the door. For example, you might try something along the lines of: "I am the most qualified person on the planet for this job. I will charm, captivate, and shine."

5. **The you nobody knows.** Don't be afraid to flash a little personality during your meetings. Part of your job is to be "the most memorable job candidate." So use interesting language and the occasional animated gesture to make your case.

6. **Rephrase the key points covered in the meeting, to show that you listened.** "As you suggested, I will call you on Tuesday morning to find out my next steps. I look forward to talking to you again on Tuesday."

7. **Promise yourself a reward for an interview well done.** "If I perform brilliantly, I will take myself out for a fantastic lunch afterwards." Then, follow through. After all, you're worth it.

219. I heard through the grapevine that working at your last company was very stressful for you. Pam Plunkett told me that you might have even had a bit of a nervous breakdown. Is that what happened?

A. My last job was quite anxiety-inducing, thanks in part to the fact that the criteria for measuring people's performance kept changing. Some management consultants were brought in to "reengineer" the company, and we were forced to make major staff cuts that ultimately hurt the bottom line. But I am delighted to report that Pam Plunkett's rumor about me is false. I didn't have a nervous breakdown...I just felt a little under the gun, as did Pam, along with everyone else on staff.

EXTRA CREDIT

Don't get defensive. If you hear an unattractive rumor about yourself, take a step back, listen to the allegation, and if it's false, don't be afraid to politely say so.

220. Many years ago, I worked at your former company, and I found the working conditions abusive. Did they get to you after a while too? Are they the reason that you left?

A. Well, I found the corroded carpet, the plastic plants, and the stale, airless environment, er, not all that conducive to creativity. But I can't honestly say that I thought the working conditions were abusive. What was your experience there like?

Inside Information

Learn to recognize which questions need thorough, detailed replies, and which ones are really more like "ice breakers."

221.
I used to work at CCR, and when I left, they really stiffed me on the severance package. Did you manage to get a good severance package?

OOPS!   **TRICK QUESTION SIGHTING.** See box below.

When Interviewers Ask Questions They Have No Right to Ask

By their nature, human beings are curious. And interviewers are no exception.

Still, certain lines of inquiry go beyond what any interviewer should ask. Questions about your severance package aren't illegal, but they are sort of tacky. However, before you seethe about being asked this type of question, consider if there is a way to turn it to your advantage. Let's say that the standard severance package for X years of service is two months plus vacation pay for the weeks you never used. Did you negotiate a better severance package? If so, why not tell your interviewer about it? Companies usually set aside a little more money for:

1. Those whom they feel were cut "unfairly," and

2. Those who negotiate for more money.

The fact that you got more money may well mean that the company valued your contributions more than other departing employees. See the answer that follows.

A. Well, Bill, as you know, the standard severance package for someone at my level was two months. But the company did a little better than that with me. I ended up getting four months. All in all, I thought that was pretty generous of them, and probably an indication that they thought highly of me.

222. From your resume, I noticed that you worked for two companies that no longer exist. You really pick them! What were the circumstances that lead to the demise of both organizations?

A. First of all, I hope that you're not a fatalist! I promise that if you hire me, your company will *not* go under. All joking aside, the first company was probably not managed all that well. Our clients were very pleased with us and kept giving us more and more projects. And I suspect that the company was undercharging them for the number of man-hours that we put in.

The second company was a "boutique" offshoot of a very successful firm. The firm wanted to find a way to service small clients in the under-$2-million category. The same year that the boutique started, a lot of those small clients ended up merging with other small clients, suddenly placing them in the over-$10-million range. If the boutique had employed more financial people and fewer creative types, they probably would have been able to canvass for small clients more effectively. But they didn't. Still, my clients at both companies recognized my strong contributions.

It doesn't seem like your firm has the same types of financial concerns. Your company is financially solvent, and from everything I've read about it in the trades, could probably use a few more creative types like me.

Are You a Big Risk?

An old adage warns that "the past is the precedent for the future." And many interviewers secretly believe this to be true. If you were fired from your last job, your interviewer may feel that this fact makes you a bad hiring risk. When confronted with this type of question, you have three choices:

1. Demonstrate that the situation at the new company is so different from your former company that the two can't possibly be compared. Then use your wits to illustrate why you deserve the job.

2. Show that your past mistake strengthened you in some way, so that you're a better, more seasoned, more valuable employee today.

3. Prove that your past mistake was a one-time-only aberration, and not "a pattern" that your interviewer needs to worry about.

What's the fastest way to get to the executive suite? Review the answers that follow, and practice, practice, practice.

223.
At your last company, it sounds like you inherited a department that was a real mess. And I totally understand why you were booted out. But at this company, the situation is identical. The _____ department has still not recuperated from Steve Mercier's sudden departure.

A. Well, there is one big difference, and that is that I'm not on staff yet. So we can work out how to solve the problems in advance of my coming on board.

Together, we can diagnose what Steve Mercier brought to the department, and how his departure impacted it. We can identify the holes he left here, and figure out how to fill them. I would even be willing to complete a self-diagnostic of my strengths and weaknesses, so that we can compensate for my weaknesses in the hiring process.

Perhaps you should bring me on as a consultant for a month so that we can get to the bottom of this together. At the end of the month, we can honestly assess whether or not I'm the right person to fill the slot. In the meantime, I would create a blueprint for you of how to solve the immediate problem, plus map out the steps that your company needs to take to avoid this sort of mess in the future.

Why This Technique Works

1. You've acknowledged the fact that you have certain weaknesses, but the company can hire around them.

2. The company has nothing to lose by taking you on as a consultant. Meanwhile, you have everything to gain. You're a problem-solving genius.

224. From your resume if looks like you were fired twice. How did that make you feel?

A. Well, after I recuperated from the shock both times, it made me feel stronger, actually. Our field is notorious for treating people as if they are totally dispensable. Let's face it, there are no unions to protect workers. There are no contracts, except at the highest executive levels. And consequently, a lot of companies have no compunctions about hiring people the minute that they pick up new business, and laying them off the second that a client walks out the door.

It's true that I was fired twice. But I managed to bounce back both times and land jobs that gave me more responsibility, paid me more money, and were at better firms. Your clients are happy and stable. Your bottom line is healthy. And the morale here is very high. In fact, your company is by far the best place that I've ever applied to. Therefore, it's the next logical step in my career advancement.

I've been exposed to the "seamy underbelly" of this business, but I'm still passionate about working in it. Let's talk about your openings, because I'm dying to work at a company of your caliber, and I've got the skills and experience that you need.

Why This Technique Works

1. Your past experience made you stronger without taking away your contagious passion and enthusiasm.

2. Your rationale for why the company is the next step in your career progression is both logical and engaging. You've mastered "The Discreet Charm of the Interviewee."

225.

So, basically, you've been unemployed for two years. Why should I hire you?

A. I'm delighted you brought that up, Eileen. When I was let go from DDL, I took the opportunity to reinvent myself. I figured that one of the things that had held me back in my career was never having a good, solid foundation in business skills. I got my first job right out of college, and was launched into our business at the tender age of twenty-one. I learned it by being thrown into the "shark pool," and most of my mentors had no scholastic training either. I've taken the last two years off to complete my MBA. Of course, I've been going to school at night, so I'm not quite "there" yet. But after another year of night classes, I will have my degree.

In the interim, I've learned the fundamentals that I always felt I was lacking—accounting skills, an understanding of economics, and even some marketing. You should hire me because I am far more skilled now than I was just two years ago, yet my price has not risen a penny.

EXTRA CREDIT **Talk about your grade point average at business school (assuming that it's high). Or discuss a case study from your last company, where having your new business skills would have lead to an even more successful outcome.**

226. Do you think that the past is any precedent for the future? You were let go from your last firm, right?

A. Yes. I do think that the past is precedent for the future, even though I was let go. Let me explain. I worked successfully at five jobs in row, never losing my job until this last time around. I am a diligent worker and also a caring boss. Every employee I've ever managed is pulling for me today to get this job, so that hopefully I can bring him on board down the line. I've also gotten along with every boss that I've ever had, even the one that had to let me go from my last position. So, yes, Merle, the past *is* precedent for my future performance. And if you hire me, I will dedicate myself to bringing in new business, and also a sense of team spirit to your hallways.

Why This Technique Works

1. You're not just a beloved manager, you're a coach; and you have many diehard fans.

2. You sound like both a nice guy to work for and to have working for you. And in the Interviewing Game, nice guys finish first.

That's a Wrap

1. If you are asked why you were fired, try to position it as a layoff. If you can't, strive to show that a new boss came in who changed the firm radically from what it had been. You were simply at the wrong place at the wrong time. Do your best to praise any ex-bosses who let you go, instead of casting blame.

2. If your interviewer wonders why you quit, prove that the situation was untenable. But also show that you tried to stick it out for as long as possible. If you have a good relationship with some former clients, stress that you can bring in new business to the company.

3. Did you see the ax coming? Generally, it's wise to claim that you did, because it shows that you have honed an important survival skill. Share what you did to prevent the ax from falling, why it didn't work, and what you gained from the experience.

4. Interviewers are naturally curious. If you're asked "What really happened?" tell the truth. Then, steer the conversation to why you deserve to be hired. If humanly possible, be playful about your answers without being superficial.

5. "The bigger the risk, the bigger the reward," except if you're the person who's considered a big risk. If your interviewer is worried that he can't hire you because you were fired, demonstrate how the experience strengthened you to make you a more desirable employee. Alternatively, position losing your job as a "one-time event," or prove that the new company is so different from your old company that there is no way you will be repeating the past.

CHAPTER 10
Your Turn

A successful job interview is simply a productive conversation. Sometimes, depending on the personality of your future employer, this conversation may seem somewhat one-sided. For these situations, you should arrive with an arsenal of questions to ask—just in case.

Here's a brief anecdote to prove my point. When I was right out of college, I completely blew my chances at a terrific job simply because I had no prepared questions of my own. The job was at *Vogue* magazine in their Promotions Department. During two summer vacations from college, I had worked as something called a General Rover in all of the different editorial and promotional departments at Condé Nast. I had a fantastic track record at the company; a portfolio of feature stories that I had written for my college newspaper (the *Brown Daily Herald*); plus I had kept in touch with Condé Nast religiously throughout my senior year. When I finally had the interview, my would-be boss socked one seemingly innocent question to me at the very end: "Do you have any questions?" she asked. I learned the hard way to always come prepared with questions!

There are five types of questions that you should ask:

1. *Questions to Start the "Conversational Ball" Rolling.*

2. *Questions That Show You Studied the Company.*

3. *Questions about the Internal Structure and/or Job Description.*

4. *Questions That Help You Decide If the Company's a Good Fit for You.*

5. *Questions That Put the Ball Back in the Interviewer's Court.*

In a normal interview (okay, maybe there's no such thing as "normal"), you may want to ask *one* favorite question from each of the categories that follow. With a particularly tight-lipped interviewer, however, it's probably a good idea to ask several questions from each of the following sections.

Questions to Start the "Conversational Ball" Rolling

At the heart of any interview is one simple question that is very much on your interviewer's mind. "Can I see this person working here?" he wonders to himself. If he isn't asking you questions that will help him arrive at an answer, it's your job to draw him out. Bear in mind that any questions that you ask need to be "softballs," because you want to make your interviewer feel comfortable being around you. The following questions should help your interviewer relax and open up in your presence.

 Where do you see your business going in the next five years?

Why This Technique Works

1. Everyone has an opinion about this, and your interviewer's response will definitely give you insights into his personality and ambitions.

2. You'll learn enough about the company to springboard onto other questions.

 What are some of the problems your company faces right now? And what is your department doing to solve them?

 How long have you worked here, and in your opinion, what are some of the strengths and weaknesses of the organization?

 EXTRA CREDIT

Be a problem-solving maestro. Always tell your interviewer how you can help him solve his problems.

Where did you work previously, and for how long? Compared to that company, do you find this one better or worse, and in what ways?

What type of employee tends to succeed here? What qualities are the most important for doing well and advancing at the firm?

EXTRA

CREDIT

If your interviewer is well known in your field, she may be slightly miffed if you don't know where she used to work! So try to find out this information before your appointment, and then modify your question accordingly (e.g., "I know that you worked at CCP for five years. Do you find working here better or worse, and why?")

How would you describe your management style, and what are you looking for in an employee?

EXTRA

CREDIT

Once your interviewer tells you what she's looking for in a candidate, picture that person in your mind's eye. She/he should look a lot like you.

Play Twenty Questions with Yourself

While these questions are all valid, you should do as much research on
the company as possible in advance. Play Twenty Questions. Write a
list of questions that you want to ask your prospect. Then, try to answer
them by going on the Internet, reading articles about the company, and
asking any friends of yours who work there for the answers. Armed with
that knowledge, then go back and rewrite your list of questions to show
your prospect that you have done your homework on the company, and
still have questions!

Questions That Show You Studied the Company

What's the best way to make your interviewer feel like you belong at his
firm? Ask him questions that aren't generic. Subscribe to trade publications from your field and their web counterparts. Work your own friends
and family for any and all connections. Ask everyone you know if they
know anyone who works at the firm, or even at one of its competitors. If
a headhunter is representing you, pepper him with questions about the
company's recent history. Then take that information and weave it into
your questions—to show that you know almost as much about the company as the people who actually work there.

233.

I researched the XYZ project thoroughly,
and was extremely impressed with how
your team turned a losing proposition
into an incredible success story. Can you share another case study
with me...something your department is proud of?

How Interviewers Size You Up

For simplicity, the checklist that follows assumes that you are a woman looking for a job; but if you are a man, please note: the identical check list will be running through your interviewer's mind during your first meeting. Please substitute the appropriate pronoun.

1. Do I like her?

2. Will she get along with her bosses, coworkers, customers, suppliers, clients, and vendors? How will the notoriously difficult Sherri react to her? (Oh, why is Sherri always such a pain in the butt?)

3. Does the candidate look like she belongs at the company? Can I send her to meetings with confidence?

4. Is she a "good value"? What does she bring to the table? (Hmm...I wonder if I can get her to bring her price down by $10,000?)

5. Does she have the right credentials for the position?

6. Is she a risk? Is she a little bit immature, or would she be perfectly fine if she would just take off those clogs? (Who wears clogs to an interview?)

7. Can I see her as a principle in X years?

8. Is this a high-impact individual? Can she make a difference here?

9. How does she stack up against the other candidates that I've already interviewed for the job? Do I like her more than the CEO's nephew? (Come to think of it, I didn't really like that guy all that much.)

10. Do I think she has enough going for her to recommend a callback interview?

Always try to ask the type of questions that make interviewers beam with the joy of happy memories.

234. I noticed that you teach a night class at NYU School of Continuing Education. How long have you been teaching, and what are some of the things that you've learned from the experience?

Why This Technique Works

1. You brought up the fact that your interviewer is an acknowledged expert in his field before he did.

2. You've got a real knack for asking the type of questions that interviewers love to answer!

235. How has the new management structure impacted the day-to-day process here? What changes have they made at the company?

 **236.** What are your plans for combating Japanese competition in the full-size pickup market?

 EXTRA **CREDIT** Ask questions that are simple, direct, and show that you've done your homework without a great deal of elaboration. Your interviewer can't fail to be impressed and to take your job candidacy seriously.

---

237. I read your CEO's letter to the editor in *Business Week*. How did his insights about the emerging Hispanic market impact your Hispanic subsidiary? Did they end up winning a lot of new business as a result?

Reorganizations, New Management Structures, New Bosses: The Truth Serum of the Executive Suite

When changes are afoot at a company, every single person on staff is obsessing about them nonstop. So, when you bring up the topic that's most on your interviewer's mind, you are really likely to hear the inside scoop. This is incredibly valuable information to have for your job search!

Here are some tidbits of information that you may want to politely inquire about:

1. How has the change personally impacted your interviewer? Did he gain or lose more business as a result of the reorganization?

2. Did your interviewer inherit some new people on his team? Sometimes, in a merger, entire new teams of people from the acquired company will be added to the roster of the successor company practically overnight. Of course, the opposite can be true, as well.

3. Was the transition smooth or incredibly bumpy? How do current clients feel about the change?

4. Did anyone from top management leave the company? Who stepped in to fill the void?

5. Is the reorganization over yet? Like the proverbial "fat lady" who sings at the opera before the final curtain falls, top executives at a company often send an unmistakable signal to their staff at the end of a reorganization. For example, there may be a company party to boost morale. If you are comfortably employed somewhere else, it's not always smart to jump ship if more changes are still in the works. On the other hand, coming on staff just after a major "housecleaning" has taken place is often the best time to start.

While you will want to learn everything that you possibly can about impending changes at the company, you must also respect your interviewer's right to privacy. If he doesn't wish to disclose any information, you need to accept that, and simply concentrate on proving why you are a talented worker to have on staff.

Questions about the Internal Structure and/or Job Description

You simply cannot arrive at an interview, all bright-eyed and enthusiastic, with the attitude of "put me anywhere, I know that I'll fit in!" The following questions attempt to nail down the specifics of the open position. Often, it helps to get an "überview" of the entire reporting chain of command, and then drill down to where you will fit in. You don't have to ask your interviewer all of these questions. In fact, take care not to, because you don't want to overwhelm him. Simply lob him one or two of the following questions, and see where the conversational ball bounces.

 Who would I be reporting to? Are those three people on the same team, or are they on different teams? What's the "pecking order"?

Look Into the Mirror of Your Soul

You've lived with yourself for X years. You know yourself better than any other person on the planet. You know the types of jobs where you do well and thrive, and also the types where you flounder. Sometimes, in "multiple-boss situations," there is a certain disorganization inherent in the organizational structure. Perhaps there are two or three bosses who are all doing the same job. If so, it's important to identify this in advance, take stock of the conceivable miscommunications, and honestly ask yourself if you are up to the challenge.

By all means, get the job offer first, and then decide if you really want it later. But unless you are a junior, recognize that having multiple bosses can sometimes lead to confusion and the inability to perform the job to everyone's satisfaction. Clarity in a job interview leads to better career choices. Asking the right questions can help you figure out if this is the right position for you.

Discretion Is the Better Part of Interviewing

Even if you and your interviewer are sitting in a veritable "cone of silence," there are some questions that you should not ask him. Here are three questions that you can probably live without knowing the answers to, until after you are on staff:

1. Review Questions—What is the employee review process like? How often are reviews conducted, and are they attached to raises? Is there a probationary period for new employees, say three months?

2. Personal Days and Vacation—How many personal days will I be given? What happens if I don't take all of my vacation time? Will it be carried over?"

3. Office Space—I noticed that you basically have an "open office" here. Are new employees ever given any of the internal offices? Or are those offices only reserved for the top managers? (Incidentally, the answer is "yes," and the French Revolution paled in comparison to the internal warfare that's being waged over those offices.)

In short: don't worry about when you'll be getting a raise, your first day off, or an office until you're already working at the company.

239. How do you handle new business pitches? Who gets involved in generating new business at this company? Is there a team in place, and do they "cull" employees from different teams, depending on the business that your firm is going after?

Inside Information

"Star" performers are usually anxious to get involved in the new business effort, even if they are not technically on the new business team. When you ask about new business, you're signaling that you're an A player.

240.

Can we talk about the management structure? How do the teams work? Are you still doing the work, or are you mainly "coaching" others who are doing it? And how do you feel about that?

Coaches vs. Players (aka Those Who Oversee the Work vs. Those Who Do It)

In the old days, circa 1980, when most companies still had hierarchical structures, there was a natural progression from juniors and mid-level people who would "do the work" to managers who would supervise it. As you moved up the corporate ladder, you would eventually find yourself in a position where supervising others would take up so much of your time that you were basically a coach rather than a player. With all of the shakeouts that have been happening during the past years, many companies have moved to flatter internal structures where this is no longer the case.

Make no assumptions. Ask your interviewer how things work at his company. It's also vital to understand how he feels about his role. Is he a coach who misses doing the work? Or does he truly enjoy supervising his staff? Does he feel beleaguered because as a manager he's expected to supervise an army of people and *still* do the work? Ask the questions, and modify your sales spiel, based on what you discover.

241. When you're away, who's minding the store? When you are pursuing new clients, who oversees the day-to-day work? What percentage of your time do you spend on generating new business? Do you mainly focus on that or on the day-to-day maintenance of your current clients?

EXTRA **CREDIT**

Ask if speculative work is generally shown in a new business pitch, or if most new clients are brought in through previous relationships.

Why New Business Is Your Business (Even If It Technically Isn't)

New business is the lifeblood of an organization. And it simply isn't possible to keep servicing the same clients, hoping against hope that they will never leave the fold. As surely as fall follows summer, there will be client attrition at some point, and then the company will be forced to pitch new business. When you ask questions about generating new business, it proves that you have your eye on the big picture, and are not simply a little worker bee, blissfully unconcerned about important matters like profitability. Another key question you might ask: "What percentage of new business pitches has your company won during the past two years?"

242. Who are the players? How many people would I be managing, and can you describe them to me a little? How well do they get along with each other? Do they need someone to organize their time or do they basically self-manage?

243. Do the managers here supervise the work-flow, the work product, or both? Who was the last person who held this position? Was she liked and respected? Why did she leave the company?

The Smartest Interviewees Insist on Meeting Those They Will Manage

New bosses are the bane of most staffers' existence. Why is that, exactly? It's because, so often, new bosses tend to come on staff, all blustery and self-important, and inadvertently shake things up due to their ignorance about the "real way that things work" at the company. And every once in awhile, the old-timers despise a new boss enough to band together and conspire to make her life a misery.

However, with a little bit of foresight and intelligent planning, you can head off this situation by meeting several of the key players whom you will be managing in advance. Simply ask if you might, and often, your wish will be granted.

Won't meeting everyone prolong the interview process, you ask? Yes, it will, but it's a good idea to do it anyway. Meeting the people whom you will be managing can help you build alliances before you arrive at the company. It can also help you conduct a diagnostic of the organization that will provide an invaluable road map for the actions you will need to take once you are situated.

Don't forget to find out what the process is. That way, you can help to ease the process, instead of standing in the way.

Questions That Help You Decide If the Company's a Good Fit for You

Finding a new job is like buying a really great suit. While the name of the brand is important, the most critical thing is the fit. Even having a really prestigious organization on your resume will do little to enhance your career if you are looking for certain features that it simply cannot provide. For example, if you desperately desire formal training and the company doesn't have a real training program in place, you will not be happy. Similarly, if you want nothing more than to "cut your teeth" on real assignments, and the company insists on textbook training and "classroom" sessions, you will be chomping on the proverbial bit of your patience.

If you are right out of college or business school and you are going for your very first job, take a week off from your search and ask yourself what you really want. Come to terms with it. Embrace it. And then on your interviews, try to figure out if the company can give it to you.

244.
What type of training do you have at your company? Does the training focus on past business case studies, current business problems, or both? Is it run by someone on the inside or a management consultant? How are employees "graded"? And what decisions are made as a result, in terms of placing new employees in their first assignments?

245.

If I go to night school for my MBA, will it help me advance more quickly at the company?

Inside Information

Many employees complain that there are no mentors any longer. But if you are a woman, and the company where you are interviewing happens to have a lot of women in top management, there might well be a mentoring system in place. If you are meeting with a woman at a female-friendly company, you might also ask if she had a role model or mentor at the company who helped her get ahead.

246.

Is there a mentoring system at your company? How are mentors selected, and can you give me an example of how the mentor-new employee relationship works?

The Pros and Cons of Taking a Less-Than-Perfect Job

If you graduated from college without a job offer, you may find that your prospects look a bit bleaker than you had hoped. Perhaps you are living back at home with your parents, chafing for your own apartment. You've been reading the classifieds every day; you've been replying to the recruitment ads listed on monster.com and hotjobs.com. You had a couple of interviews that didn't lead anywhere; and now finally, one of them seems to be heading towards a real, live offer. Naturally, you jump at the chance, right?

Not so fast. Before accepting the job, do yourself a favor and write a serious "pros and cons" list. Be honest with yourself. Is the job giving you at least 80 percent of what you desire? If so, take it, jump for joy, and start looking for that first apartment away from home. But if the job falls short, remind yourself that you don't have to accept it. After all, unless you are up to your eyeballs in college loans, you can afford to be a bit selective.

If you've reviewed your list, and have decided that the job, while far from perfect, is "good enough for now," then at least map out a timeline for when you will begin looking for another position. Most companies today have precious little loyalty to the people whom they hire. So follow the words of the immortal bard William Shakespeare, and "to thine own self, be true."

247. Is CCR a company that's upwardly mobile? For example, if you put me in Product Control, and I prove myself there, do you think that you might eventually move me to Sales? Or, let's say that I love Product Control and want to stay there. How are decisions made, in terms of putting employees on new assignments and tasks?

A Job in the Hand Is Worth Two in the Classified Section

In the game of bridge, there is a saying, "one peek is worth two finesses." If you don't happen to be a bridge aficionado, this motto explains why you should never let your opponent see the hand of cards that you are holding. In the example given above, the question works because you have countered the idea that you might want to move into sales with the equally likely possibility that you might wish to stay in product control for many years. You are simply inquiring how employees move laterally within the company.

But if you are applying for a job in one department when your real interest lies within a totally different area of the company, broach the topic very cautiously. The *last* thing that you want your interviewer to think is that you really aren't interested in the job that he can offer you now.

Would you be able to show me an example of some work that you're particularly proud of?

EXTRA

CREDIT

Not every company is proud of the work that they do. But there is a simple way to figure out if they are. Arrive at your interview ten minutes early, and survey the posters that are hanging on the walls of the hallway and reception area. If the company has some of its work hanging prominently on display, then asking to see more of it is a wonderful idea. But if, after casual inspection, you can't find even one example of the work that the company does, it's often better not to inquire about it. Follow the old adage, "ask no questions, and they'll tell you no lies." (But do investigate the company's website to see for yourself why they chose not to showcase their work in the office.)

Questions That Put the Ball Back in the Interviewer's Court

Hopefully, you used the preceding questions in this chapter to engage your interviewer in a lively and productive conversation. She opened up to you, and you both felt stimulated by the exchange of ideas, insights, and information. Maybe for a few minutes, the two of you even found yourselves in the delightful "interviewing zone." But now it's time to very casually sneak a peek at the clock on your interviewer's desk or wall. (Don't look at your own watch…You don't want her to feel like you're bored.) If you are thirty or thirty-five minutes into a one-sided interview where you've asked most of the questions, it's that magical moment when you really need to set the meeting back on course. You need to gently steer your interviewer to ask you those questions that she should have previously. Here's how to politely redirect her down the primrose path.

249. Do you have any questions that you would like to ask me? I brought my resume (and/or portfolio) with me today if you would like to take another look at it. (Then, pull it out.)

Why This Technique Works

1. In the gentlest of terms, you have politely reminded your interviewer that you were called in to demonstrate your job suitability, and your resume and/or portfolio are your strongest selling points.

2. Your question will encourage your interviewer to ask you some questions.

250.
Well, I think it's pretty clear that I would *love* to work for you. So tell me, Brad, what are my next steps?

Why This Technique Works

1. You've tossed out a "feeler" to your interviewer. If he still has any unresolved questions or nagging concerns about you, he'll tell you.

2. But chances are, he will say something that's politely encouraging, such as: "It was wonderful to meet you. And you'll be hearing from us very soon."

251.
How long do you think it will take to make a decision about me, and is there anything I can do to help you make it?

Red Light, Green Light, or Yellow Light

Call it a hunch, ESP, or simple intuition. Most job candidates have an innate sense of how well they performed on a job interview before the elevator even arrives to whisk them out of the building. They may not know how their competition will stack up, but they usually have a very clear idea of which portions of the interview they aced, and also, where they might have done better.

After a bit of interviewing practice, your intuition will become razor sharp. But even if you're an interviewing novice, it's generally a good idea to take a leap of faith and believe in your gut instinct, until proven otherwise.

Clueing into your intuition can really help you with the next phase of pursuing the job. Let's try it, with an exercise called: "Red Light, Green Light, Or Yellow Light."

At the end of your interview, ask yourself if the meeting that you just had was "red, green, or yellow,"—yes, just like the colors of the traffic lights.

If you feel that your interview was a "red light," it means that the search for this job stops now. On some primal level, you know that you will not be offered the position. If this is the case, ask your interviewer what your next steps are anyway, and resolve to give it your best shot by following the advice in the next chapter.

Was your interview a "green light"? Then it's probably a "go." Congratulations. Follow up with a killer thank-you email, and anticipate that your interviewer will get back to you shortly with your next steps.

What if your interview was a "yellow light," otherwise known as a "firm maybe"? If the company will be continuing to meet other candidates, or if you feel, in your heart of hearts, that some of your responses could have been sharper, ask your interviewer if he would be open to you emailing him occasionally, say, every two weeks, until a decision is made. Chances are, he will honor this simple request, and it will keep you in the running. Then, try to bolster your case with brilliant follow-up letters and the periodic phone call.

That's a Wrap

1. If your interviewer feels uncomfortable asking you questions, you need to reverse roles with him and ask some questions that will make him open up to you. Take care to keep your questions easy, and also not to behave like a drill sergeant. Play Twenty Questions with yourself, not your interviewer.

2. All questions are not created equal. Those that demonstrate that you've researched the company put you in your best light and make interviewers take your candidacy seriously. If the company has recently reorganized, be sure to ask about it! Alternatively, questions that reveal you know some great fact about the person interviewing you also receive very high marks. Remember always, you are selling yourself to a "target market of one": your interviewer.

3. Asking about the internal structure of a company or details about the specific job description can also help you position yourself as the ideal candidate. If you're going to be working for several bosses, it's important to understand the lay of the internal land, also known as the "pecking order." If you're going to be managing several people, it's a good idea to try to meet with them.

4. Often, an interviewer will say, very politely, at the end of a meeting, "if you have any more questions about the position, feel free to contact me." But it's frequently awkward to follow up about things that you should have asked in your initial meeting. Use your interview to figure out if the job is right for you. After all, it's your career. Think about what you're really looking for in the job, and then determine if the company can come through.

5. In a one-sided interview, it's important to keep a discreet eye on the clock. If, after thirty or thirty-five minutes, you're still the one who's asking the majority of the questions, then you need to gently redirect your interviewer back on track and encourage him to ask you some questions of his own. Mentioning that you brought an extra copy of your resume or portfolio to the meeting can help you accomplish this mission seamlessly.

CHAPTER 11

If Only I Had Said X Instead of Y, I'd Be Hired (Or, How to Change Your Answers After the Interview)

If you flubbed one or two of your answers in a job interview, do not despair. It's still possible to revise your answer, post-interview. You will need to write a thank-you email or letter to the person whom you met. This gives you a real opportunity to explain the answer you gave a bit more, add some depth to it, or even, to completely reverse yourself and give an entirely different answer, if you so choose.

When employing this approach, the trick is to pull it off without sounding either defensive or wishy-washy. This is a bit of a feat, but with some practice, you'll soon become adept at it. The effort is well worth it. For starters, it's a lot more productive than banging your head against the wall and chastising yourself for your lackluster performance. And nothing feels better than landing a job that you were certain would be offered to someone else!

There are five types of "if only I had said X instead of Y" answers:

1. *Answers Where You Didn't Really Answer the Question (Or Said Too Little).*

2. *Answers Where You Said Too Much.*

3. *Answers That Were Generic and/or Lame.*

4. *Answers That Must Be Revised Due to New Information.*

5. *Answers That You Flat-Out Flubbed.*

Together, we'll explore the original answers given and how to successfully turn them around in your follow up communications. Above all, have confidence that you can bring up your score. In order to persuade someone to hire you, you really do need to believe that you are worthy.

Answers Where You Didn't Really Answer the Question (Or Said Too Little)

Your interviewer asks you something. You nod your head intelligently and proceed to answer the question…or so you think. Hours later, as you are replaying every word of the conversation in your head, you have a thunderbolt. With a start, you realize that you didn't actually answer the question that your interviewer was asking. Or you did, but your answer was superficial beyond belief. You call all of your friends to ask what they think. Two of them tell you that you're overreacting. But your best friend on the planet doesn't happen to think so, and neither does your mother. What do you do? You read the Q &A's that follow for inspiration, and then shoot your interviewer the best follow up email that you've ever crafted.

252.

What is your favorite book?

A. Well, I've learned quite a lot from several books. Dale Carnegie's book *How To Win Friends and Influence People* taught me the importance of giving people sincere appreciation, and I really want you to know how much I appreciate the opportunity to work at your excellent organization. I read *How Would You Move Mount Fuji?*, and I want to thank you for not asking me any of those trick questions they ask job candidates at Microsoft. I also read both *Thriving on Chaos* and *In Search of Excellence*, which I am certain will help me here when you offer me this job.

EXTRA CREDIT

Your answer wasn't terrible, but it made you sound like a "one-trick pony," the kind who only reads business books, and has no time for "a life" outside of the office. Meanwhile, your interviewer wasn't even asking you which business books you had read, just what your favorite book was. You need to send him an email that answers his question (and addresses his concern) in a charming way.

Email

Dear Richard,

I greatly enjoyed meeting you this afternoon, and I am thrilled about the possibility of becoming marketing director at American Express. We spoke at length today about why my background at Visa and Discover would make a great "fit" with your company. But a really great marketing director also needs to be in touch with what's happening in the world of popular culture, or else how can one be expected to come up with the ideas and brilliant insights that touch people's hearts and minds? Towards that end, I wanted to share with you some of the books that I have been reading purely for pleasure:

1. The Devil Wears Prada
2. Bergdorf Blondes
3. Bridget Jones Diary

You won't find any of them on the suggested reading list at a university. But I do think they will help me gain a privileged entree into the elusive female mind, which can only help me with American Express's new challenge for next year: marketing to women. I will follow up with you early next week to find out your decision.

Cordially,

Blake Peterson

Inside Information

While it's a good idea to try to improve on your answers sometimes, take care not to overreact. Really consider whether your interviewer even noticed your flub before writing an entire email trying to correct the misimpression. If it was a minor gaffe, it may be smarter to write him an email about an entirely different topic. If, on the other hand, you feel strongly that you need to revise your answer, follow your instincts. You're probably right.

How to Write a Thank-You Email

Thank-you emails give you a real opportunity to build on an idea that surfaced in your interview, relate a story that you forgot to mention, and position your name in your interviewer's crowded memory bank. However, these emails need to be cleverly articulated. If there are several different points that you wish to make, it's often better to send your interviewer two emails, rather than one where all sorts of ideas hang together disjointedly. Take care to space these emails apart. Wait at least a week before sending your interviewer a second follow-up email, lest he sniff the whiff of desperation on you.

Here are some points to cover:

1. Thank your interviewer for inviting you to the interview.

2. Mention a topic that the two of you discussed in your meeting and try to briefly expand on it to show why you are ideally suited to work for the company.

3. Reiterate what the interviewer told you about following up, or suggest a date when you will contact him again to find out how to proceed.

4. Close. The follow up email is really a faster way to send an old-fashioned letter. It's perfectly acceptable to close your email with the same type of language that's customary in a formal letter—"cordially," "sincerely," "best regards," or simply "best."

 Can you give me an example of a time when you went the extra mile?

A. As the client coordinator at CGY Color Labs, it was my responsibility to help our corporate clients create gorgeous enlarged C-prints for their meetings and presentations. I would do whatever it took to make sure that their materials looked polished; and two nights out of five, this meant staying at CGY until the wee hours of the morning. Chinese takeout became my staple, and once or twice, I even had to buy a new shirt on the morning after because I had literally stayed at the office all night.

Why This Technique Could Be Improved

You're obviously dedicated, but your interviewer asked you about a specific time when you really exerted yourself for your clients. Why not describe one, with the email that follows?

Email

Dear Shen,

Thank you for meeting with me today and telling me more about the opening at RST Color. I thought some more about our conversation, and wanted to let you know of a time when I truly "went the extra mile" for one of our clients.

One day, several months ago, our machines at CGY were on the blink. Our General Foods client was very upset because one of our sales reps had told him that meeting his deadline would be impossible. I checked out the glitch with the machines, and realized that there was only a fifty-fifty chance that they would be up and running in time to get out our client's materials. I promptly called him and asked if he would mind if I sent his job out to one of our competitors. He said, "Do whatever it takes." I hand-delivered his charts to one of our rivals, and then stayed there until 3 o'clock in the morning to check the color of the C-prints. We didn't end up making a dime on that assignment; but we earned our client's loyalty to us for life. Looking forward to finding out if there might be a spot for me at RST.

Cordially,

Charlotte Kearns

EXTRA CREDIT

Don't let the dust settle. How long should you wait before sending a thank-you email? Twenty-four hours, max. Email is a 24/7 medium. If you are going to wait longer than a day, you may as well send your prospect a handwritten note via snail mail.

254. Do you consider yourself a good problem solver?

A. Oh, yes, most definitely. In our business, you really have to be. There are always scheduling screw-ups, staff upsets, and clients in an uproar. When things get particularly chaotic, I just try to stay calm by reminding myself that "today, too, will pass."

Why This Technique Needs Work

It's good to imply that you solve problems on a daily basis, but you will get far more leverage from an answer that drills down and discusses one specific problem that you solved.

Email

Dear Marjorie,

It was wonderful meeting you and hearing more about your chain of luxury spas and beauty retreats. Yesterday, you asked me if I was a good "problem solver," and so I thought I would tell you about a particularly harrowing problem that I fixed. There was an employee at EasyLife Spa who used to steal products from the salon. During Inventory, there would always be these glaring discrepancies between the number of shampoo bottles "on the books," versus the number on the shelves.

Then, one day, one of our best customers started screaming about how her personal stash of blonde color shampoos was missing from her cubbyhole. Suddenly, I realized that the "thief" must be blonde...who else would need a blonde color shampoo?

I asked all of the blonde stylists to work the following Saturday (and gave the brunettes and redheads the day off). I then "planted" one bag of blonde color shampoos at a particular station that was only shared by three of our hairdressers. When that bag was missing, I knew that I had narrowed down the pool of potential culprits to three.

After that, I just made certain that the three blonde hairdressers were never working the same shift. I planted one additional bag of blonde color shampoos at their station. When this bag was also stolen, I knew for certain who the "problem employee" was. I put her on probation, and fortunately, that was enough to stop her from filching any more shampoos. I will follow up with you early next week to chat about my prospects.

Cordially,

Michael McKinsey

The Spin Doctors

Exactly one nanosecond after a political debate ends, spin doctors from both parties adamantly insist to the press that their candidate "won." While some of their methods may seem heavy handed, spin doctors know that the contest "ain't over until it's over." The debate, per se, was only the beginning; the media's reaction to it plus the public response are almost as important as the debate itself.

You are also on a "campaign" for a particular office (hopefully, windowed). The interview is the centerpiece of your campaign. But through rigorous follow-up communications, it is possible to counter a mediocre showing at your initial meeting.

255.

What are the most important rewards that you expect in your career?

A. I enjoy training others to sell computer services. It's a joy in and of itself. I particularly love the moment when I see that one of my students really "gets it." The confusion vanishes…and I always feel justified that this is truly what I was meant to do with my life.

How This Technique Could Be Improved

Your answer is on the right track, but needs to be tightened to really turn it into a "home run." See the follow-up email.

Email

Dear Paul,

When I got home today after our meeting, it suddenly hit me. I told you why I love training salespeople, but I didn't really capture the genuine pride that I feel in their accomplishments. And so, I thought I would take the opportunity right now to tell you about an ex-student of mine. Her name was Cynthia, and when she first arrived in my seminar, her boss, Scott Smithers, told me that he had "no hope" for her survival at JYT Systems.

Cynthia had been trying to sell a package of computer services to businesspeople to help them generate PowerPoint presentations. The problem was that Cynthia had never had to develop one of these presentations herself, thus had no clue about some of the problems that businesspeople would encounter. Instead of launching right into the selling points that she should make, I gave her a homework assignment. "Take my sales materials," I told her, "and develop a PowerPoint presentation on how to sell these computer services."

Cynthia studied night and day, and, against all odds, crafted one of the finest PowerPoint presentations that I had ever seen. Going through the exercise herself made her lose all self-consciousness when it came to helping others. She became a master saleswoman, and her boss asked me to make the exercise that I had given Cynthia a mandatory part of my training.

Seeing "the light go on" in my students' eyes is the reason that I gave up a lucrative career selling computer systems to help others sell them. I look forward to bringing my expertise to your firm in the very near future.

Cordially,

Nadia Thompson

Is It Really Possible to Change Your Grade Post-Interview?

It all depends on what kind of a flub you made, how much your interviewer "counted it against you," and how cleverly you follow up to change his impression. You may not be able to improve a B showing in an interview all the way to an A. But you can try, and depending on how your competition follows up (or fails to), you may actually have a shot. If you need any inspiration, go rent the movie *Clueless,* and watch how the character Cher manages to persuade her teachers to give her much better grades after her report card has already been sent home. "Honey, I couldn't be happier than if they were based on real grades," her dad says.

256.
Tell me about a time when something bad happened to you in your personal life.

A. I was rejected from all of the Ivy League colleges where I applied, which was quite a blow to me at the time. I was a straight-A student in high school, and had gotten very high SAT scores, double 700s. So it was very humbling to only be accepted by my "safety school," Trinity College.

Email

Dear Marianna,

I am so excited about the possibility of coming to work for you, and look forward to finding out my next steps. In the meantime, I thought that I would tell you some more about why I believe that my early setback (not getting into any Ivy League schools) actually helped me to become a terrific events manager. I learned from an early age to "expect the unexpected," and to be prepared for any crisis.

Last month, when I put together a party for the UJA, Mel Brooks was supposed to be our guest speaker. But in the eleventh hour, Mr. Brooks wasn't able to attend the function. The party invitations had already been printed, and I really think that the average events planner would have freaked out. Instead, I worked the phones and was able to persuade Robin Williams to stop by for the evening. It was one of the most successful events that the UJA ever held, and contributions to the cause doubled.

If you hire me to be your events manager, I'm confident that I will be able to pull a similar "miracle" out of my hat. I look forward to chatting with you soon about this exciting possibility.

Cordially,

Ivy Knowles

Answers Where You Said Too Much

Once a sentiment is "out there" in the universe, it can be very difficult to pull it back into a response that can help you bolster your case. Still, with a certain amount of ingenuity, you can prevail. Recognize that in situations where you said too much, you are definitely "starting from behind" in your interviewer's eyes. But black sheep, dark horses, and interviewees who have put their foot in their mouths still sometimes find a way to salvage their job hunts!

257. I understand that you want to break into this company. But I'm not in the right department to help you. Why did you contact me instead of our human resources manager?

A. Well, quite honestly, Adam, I heard through the grapevine that Mimi Vanderling could be a little difficult to reach. And so, I was hoping to meet someone else in the company first…and hopefully have that person talk to Mimi on my behalf.

No, No, No!

Your answer wasn't a mere "no-no." It was a triple no, for the following reasons:

1. You practically bad-mouthed the HR manager of the company before you even had a chance to meet her. And you want her to give you a job?

2. Your interviewer asked why you contacted him, and you didn't give him a compelling reason. (Hint: Saying that you contacted him because Mimi's impossible to get a hold of is *not* a good reason.)

3. You came off sounding manipulative, and modern-day Machiavellis don't make terribly attractive job candidates. You need to write a really strong follow up email to counteract this impression.

Email

Dear Adam,

First off, I want to thank you for agreeing to meet with me today. The world of purchasing has often been closed to "outsiders" like me, and I can't tell you how much I genuinely appreciated your taking the time to sit down with me and tell me more about the exciting projects that have been going on in your department. I know that you are a genuine expert in the field, and I consider myself privileged to have finally made your acquaintance. Your offer to put in a good word to Mimi Vanderling was very kind, and I look forward to following up with both you and Mimi in the very near future. As you suggested, I will call Mimi when she gets back from vacation on Tuesday, and then contact you later in the week to apprise you of my progress.

Thanks again, Adam!

Perry O'Connor

258. What adverse factors have kept you from progressing faster?

A. When I had just graduated from business school, I joined LMP as a consultant. My pay package was probably 25 percent less than what I was worth, but I was very impressed with the caliber of the LMP staff, and I was jazzed up about the opportunity to learn from some of the best people in the business.

I was promoted almost every year, and had the chance to take on more responsibility in managing client relationships. As I climbed the corporate ladder, however, I began to realize that I would probably never make it to "principal" at LMP. People who were promoted to that level generally got there by kissing up to their managers, rather than by any real contributions they had made to the firm. The economic slowdown didn't help either, as we were suddenly under tremendous pressure to meet unrealistic sales goals. My bonus last year was a bit off, and so I started to look around.

Mayday! Mayday!

This is *way* too much information, and it's also riddled with false logic. If the people at LMP really were the "best in the business," then why would they suddenly start giving their staff unrealistic sales goals? You are not going to be able to correct this answer in your follow up communications, because you've already said much too much. If you find yourself in this situation, the best thing to do is to backpedal gracefully…right there in the interview.

Backpedal A. You know, there have been a lot of changes in the leadership at LMP recently, creating some managerial "hiccups." The company has a long and celebrated history, and so I'm certain that this is just a minor aberration, rather than a sign that anything's seriously wrong there.

However, I'd rather work as a consultant for a really prestigious firm such as yours. I've done well at LMP for five years, and I would love to bring my consulting skills to a company where I can continue to learn and grow.

259. What are your other job possibilities? How do you feel about them?

A. Well, I can always go work for my daughter at her baby accessories store. Although, truthfully, I'm a little concerned that working for my 40-year-old kid is going to make our family even more dysfunctional that it is normally.

EXTRA CREDIT Loose lips sink ships (and job offers). Why bring up the fact that your daughter owns the baby accessories store? It will just make your interviewer wonder if your daughter will be paying you for your time (and, if not, why he should!). Turn on your laptop, and start cranking out your email.

Email

Dear Roger,

Thank you for talking to me today about the fashion-merchandising program at The European Man. As you know, I used to follow retail stocks when I worked on Wall Street, and, over the years, had the burning desire to switch over to the retail side numerous times. I have also shopped at your store so often that it's no exaggeration to say that I know your merchandise inside out!

While I do have some other offers on the table, I would vastly prefer to work for your fine establishment. In fact, working for you would help me fulfill the dream of a lifetime. I will call you next week to find out my next steps.
Cordially,
Andy Blair

 **What were the most rewarding aspects of the job?**

A. I was allowed to jump from department to department for a couple of years to "find myself." I worked in seven positions at Zel Labs since I started just a few years ago. I was in their training program, which offered rotations every three months. This helped me find a great manager whom I really respected, and I simply attached myself to her "like a sponge" and absorbed everything that she had to teach me. An article that I once read claimed that Zel was one of the best places for a woman to work, and truthfully, I found that to be the case.

Can I Take That Back, Please?

Your response was so deferential to your current place of employment that you've given your interviewer no gripping reason to "rescue" you from your job. Why should he hire you when you're blissfully employed, when so many others would kill to come work for him? Your follow up email really needs to make the case that you are ready for a change.

Email

Dear Steven,

Now that I've finally had a chance to meet you after all of these years, I wanted to let you know how much I would really like to work for you. As a place to learn the ropes, Zel Labs was fantastic. But in the past year or so, I find that I have been anxious to find a permanent home at a biotechnology company like yours. I know that your company is making huge strides in cancer and leukemia research. (My grandfather died of leukemia, so this has always been a cause that's close to my heart.) I would consider it a great honor to work for your company. I will call you early next week to find out if I might be able to.

Best,

Jenny Jones

Answers That Were Generic and/or Lame

Generic answers let your interviewer know that you didn't care enough about the position to research it properly. This is not a clever job-hunting strategy. Your interviewer may feel miffed that you didn't take the job interview seriously. And today, you can count on the fact that there will be at least one competitor of yours who will manage to answer the identical questions in a way that proves he really deserves the job. Never ever give a generic answer. But if you do, make every attempt to compensate for it after the fact.

261.

What criteria are you using to evaluate the company for which you work?

A. I'm happiest in a fast-paced environment. I like to work long and hard, and I'm a true believer in the team concept. I enjoy being around high-energy people. They seem to bring out my competitive spirit, challenging me to be my best.

EXTRA CREDIT

Your answer gets a "B" for "boilerplate" and lacks the oomph it needs for you to get a call back interview. Add some pizzazz to your answer with the email that follows.

Email

Dear Jane,

I can't thank you enough for sitting down with me yesterday, and telling me more about life on the inside of Zee Foods. I am keen to join your Condiments Division and help find a niche for condiments in cool colors—purple mustards, white ketchups, and pink onion pastes. As a business analyst for desserts and snacks, I've worked long hours, especially during planning and budgeting weeks. I know how to write a presentable deck, analyze P&L, and help create the kind of strategic platforms that will propel Zee Foods into a number one brand. I look forward to working closely with the high-impact staff at Zee, and will call you early next week to find out my next steps. In the meantime, did you happen to read the article about Beatrice Foods in BrandWeek? I've attached it for your convenience, in case you missed it. Looking forward to chatting with you next week.

Sincerely,

Emma Wilson

262.

What have you disliked most about your past jobs?

A. I didn't always feel as if I was allowed to grow on the jobs. I fulfilled my directives pretty well and received raises and promotions regularly, but I wasn't actually learning anything new after awhile.

Why This Technique Doesn't Work

As master communicator David Ogilvy used to say: "You can't bore anyone into a sale."

Email

Dear Frank,

What a sincere pleasure it was to meet you this morning. I was very taken with those excerpts that you quoted out of your company's handbook, and I really believe that your firm is poised to grow, thrive, and take on the "lumbering giants" in our field. Naturally, I want to be right there, alongside you, learning and growing. As we discussed, there is plenty of room for a new type of "home concierge" service, and I look forward to helping you find the prospects who have been dissatisfied with theirs, pitching your company to them, and developing a thriving client base. I will call you on Tuesday morning at 10 a.m. to find out my next steps.

Yours truly,

Eleanor Mackenzie

263.

What one person had the greatest influence on your life? Why?

A. The headmistress of the all girls' school I attended always made me feel that I could be anything I wanted to be. She was a true role model, and I genuinely respected her.

Blah, Blah, Blah

Your answer wasn't memorable or unique, and it probably didn't impress your interviewer enough to recommend you for a position. Strengthen your response, by revealing more about this important mentor.

Email

Dear Sandy,

I am ecstatic about the possibility of coming on staff at Women to Women. Today, when I got home from our meeting, I happened to catch the "Women in History" program on your excellent network, and it reminded me again of my own dear headmistress, whom as you know, was one of the biggest influences in my life. She was fond of saying that "99 percent of the obstacles we would ever face were in our own minds." Her gem of wisdom kept me going over the years, through Vassar, Wharton, and my first couple of jobs in children's television programming. I look forward to hearing about my next steps from you, since, "in my mind," I'm already working at Women to Women. I will call you next week, Sandy, if I don't hear from you first.

Regards,

Becky Meyers

264.

What qualifications do you have that make you think that you will be successful?

A. Well, Cara, as you know, I've been working in a four-diamond hotel, and I believe that I really do provide four-diamond service to our guests. I have learned how to make our visitors feel at ease and supremely well taken care of during their stays.

Yawn!

Your answer is going to make your interviewer want to reach for one of those fluffy pillows that you always get at four-diamond hotels, and catch some shut-eye.

Email

Dear Cara,

Thank you for meeting with me today and telling me more about the Corporate Accounts Manager position. I am eager to transfer to your premier hotel chain, and wanted to follow up with you about my qualifications. As the catering manager at my last hotel, it was my job to arrange wedding receptions in the Blue Room.

At one of these parties the bride lost her engagement ring! She ran up to me with tears streaming down her face, and it was my job to figure out how to search the room without disrupting the festivities. I approached the band, and asked it to play some "happy music" that would get everyone in the room on the dance floor. Four dances into the set, I found the bride's ring. She had inadvertently slipped it off her hand while her groom fed her a piece of wedding cake; and, fortunately, her ring was sitting right there on the wedding cake table!

I always strive to give Four Diamond service, but on that day, I think I gave the bride four-diamond service, plus one extra diamond: her 2-carat, square-cut diamond ring. I will call you early next week to find out my next steps.
Best regards,
Daria Wilson

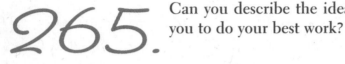

265. Can you describe the ideal conditions for you to do your best work?

A. I always want to feel like a valued asset. I'm interested in working at your company because, while the hours will be long and hard, I know that there will be plenty of opportunities for advancement.

EXTRA **CREDIT** If an answer is right out of "the Q&A handbook," it's not good enough! Find fresh ways to prove that you will be a productive and valuable member of the team.

Email

Dear Marvin,
I wanted to get back to you on the conversation that we had this morning, and tell you a little more about why I feel SST would be the perfect company for me. As you know, I met with Sara Cloverdale last Tuesday, and felt like we bonded immediately. Sara told me more about some of the initiatives that are taking place on her team. I know that she will make a superb mentor and role model for me, and I am very excited about the possibility of following in her footsteps. As you suggested, I will follow up with you on Tuesday to meet the rest of the team.
Best,
Claire Crossing

Answers That Must Be Revised Due to New Information

You've done the unthinkable. You gave your interviewer the *one* answer that he didn't want to hear. Ironically, if you happen to be extremely organized, you may find yourself blowing more than the occasional interview. Why? Wasn't being disciplined and doing your homework on the company supposed to prevent that very scenario? The simple answer: yes, but other people may not be as organized as you are. So it's entirely possible that while you left "no stone unturned" in your efforts to uncover everything about the position, your headhunter didn't. Hence, you are caught off guard by some fact about the position that you didn't know in advance.

The best thing to do is stay flexible during your meeting. Don't dismiss a job just because you discover something negative about it. Keep the door open, at least until you can plot out your next move. Failing that, here's how to reverse your original answer in your follow up email.

266. Are you looking for a permanent job or freelance?

A. Oh, I definitely want a full-time job. I've been freelancing for a while now, and nothing would please me more than finding a full-time job at a great company like yours.

Oops!

The second that you got home, your headhunter called to tell you what she should have told you before your interview: the job is for a consultant to fill in for someone for a couple of months. There is no full-time job. It's time to change your response, with the email that follows.

Email

Dear Stewart,

Thank you for meeting with me today and telling me more about the freelance position on DGX Toys. I would relish the opportunity to come on as a consultant for you for two months and fill in during Maria Grunwald's leave. In fact, nothing would please me more. The toy convention is around the corner, and it sounds like you could certainly use someone to help you set up your booth, double check that all of the promotional materials are in place, and ensure that your fall sales drive leading up to the big Christmas selling season goes off smoothly, without a hitch. I will call you next week to follow up.

Thanks, Stewart.

Best,

Victoria Simmons

 **. Did the recruiter mention that one-third of your time would be spent in our Ontario office, and how do you feel about that?**

A. No, she definitely didn't! I had no idea that this job would involve so much travel. Can you tell me more about how your headquarters works with the Ontario office?

How to Repair This Interview Blooper

1. Take a deep breath. Exhale.

2. Listen carefully to what your interviewer tells you about the Ontario division. Instead of fretting about how all of that travel will affect your relationship with your new gorgeous boyfriend (or girlfriend), picture all of the frequent flyer miles you will rack up. Gee, after six months at the job, you might even be able to fly to Europe with your honey for free.

3. Tell your interviewer that you find the prospect of being the Ontario liaison thrilling. (When you get home, you can always politely decline the job, if you decide otherwise.)

Spell-Check Your Emails

Nothing takes away points faster than a glaring typo on one of your emails. Here's how to write a "foolproof" email.

1. Type your email first on a blank document, and spell-check it once using your computer software.

2. Print out the document, and check it one more time to catch any typos that spell-check missed (due to usage confusion, or words that can be spelled two different ways).

3. Cut and paste that document into your email.

It will definitely take you longer to write your emails in this manner. But the extra care that you take is bound to show.

Answers That You Flat-Out Flubbed

It's been called the "Fight or Flight Syndrome," and it perfectly captures how human beings react to stress. Let's suppose that your interviewer asks you a question that is far too difficult to answer on the spot. Chances are, you're not going to get into a heated debate with him about how unfair the question is! Instead, the "Flight Syndrome" kicks in. You can't think of anything to say...because all you want, at that very moment, is to flee from your interviewer. So you choke, and—what do you know—your meeting ends early.

When you have the urgent desire to hightail it out of your interview, recognize that this is a natural reaction to stress, and have confidence that you will improve on your answer once you have calmed down.

 This division was the brainchild of our CEO William Wentworth. But after William passed away a couple of years ago, the "fire" went out of our company's belly. And this department has been limping along for the last three quarters. What would you do to improve profitability?

A. Wow! That's sort of a tough question to answer right here, on the spot, Clark. I wonder if you might give me twenty-four hours to create a proposal for you about how I would turn things around?

268b. No, Cal, that's really beyond the call of duty. I'm asking you, off the top of your head, what would you do?

A. Clearly, your CEO had a vision for this department, which is either deliberately not being followed by the top managers, or more likely, isn't completely understood by them. The key questions to ask are:

1. Did William Wentworth's vision really work when he was still around to manifest it? If it did, then the managers of your company simply need to be retrained on how to fulfill his directives.

2. But if there was some flaw in William Wentworth's vision, or if economic factors have changed so dramatically in the past few years that his idea no longer works, then the top "visionary" at your company needs to work out a completely new purpose, and possibly, revamp your organizational structure to make this department functional again.

I have consulted for several companies who found themselves in this very predicament, and would be delighted to help your visionary create a strategic plan that would help get your department back on course.

The 5 Things to Double Check Before Letting Your Thank-You Email Fly

1. The spelling of your interviewer's name. Can you spell "careless"?

2. The spelling of the name of the company where you are applying. You would be surprised how many times candidates completely batch this spelling! (Incidentally, the word "batch" was supposed to be "botch.")

3. The spelling of your interviewer's email address. You want your email to reach him, right?

4. The spelling of your own name and email address. Should your interviewer wish to contact you via email, you want to make it as easy for him as possible.

5. Check the "Copy Message To Sent Folder" box at the bottom of your email. It's enormously helpful to have a record of your email, the date that you sent it, and your contact's email information. This will prevent you from "over-communicating" to your prospect because you can't remember the exact date that you followed up with him.

269a.

This is a family-run business where family members are given all kinds of latitude and room for error. Staff members who don't belong to the Berlinger clan really aren't given the same consideration. You would be reporting to two Berlinger brothers who never see eye to eye on the future of the business. What makes you think that you'll be able to cope?

A. I will simply have to do more homework on the marketplace and be unbelievably thorough about my recommendations. I've been very adept at avoiding political confrontations in my past job as an import/export manager at Peruvian Foods International, and...

269b.

Yeah, but Bobby Berlinger believes that we're in the high-end gourmet specialty foods business, while Bertrand Berlinger feels just as strongly that our specialty foods should become more mass market, appealing to middle class housewives. You'll be slaughtered in a vicious sibling rivalry war.

A. May I take a quick walk to your water cooler down the hall, and clear my thoughts for a moment? (Then return and give your interviewer the answer that follows.)

Alt. A. At some level, both Bobby and Bertrand Berlinger must recognize that Berlinger Foods International can't sustain its growth by being "all things to all people." If your company only imports high-end gourmet foods, there's a limit to how many customers your company will attract, given the decline of gourmet home cooking in households across America. It's no secret that the middle class now eats at restaurant chains three times a week.

At the same time, it's unrealistic to assume that Berlinger Foods is going to evolve into a company that makes everyday household food products like mayonnaise. Your price points are simply too high for the average American woman to swallow.

I think that we can bridge the divide, however, if we start targeting your specialty foods to restaurant chains. The items will continue to have an upscale, gourmet, high-end vibe to them, but their distribution will double or triple. American housewives will be introduced to your products in the places where they eat out all the time. And then, when it comes to cooking their own dinners, they will be able to justify splurging on Berlinger Foods at their local supermarkets. Bobby and Bertrand's goals can both be achieved.

Why This Technique Works

1. Given a choice of "black" or "white," you found a new "gray" area to explore that has a lot of promise.

2. Wisely, you stuck to discussing the things you know, rather than being sucked into the quagmire of a family squabble that consumes most outsiders.

270. What are you looking for in your next job?

A. I am unbelievably excited about the opportunity to work on the HKT account. I've always had my heart set on helping them target the suburban Dallas market, which I understand has been challenging lately. I read a very interesting article about HKT in the *New York Times,* and…

271.

Did the article happen to mention that we lost the HKT account?

Time for Some Fancy Footwork

1. First, remove your foot from your mouth and put it back firmly on the floor.

2. Say something that acknowledges your error in a genial way, such as: "Wow! I'm so sorry, Mack, I hadn't the slightest idea. I've been studying your company so thoroughly because I am really 'hungry' to work here, but I guess I just missed the obvious. Your account loss wasn't even mentioned in that article! But I would love to hear more about it from you right now. When did it happen exactly? Were you surprised? And how did your staff react to the news?"

---

3 Gaffes No Follow-Up Email Can Fix

1. **You showed up late.** That was tacky, but re-apologizing for your error via email is worse. It will just remind your interviewer why she shouldn't hire you.

2. **You made a joke in the interview that wasn't funny.** Not only didn't your interviewer laugh, he actually took the joke seriously. Splat! (That's the sound of you reliving the moment over and over again in your head, as you mentally try to pick yourself up off the floor.) Don't bring your interviewer down along with you by revisiting your error in an email. Just get over it, okay?

3. **Your cell phone rang during your interview.** Yikes! Real quickly: here's the Murphy's Law of cell phones. Even if your cell phone never rings, it will during your interview. That's why you have no choice but to keep your cell off. But now that your interviewer has grave doubts about your business etiquette, there's really no point in apologizing for your cell. Just hope that the rest of your conversation impressed him enough to ignore your cell phone gaffe.

3. After you get the lowdown on HKT, ask your interviewer which accounts you would be handling. Then, make the case for why you deserve to work on those pieces of business.
4. Do not allude to your mistake in any follow-up communications.

272.

How well do you deal with quicksand, Marcia? With all of the management changes that have been going on here, you'd basically be a moving target.

A. Really? Gosh, Alan Sandbanks (my headhunter) didn't tell me anything about this. Given all of the management upheavals, are you still looking for a new director of customer sales at EER AudioTrax?

Why This Technique Doesn't Work

1. You sound like you're painfully out of the loop. It's okay to ask your headhunter for the scoop on a company, but it's not okay to rely exclusively on that information.
2. Your interviewer asked how well you deal with change, and you didn't answer the question.

Email

Dear Larry,

I was surprised to hear from you that EER AudioTrax is going through so many internal changes because it sounds exactly like the company where I presently work. I feel like the management structure here is always in motion. Hardly a quarter goes by without a mini department shakeout of some kind.

Still, I have managed to stay focused in spite of all of these changes. In our business, we have so many important challenges ahead of us that it's never a good idea to get distracted by internal politics. If you hire me, I will be able to expand your list of retail partnerships significantly, so that audiophiles the world over will come to us first whenever they want to hear their favorite magazines and books on tape. As you suggested, I will call you next week to see if I might be able to meet with Daniel Richards.

Cordially,

Marcia Metters

---

3 Other Ways to Choke and Recover

1. You gracefully walk into your interviewer's office wearing your perfectly appointed T-strap pumps, and *whoa!*, proceed to slide across his recently polished hardwood floors, landing firmly on your butt.

Recovery Line: You know, I always like to make an entrance.

2. As you delicately perch on your interviewer's chair, a spring pops. Striving to catch your balance, you knock over a small paperweight on his desk.

Recovery Line: Well, now that I know that I have your attention…

3. You gaze into your interviewer's eyes and answer his question perfectly, but call him by the wrong name. He corrects you.

Recovery Line: I'm so sorry, Edgar. I had a lobotomy yesterday, and I guess I haven't fully recuperated.

Inside Information

Never forget the cardinal rule of selling yourself: once you've made the sale, stop selling. Don't give your interviewer the chance to change his mind!

 **How do you spend your vacations?**

A. Well, I've been spending this vacation looking for a job, of course. But, when I was growing up, my Dad used to work at Royal Caribbean, and so, I actually spent many of my winter vacations taking cruises with my family. For eighteen years, I heard all about the cruise industry at the dinner table, and I think that my innate understanding of it will help me develop into an excellent account executive.

Why This Technique Works

1. It's smart, clear, and leaves little doubt that you know the cruise industry a lot better than any outsiders.

2. But don't guild the proverbial lily by sending your interviewer a follow up email that hits the same theme. Find something else to write about.

274.

Let's discuss your extracurricular activities. I see from your resume that you like to tap dance?

A. Yes…and when you hire me, I'll do a tap dance.

You sound like you would be a fun person to have on staff. But don't expand on your hobby in your follow up email. Instead, write an email that proves beyond the shadow of the doubt that you have the qualifications your interviewer is seeking.

275.

Did you happen to bring an extra copy of your portfolio with you today? Our HR department inadvertently sent it back to your headhunter, and I'd really like to take a look at it.

A. No, Stella, I'm sorry I had no idea that this had happened. In fact, I actually checked with Carrie Stevens this morning, and she told me that my book was still here. But I'll be happy to swing by Carrie's office on my way home today, pick up my portfolio, and then hand-deliver it to your receptionist later this afternoon.

If you are willing to go this far out of your way before you even get the job, it's a good sign that you will be unbelievably dedicated at the job. Follow up with an email to double check that your interviewer received your portfolio.

Email

Dear Stella,

What a pleasure it was meeting with you today and hearing more about the open position at BFG, along with some of the challenges your department is facing. True to my word, I stopped by Carrie Stevens's office, picked up my portfolio, and dropped it off for your terrific receptionist Mary Witherspoon this afternoon. I had looked forward to taking you through the work in my book, although, in a way, this will be the true test of its powers of persuasion. As a former colleague of mine used to say: "Your work always needs to sell itself. It's not like you'll ever be sitting with it to explain it." I look forward to hearing your feedback on it. And I will call you next Tuesday to find out more about what you thought, along with what my next steps might be.

Best,

Courtney Andersen

That's a Wrap

1. If you realize that you didn't answer your interviewer's real question, it's time to carefully craft an email to him that will. Was your answer too superficial? Answers that barely skim the surface of your experience make you look like a total lightweight. If you encountered "interview interruptus," send your interviewer a thought-provoking email that will respond to his question in a deeper, more meaningful way.

2. Did you say too much in your interview? It's hard to take something back once it's out there, but sometimes, there is a graceful way to move your relationship with your interviewer forward, anyway. If you possibly can, try to correct your faux pas in the actual interview. Failing that, find a way to send your interviewer an email that eloquently explains why you are the ideal candidate for the job.

3. Generic answers to questions prove that you don't care enough about the job to merit it. If you give a generic answer by accident, follow up with an email that's extremely detail-oriented (and pray that your competition doesn't follow up).

4. Sometimes, being overprepared cuts against you in an interview, if your sources were misinformed. Try to stay open-minded, as new facts are revealed about the position, so that your interviewer will feel like you are genuinely interested.

5. Even interviewing protégés have occasionally flubbed a particularly tough question. If you feel your answer getting caught in your throat, recognize that the "Flight Syndrome" has kicked in, and ask your interviewer for a five-minute break to catch your breath and silently collect your thoughts. Then, come back and deliver the job-winning response.

CHAPTER 12
Special Situations

By now, you've probably mastered the formal job interview (and have even started coaching some of your friends). You dress for the part. You converse with natural ease and grace. And very few questions even rattle you.

Unfortunately, not all job interviews take place in someone's office after you've had an entire week to prepare. Some interviews are virtual (even if they're conducted via old-fashioned technology); some interviews are informal; some interviews are unexpected; and some interviews are really job-saving strategies. Still, the more clearly you can anticipate the types of questions that you will be asked on these interviews, the better you will perform.

There are five types of interviews that are really special situations:

1. *Phone Interviews.*
2. The *"Last Interview."*
3. *Informational Interview.*
4. *One of the Bosses Never Met You.*
5. *Interviews to Keep Your Job.*

How do you deal with these special situations? First, learn to recognize when you happen to be in one of them. Anticipation is the key to success. Recognize that there's no such thing as an informal chat with someone who's empowered to hire you or who holds your destiny in his hands. Second, take stock of your own progress. Resolve to learn from what you did right. Here's how to contend with those special situations that are uniquely harrowing to even the most practiced interviewees.

Phone Interviews

If you apply for a job at a company, and someone calls you to set up a phone interview, first, realize that this is really a prescreening technique. The purpose of the phone interview is not to hire you, but to vet people from the process. And just like in the reality TV show *Survivor,* some people will not make it to the next round. On the phone, you will hurt yourself far more by saying too much, rather than too little. Remember that from your standpoint, the only purpose of the call is to get your interviewer to grant you an in-person meeting.

276. How much money did you make at your last job?

A. My last salary was pretty typical for someone in my position. And I promise to tell you the exact number when we meet in person. Are you available to see me on Tuesday at 10 a.m.? I would love to continue this conversation face-to-face.

EXTRA

✓

CREDIT

Don't ever reveal what your last salary was during a phone interview. You don't want it used as an excuse to eliminate you in round one.

277. So, what did you think of _____ (your last place of employment)?

A. That's a very interesting story, Marla, and I can't wait to tell you all about it when I see you. I feel like we probably have a lot to talk about, and it's no secret that I'm dying to work at your company. By any chance, would you be free to see me this Wednesday at 11 a.m.?

Be a Phone Tease

Promise your interviewer the moon, the stars, and even the inside scoop on a company if necessary, but work that phone to get an in-person interview. (However, when you finally do sit down with the person, take care to withhold any information that is negative. Those with the gift of gab know when not to blab.)

I Just Happen to Be in Your Neighborhood

The fact that you don't live in the same city adds some cachet to your cause, and makes interviewers more open to granting you a meeting on your schedule. So never hesitate to let an interviewer know when you're going to be in his 'hood.

 Are you really willing to move all the way from Pittsburgh to Albuquerque for this job?

A. You bet, and as a matter of fact, I'm going to be in Albuquerque next Thursday. I was wondering if you might have a few minutes to sit down with me that day at around 11 a.m.?

EXTRA CREDIT Some companies are wary of hiring candidates from out of town due to hefty moving expenses. If you suspect that this is the case, you can always claim that you are planning to move—regardless of whether you are offered the job.

279.

I'm sort of a Luddite, and so I really need someone on staff with good computer skills. Are you familiar with Quark, Photo- shop, Illustrator, and M-Design?

A. Yes, and I actually trained a lot of the studio designers at my company how to use them. Would you like to see an example of a presentation that I designed in Adobe Illustrator? I could email it over to you right now while we're still on the phone and you could ask me any questions about it that you'd like. Or, if that doesn't work for you, would you be able to meet me next Wednesday? I would love to show you my portfolio.

Why This Technique Works

1. Computer illiterates generally admire designer geeks (and geekettes). Offering to shoot over the presentation on the spot is a technique that's both hi-tech and hi-touch.

2. If your interviewer really is the Luddite that he claims, he probably won't want you to email him your presentation. Instead, he'll invite you to come and meet him in person.

Don't Put Your Interviewer in Cell Hell

Welcome to cell hell, a scary place where connections are frequently muddled, voices fade in and out, and people can be cut off mid-sentence without even realizing it. If you are anticipating a phone interview, always give the company the phone number of your land line, and hang out there to wait for their call. Cell phone technology is still not as perfect as your landline at home. You don't want this all-important phone call interrupted by the din and roar of traffic or other pedestrians.

Never claim that a contact of yours suggested that you stop by for an in-person meeting unless he really did. But if he did, why not pass along his words of wisdom?

280. So, how do you know Billy?

A. Billy and I used to work together at PNT International. I have tremendous respect for Billy's talents, and when your job opening came up, he actually called and urged me to apply. Billy also thought that it might be a good idea for me to stop by and say hello to you. Do you have any time for a quick "meet and greet" on Tuesday at 10 a.m., because nothing would please me more?

The Art of Giving Good Phone

If talking to a total stranger on the phone is not exactly your forte, suggest a date for the phone interview that is a full two days later than when you first receive the call to set it up. (Never take a spontaneous phone interview!) Then, follow the three rules of giving fabulous phone:

1. **Think about the questions your phone interviewer is likely to ask.** Write down your answers to them in advance. (Your interviewer won't be able to see you referring to your notes, so why not take advantage of the situation?)

2. **"Sound bite" yourself.** Most of the time, questions over the phone are identical to the ones that you would be asked in person. But your answers need to be a lot shorter, just long enough to keep you in M-Design the game.

3. **Close the sale.** Always suggest a date and time for a real, live meeting at your interviewer's office.

The "Last Interview"

After you've aced several interviews at a firm, there is often one last person whom you will be asked to meet. In essence, this person is the "pope" of your job quest: he needs to give you his blessing. If he deems that you are worthy, then you will be offered the job. (And you can say "amen.") This one last interview is critically important. So even if you're told that it's "just a courtesy interview," nod your head courteously, and proceed to study for this interview as diligently as you have for all of the others.

281. Are you 100 percent certain that you'll be able to turn things around in our department?

A. Let's put it this way, I'm 99.9 percent certain. But I always like to leave a little room for error and not "over-promise." In my past three jobs, I turned around driftless, lumbering departments. I'm willing to make the tough decisions that you need and really make sure that everyone at your company is pulling their weight. But while I'm tough, I also have a reputation for fairness. I don't make rash, impulsive decisions. I take a long time to make a detailed, thorough assessment. And then, when I have to make cuts, at least I'm certain that I'm making the right ones.

EXTRA CREDIT

You'll sway more interviewers if you position yourself as a compassionate reigning monarch, rather than a ruthless dictator. After all, everyone would rather serve the former.

**282.** So far, you've dazzled every single person on our team. But I'm a little pickier than they are. Let's pretend that I never heard anything about you. Why should you work here?

A. Well, I'm very intrigued with your business, Jonathan. On the one hand, you've been providing essentially the same service to people for the last sixty years—emergency towing when their cars break down. On the other hand, the business has been gradually evolving and changing as luxury cars have started to offer towing services as well, but through your organization. I look forward to the challenge of continuing to give your customers the "peace of mind" they've come to expect along with new and exciting members' packages. As you know, I'm no stranger to the travel package and promotions business. At my last job, I picked up the skills to generate the types of promotional ideas that you need to move your business forward today.

283. Well, since I'm the "last stop on the hit parade," I just thought that I'd call you in for an informal chat. Do you have any questions?

A. Well, Marla explained the internal structure of LTL really thoroughly; Audrey outlined every detail about the job; and Phillip gave me the "heads up" on your vendors, suppliers, and partners. So I feel comfortable that I understand the position along with what everyone's expectations will be. I do have one question about the corporate culture, though. When your entire team is sitting in a meeting with one of your corporate partners, is it customary for the most senior person to speak his mind first, or the most junior person?

Why This Technique Works

1. You've recapped what you learned about the company from each of the team members—proving that you know the job inside out.

2. You followed up with a "softball" question, which is certain to spark a lively conversation about etiquette at the conference room table.

Inside Information

If you can summarize it, you've absorbed it. Listen closely to what various interviewers tell you about the company. Then, rephrase the information to show that you get it.

 **You met with Tom, Dick, and Harriet already. Did they explain how the internal structure works? And do you understand it?**

A. Yes, I'm pretty confident that I do. From what I understand, Tom and Dick are partners who head up one mega team at PYL, while Harriet is the team leader of a second group. But Tom, Dick, and Harriet all cover for each other during business trips overseas. Our clients feel comfortable with all three managers and believe that they are all on the same team. The internal structure at PYL needs to remain "invisible" to our clients, so that they will continue to feel like things here work seamlessly, and that their needs are being attended to first.

285.

Did Sam explain that we're not in the habit of giving new hires three-year contracts? I know that you had your heart set on one... but would you settle for a two-year contract?

A. Actually, Sam didn't happen to mention it to me, and neither did Paulo Moroni. I'm fairly flexible to a point. Do you happen to have a copy of the standard contract? I would love to have Paulo take a look at it, and also my lawyer.

Why This Technique Works

1. You didn't overreact to the bad news about your contract, and wisely deferred any negotiations until your headhunter and lawyer could review it.

2. Your interviewer claimed that it was "Sam's job" to discuss your contract with you, but it's far more likely that your interviewer was supposed to do it and wussed out. Your interviewer is the "good cop." Sam is the "bad cop." See chapter 7.

Informational Interviews

Sorry to inform you, but most informational interviews do not lead to full-time jobs. These interviews are usually granted out of the kindness of a contact's heart, and, out of consideration, need to be kept short. Treat them as genuine fact-finding missions. Basically, you want to learn if a particular career appeals to you, and if so, how to break into the field. Your contact will probably lead the conversation; but you will have to springboard off of his questions to tease out the information that you need.

286.

So, Cindy, what can I do for you today?

A. First of all, Steve, I want to thank you for taking a few moments out of your busy afternoon to sit down and talk to me. I genuinely appreciate it. Ever since I was a kid, I've been fascinated by music videos. I know that you direct them…and I was wondering if you could give me some pointers. How can I get my foot in the door of your company? Do you have any thoughts for this "director wannabe"?

Inside Information

When you acknowledge that your contact has more important things to do than to meet with you, it often relaxes him just enough to give you all the time you need.

287.

Do you want feedback on your resume, or do you just want to ask me some questions?

A. Please, Jim…let's not stand on ceremony. I'm here to learn what it takes to get into your line of work. So, feel free to be "brutally honest." If my resume needs any polishing, tell me what I can do to improve it. Is there any portion of it that isn't clear?

EXTRA CREDIT Always demonstrate that you're mature enough to handle constructive criticism. After all, you're at the informational interview to get honest feedback and advice.

288.

You understand that there's no real job opening here, right, Rich?

A. Oh, yes, of course, Christopher. I just sincerely appreciate the opportunity to hear more about designing computer games for companies. How did you get your start?

EXTRA
CREDIT

One effective strategy for drumming up informational interviews is to promise your contact that you will take only twenty minutes of his time. But if you employ this strategy, you must really keep your meeting to twenty minutes, no matter what.

289.

Boy, I hadn't heard from your dad in a long time, and so I was sort of surprised to get his call. How is your dad doing, anyway?

A. Well, you know, Dad is going to try to retire again. Obviously, he's so energetic that sometimes he has trouble relaxing. So who knows if he'll be happy in retirement? At any rate, my Dad has fond memories of working with you, and he thought that you would be the perfect person to talk to me about the fundamentals of the business. What steps do I need to take to get a job at a company like yours? Do I need to go back to school? Tell me what you think.

EXTRA

CREDIT

If you are asked about a mutual connection, give that person his conversational due, and then deftly move the interview to its correct focus—which is learning more about your chosen career path.

The 411 on Informational Interviews

Here are nine questions to ask on your informational interviews:

1. How did you break into the field?

2. Are you having fun? What's great about the profession?

3. What are some of the drawbacks of the career?

4. What qualifications do I need to get a job working at your company?

5. Who's the right person to follow up with?

6. Would you be willing to put in a good word for me with that person?

7. Do you know any people in your field who work at other companies? Would you be able to give me their phone numbers so that I might contact them as well?

8. Would it be okay if I kept in touch with you occasionally to let you know of my progress?

9. May I get your business card?

One of the Bosses Never Met You

You had six, count 'em, six interviews at the company. They finally offered you a job and you accepted it with glee. You've been working at the office for two weeks, very happily…when suddenly, some guy whom you've never seen before stops you in the hallway and claims that he's also one of your bosses. How on earth could this possibly happen, you ask yourself (erstwhile hoping that you don't look dazed and confused). Whether your newest boss was on vacation during the hiring process or was recently rotated to your team via an internal shuffle, here's how to ace the questions he's likely to ask.

290. When Milton decided to hire you, I was in Rio for a couple of weeks. Mind if I take a look at your portfolio?

A. Oh, I would love to have you review my book. I even happen to have an extra copy of it with me today at the office. Would you like me to take you through my work, or would you prefer for me to leave it off for you and pick it up later this afternoon?

Why This Technique Works

1. Your new boss may be dismayed by the fact that he never had a chance to see your portfolio before you were hired. But you've done your best to unruffle his feathers—by being friendly, cooperative, and easygoing.

2. Clearly, it would be in your best interest if you could sit down with your boss while he looks at your work. But by offering to drop off your book for him, you've exhibited a great deal of confidence. You're unflappable.

291.
I don't know if Roslyn mentioned me when she hired you, but my name is Jock, and you'll also be reporting to me.

A. And may I just say, it's great to finally meet you, Jock. Roslyn told me all about you, and I've been looking forward to putting the name together with the face. Is there anything special that you would like me to know about working for you? How often would you like me to check in with you about projects?

Why This Technique Works

1. You covered for Roslyn, which was in your best interest. You're so diplomatic, that soon you'll be issued a special license plate.

2. You sound like you're genuinely pleased to be working for your new boss, and enthusiasm is contagious.

292.
I was on a business trip when the decision was made to put you on staff. In addition to everything else on your plate, you'll also be answering my line and typing my correspondence. Can we talk for a moment now about procedures?

A. I would love to talk to you about the process. I've been very eager to meet you because I've heard so much about you. Let's find a quieter locale—perhaps your office?—where we can talk about your expectations.

293.

When you were interviewing here, the HR Department forgot to have you meet with me. Do you have five or ten minutes right now?

A. I have as much time as you can spare for me. In fact, let me grab a pad of paper and a pen, and let's go into your office to chat. By the way, my name is Lucy. It's a pleasure to meet you.

Why This Technique Works

1. You put your new boss at ease during what could have been an embarrassing moment.

2. You come off as very personable, a good quality in an ally.

The Incredibly Bad Timing of Meeting Your New Boss

Consider it a law of the corporate jungle. Whenever your new boss finally deigns to poke her head into your cubicle to introduce herself will find you smack in the middle your very first work crisis. But even if you are putting out fires left and right, it's *not* a good idea to delay talking to your new boss, even for half an hour. Do not make the cardinal mistake of telling her that you're "under a brutal deadline" to get some other boss's work out. Just stop everything that you're doing cold—and listen to what the woman has to say!

5 Possible Reasons the HR Department Forgot to Introduce You to Your New Boss

It sure would have been nice to have met your new boss before you got on staff. But since that obviously didn't happen, all you can do is to try and make the best of it. Here are five conceivable reasons why arranging a meeting between you and your new boss slipped the HR manager's mind:

1. Your boss was either on vacation or on a business trip during the time that your candidacy was being considered, and gave her "proxy vote" to someone else on staff. In her absence, she empowered that person to make a hiring decision about you.

2. While you were interviewing, there was a reorganization, prompting the boss whom you never met to switch teams. The hiring manager didn't realize that you would be reporting to this person, thus, never scheduled a meeting between the two of you.

3. Your new boss is on her way out.

4. The company is somewhat dysfunctional.

5. The company is unbelievably dysfunctional.

294.

It's a pity that I didn't have the time to meet you while you were interviewing here because you and I are going to be working together rather closely.

A. I would have killed to meet you during the time that I was interviewing! As a matter of fact, I kept asking everyone if I could. "Can I meet Tony, please? Can I please meet Tony?" Eventually, though, I really felt like I was just nagging everyone to death. So, Tony…I'm very pleased to have finally made your acquaintance. What are some of the projects that you have in mind for me?

Interviews to Keep Your Job

When there has been a reorganization and a new boss comes on staff from outside the company, the biggest mistake that you can make is not recognizing that your job may be in jeopardy. It doesn't particularly matter whether you have been an average performer or a "star" with years of glowing performance appraisals in your dossier. The reality is, new bosses often have sweeping powers to make dramatic changes. You must make every effort to impress your new boss. Regardless of how long you've worked at the company, you will need to jump through hoops right now... the way that you did when you first joined the firm.

295.

Hello, Darlene, I'm Jerry. Pleased to meet you. As you know, I'm new around here, and I was wondering what your experience has been like at this company so far.

A. Well, in general, I've enjoyed it. You know, there have been a lot of management changes since I first arrived four years ago. But hopefully, under your guidance, things will settle down and we can all get back to the task at hand—which is helping our clients' businesses grow.

Why This Technique Works

1. You haven't said anything damning—about yourself, your clients, or others on staff.

2. You've expressed an interest in getting back to work instead of getting mired in politics.

296.

I've got to be honest with you, Daryl. It's going to be my job to supervise the work… and frankly, I'm underwhelmed with the work that's coming out of your team.

A. Yeah, Roger, I happen to agree with you. I think that part of the blame lies with our clients. Their business is down…they're running scared, and their tendency is to go for our most conservative stuff. To placate them, we were forced to hire some very conservative staffers with technical backgrounds a couple of years ago; and frankly, their work has been unspectacular. But unfortunately, that pedestrian work is what our clients always seem to go for. When I heard that you were coming over here, I was delighted because I knew that you would quickly get to the bottom of this. I hope that you will count on me to help…because, honestly, if we can't produce good work, what's the point?

Why This Technique Works

1. You've pointed the finger at two things that need immediate improvement…your clients' taste level and some of your staffers' sleepy, ho-hum work.

2. You've also let your new boss know that you agree with his assessment, and that you're very willing to get behind him in his efforts to turn the place around.

The Skinny on "Cutting the Fat"

A lot of companies can be compared to crash dieters. They go through binges. In an up cycle, companies tend to over-hire. Then a down cycle comes along, and they shed employees even faster than you can drop pounds on *The South Beach Diet*.

When a new boss arrives, the top managers of the firm often anticipate that there will be some corporate "calorie counting" as well. The new boss may wish to bring in some employees with whom he worked in the past. (And "cutting some of the fat around here" may well be his justification.)

If a new boss doesn't seek you out to have a "heart to heart" chat about life at the company, wait two weeks, and then schedule an appointment with his personal assistant to stop by an introduce yourself. You must set about getting your new boss to respect you and your work. There's no point in delaying your initial meeting with him for too long.

297.

So, Robin, I understand that you worked here for twelve years and have survived umpteen management shakeouts. In your opinion, who are the strong players, and who are the weak ones?

A. Well, Mike, I'm perfectly willing to tell you…as long as you swear to me that you won't "shoot the messenger."

298.

Don't be ridiculous, Robin. Just tell me the truth.

A. Okay. I think that Gertrude, Gerta, and Gabe are absolutely fantastic managers, and the people under them—myself included—all seem to be thriving under their careful, meticulous guidance. Everyone on our team made their numbers this year, and, as you know, our goals were "through the roof."

In A.J.'s team, however, that was not the situation, at least according to the rumor mill. I don't know if this was due to A.J.'s "hands-off" management style, or if was because A.J. inherited a couple of weak players in the XYZ merger three years ago.

Why This Technique Works

1. You've protected "the good team," backing up your assertions with irrefutable proof: everyone on the team made their numbers.

2. You've casually implied that another team at the company is in trouble. But you stopped short of coming out and saying that it was the team leader's fault.

299.
Stacey...I heard that your last meeting with the LKR Group didn't go all that well. What happened?

A. You're absolutely right, Neal, the meeting was sort of a non-event. We arrived exactly on time at 9 a.m. last Friday, and the LKR Group made us twiddle our thumbs for three hours before the meeting got started. They claimed that Claudia Reese needed to be in the room, that she had a "conflict," and that we would just have to wait. Every hour, our clients stopped by the conference room, and asked us if we needed to use the bathroom. Eventually at noon, they filed in, mysteriously announced that Claudia wouldn't be able to attend after all, and told us to proceed with the meeting anyway. By that time, our energy level was totally depleted... partly because we didn't think that anyone on their side of the table was empowered to make any decisions. We presented our case...they seemed to take a lot of notes, and we left.

I was wondering if Claudia is still working for them. Do you know if she is? Because it's been two weeks since we had that meeting, and we still haven't heard a word from our clients about how they think it went.

Why This Technique Works

1. Your team was put in a trying situation by a group of rude clients. Intelligently, you positioned the meeting as a non-event (rather than a total fiasco).

2. You also gave your new boss something to probe: Claudia's mysterious absence. Your boss's radar, at least for now, is off of you.

The New Boss Gives You the Heebie Jeebies. Now What?

Approximately two months into a new boss's term, you should be able to intuit whether he likes you. If he doesn't stop by your office occasionally to shoot the breeze and find out how your projects are going, it's fairly certain that he's identified you as either a marginal player (whom he will cut at a later date) or possibly, an A player who frightens him because he perceives you as a threat.

Either way, the situation is "code yellow," and you would be well advised to surreptitiously contact your headhunter and quietly begin looking for another job. (The operative word in the preceding sentence is "quietly.")

Don't discuss your ambivalence about your new boss (or fears about him) with anyone on staff. Don't raise the red flag by disappearing for two hours every day to go on interviews. And if you happen to be the last person on the planet without a cell phone, now is the time to buy one!

Never make your job-hunting phone calls from your company's landline. Instead, leave the office building for fifteen minutes to "go grab some coffee," and then, walk to a destination that's at least five blocks away, and discreetly make your job-hunting calls from there. Ask your business contacts (and headhunters) to call you back on your cell (and keep it on "vibrate.") When you're at the office, keep your door open at all times. Be careful not to let your new boss catch you in the act of looking for another job!

Finally, it's worth mentioning that, by law, employers are allowed to read the emails that staffers send. So don't tempt fate by sending a job-hunting inquiry from your office email account. If you suspect that your new boss is "out to get you," trust your instincts.

Take a slightly longer lunch break than usual, once a week, and go home and send your job inquiries from the privacy of your own computer.

300.

According to Eric, my job description is to "shake things up around here." What exactly needs to be fixed?

A. I'm not sure if things need to be "shaken" or simply stirred. Our numbers are off; morale is unbelievably low; and the people around here are always complaining that they can't get their work done because our printers always fail in the clutch. But top management refuses to invest in new machines until our numbers get better. I can't tell you how happy I am that you've come on board because I know that you're brilliant at solving problems; and, quite frankly, we seem to be saddled with several of them

The Exit Interview: Not the Place to Vent

You may be tempted to reveal that you started looking for a job because you couldn't tolerate your boss's rants. After all, who could? The man was a maniac! Still, there is nothing to be gained by sharing this information in an exit interview, and actually, quite a lot to lose. The word will get back to your former boss, and retribution will come in the form of lousy recommendations from him at some point down the road. Whatever the circumstances were that led to you leaving the company, take care to exit graciously.

at this moment in time. Please let me know how I can help you out.

How to Have a Beautiful Relationship with Your Headhunter

Most relationships in life that are worth having take a little work. A relationship with a headhunter is no exception.

Here are five rules for creating a smooth, working bond with a headhunter:

1. **Appreciate that headhunters are incredibly loyal—their first loyalty just isn't to you.** Headhunters are paid by the companies they represent. Therefore, pleasing these companies is their top priority. If your headhunter thinks that you're the perfect fit with a particular firm, he will bend over backwards to get you placed. So do your best to impress your headhunter the very first time you meet him.

2. **Headhunters expect you to be 100 percent loyal to them.** Frequently, they will be competing against other recruiters to place candidates at the same company. If one recruiter tells you about an open position, you need to pursue it with him, and not some other recruiter.

3. **Headhunters hate to be "out of the loop."** If a headhunter helped place you in a long-term freelance gig, it's only polite to give him a jingle every two weeks, even if it's just to let him know that things are going spectacularly well.

4. **Headhunters don't appreciate being nagged.** When there isn't a particular job that you are pursuing, one phone call, once a month, is enough to keep you top of mind.

5. **Headhunters want to be appreciated.** Do you want to give your headhunter the perfect present? If you're not interested in a job that your headhunter tells you about, always recommend someone else for the position.

301.

Sorry things didn't work out, Maya. Is there anything that you would like us to know about your experience here?

A. I had a terrific run at KST and I have only positive things to say about my boss, colleagues, and clients. I was offered a great job; so naturally, I had no choice but to accept it. But I loved the people here, and I have visions of coming back to work here again in my future.

Alt. A. I always loved my job and I gave it my all. It was a wonderful experience, and I'll think of everyone here fondly at wherever it is that I end up. I would like to give your name out as a reference. Would that be all right with you?

EXTRA CREDIT

If you left under good circumstances, always try to keep the door open. If you were fired or laid off, try to leave without slamming the door on the way out.

That's a Wrap

1. In a phone interview, you can hurt yourself by revealing too much information. Keep your answers short and focused on the next step—which is getting an in-person meeting.
2. Even if you're told that it's just a "courtesy interview," the last interview that you have at a company can make or break your bid for the job. Prepare for this meeting just as thoroughly as you have for all of your others.
3. Informational interviews are reconnaissance missions. Whether you're graduating from college now and are looking for your very first job, or are trying to switch careers, informational interviews can help you figure out if the field is right for you and what it will take to enter it.
4. If someone whom you've never met approaches you at a new job and claims to be your boss, treat your initial meeting with him as if it's a job interview. Drop everything that you're doing and concentrate on making a good impression on him.
5. With restructurings and reorganizations often come new bosses. Frequently granted sweeping powers to make big changes, a new boss who doesn't like you can play havoc with your career. Set up a meeting with him as soon as you possibly can to introduce yourself, if he doesn't seek you out first.

CONCLUSION

How to Snag the Job of Your Life in Forty-Five Minutes

A job interview is like a very short date with a prospect to assess your compatibility. You will have approximately forty-five minutes to make an impression. Meanwhile, it really is not possible for anyone to get to know a perfect stranger in under an hour.

In less time than it takes to eat lunch, your prospect will need to decide how he or she would feel about seeing you five days a week, forty-nine weeks a year, for the foreseeable future.

How will your prospect make this decision? By asking you a series of questions, one or two of which might be curveballs, trick questions, or even questions that have no answer.

If you want to perform at your peak, there is no substitute for good, solid preparation. And hopefully, that's where this book has really helped you.

You've learned how to field any kind of question that can be thrown your way, including the ridiculously tough question. The how-can-they-ask-me-that question. The Killer Question. The getting-this-job-depends-on-my-answer kind of question. After all, anyone can answer the easy questions. (If you can't, time to reread chapter 1 immediately.)

You've become a pro at tackling the types of questions that need some homework done on them in advance. Maybe you've even memorized the answers to one or two of them, so that you can come off "spontaneously" in your interviews, with grace and aplomb.

In sum, you have achieved poise; and in the Interviewing Game, never underestimate the power of poise.

If you used this book to ace your first interview at the company, please give yourself a big pat on the back. You are well on your way to your dream job.

And now, a word of caution. Try to feel happy about your performance without becoming cocky about it. Interviews tend to get even more difficult in the second, third, and fourth rounds. So go back now and review your "master list" of questions and the answers that you created. Then, use the next couple of days to add to the list. Give yourself even tougher questions, and force yourself to come up with answers that are even more thorough. Also, figure out new ways of phrasing your replies to the questions you were asked already, because nothing sounds more canned than repeating the same answer verbatim to a different interviewer within the same company.

Above all, believe in yourself. Have faith in your powers of persuasion and that unique blend of charm and savvy intelligence that makes you *you*. Realize that the only way to nail your interviews is by making a strong, positive impression on the people doing the asking. Each time, you will need to make your prospect feels like he or she really "gets you." Not some overstudied, nervous Nellie version of yourself, but the real you, the one your friends love.

You now know what it takes to perform brilliantly. So go out there, and do it all over again.

That's a Wrap

1. You no longer flinch when someone asks you a tough question. Were you fired? Laid off? Downsized? Made redundant? You have a strategy for explaining what happened in a way that interviewers will embrace.

2. You don't play the "blame game." You credit all ex-bosses with what you learned from them along the way.

3. Turning your biggest weakness into a strength is a trick and you are a practiced magician.

4. You leap over obstacles that stop other candidates from getting hired. There isn't a glass ceiling in the land that you can't smash.

5. You condense your life story into memorable "sound bites." You're the hero (or heroine) of the tale, and interviewers root for you to win.

6. You've learned how to become a job magnet. You're not afraid to flash some personality during appointments.

7. You've tamed the Impossible Question.

8. Any mistakes from the past no longer haunt you because you've already erased them, or chalked them up to experience that has made you all the wiser.

9. You know that the most important thing is to come off as likeable, an attribute that helps you ace personality tests in the executive suite.

10. You dance around the prickliest, most personal questions with gusto. You know how to distract your interviewer with charm, or address his real concern if there is one.

11. You are a gifted conversationalist, and are just as comfortable following your interviewer's lead or taking charge when need be.

12. Good Cop/Bad Cop routines have become routine, and you don't feel intimidated by them anymore.

13. You're a genius at bringing a question from a distant galaxy down to earth.
14. What do interviewers want? You can prove that you've got the very qualities they are seeking.
15. You are proud to be a zealot in pursuit of your passion.
16. You'd never dream of leaving an interview without asking your prospect at least three "softball" questions.
17. When the product that you are selling is YOU, you are most convincing.
18. You don't sit around wishing that you had said X instead of Y, because you know that you can always say X after the interview in a beautifully crafted follow-up email.
19. You no longer fear the toughest "interview" of all—the one where a new boss comes on staff and is really meeting you to decide whether to keep you or let you go.
20. You are more confident now than you have ever been in your life. And you recognize that this quality alone is all that you really need to succeed.

appendix

Job Websites

Top 10 Job Listings

1. monster.com
2. craigslist.org—Look to the right hand side of the screen to plug in your city of choice.
3. hotjobs.yahoo.com
4. careerbuilder.com
5. hotmailjobs.com
6. job.com
7. ajb.org
8. about.com
9. joblink-usa.com
10. nytimes.com—Search classifieds

Nontraditional Job Listings—Outdoor, Adventure, Gaming

1. jobmonkey.com
2. funjobs.com

Diversity Hiring

1. hirediversity.com
2. latpro.com

Specialty Listings

1. jobsinthemoney.com—financial jobs
2. businessweek.com—financial jobs
3. bankjobs.com
4. dice.com—hi-tech jobs
5. energycentral.com—hi-tech jobs
6. 6figurejobs.com
7. execunet.com—six-figure jobs
8. adweek.com—advertising/marketing jobs
9. showbizjobs.com

7 Clever Ways to Research a Company

1. wetfeet.com
2. hoovers.com
3. vault.com
4. sec.gov/edgar/searchedgar/companysearch.html—When the list of the company's filings comes up, choose the most recent 10K report. This is the company's Annual Report and should include a good description of their business.
5. google.com—Find out if the company where you're interviewing has a blog.
6. motleyfool.com
7. http://finance.yahoo.com—If the company's public, you can search for information about its stock, and then check out the company's message boards. You will need to know the symbol for the company's stock, but this extra step is well worth it.

Giving Good Phone

1. quintcareers.com/phone_interview_etiquette.html

In-Person Interviews

1. jobsFAQ.com/interview/behavioral-interview.html

For Women, Career Changers, and People Reentering the Job Force

1. womensjobsearch.net
2. 9to5.org
3. careerchangenetwork.com
4. aarpjobs.com

For College Grads

1. collegegrad.com
2. jobweb.com

Interview Dress Dos & Don'ts

1. quintcareers.com/dress_for_success.html
2. worktree.com/tb/IN_dress.cfm ("Dressing for Success")

Personality Testing

1. paladinexec.com—Look up Myers-Briggs Type Indicator (MBTI) Instrument.
2. lrandc.com/onlinediscrequest.html—Free online DISC test.
3. advisorteam.com/temperament_sorter/register.asp?partid=1—The Keirsey Temperament Sorter II.

Advice

1. artofselfpromotion.com
2. interview.monster.com
3. careerjournal.com

Trend Spotting and Staying Up-to-Date

1. keepmedia.com

Job Hunting Savvy

1. vickyoliver917@hotmail.com

Inside Information

If you get stuck on your job search or you just need some friendly advice, you can email me once. And I do promise to return your first email. So save it for a time when you could really use the help! Good luck with your job search.

index

A

A players vs. B players 132
accomplishment, most difficult 16
accomplishment, most out-standing 20
accomplishment, recent 16
advertising industry 23
advertising, word-of-mouth 95–96
age barrier 61, 62–69
age, questions about 171–172
animal question 232–233
anti-discrimination laws 82
assertiveness 188–189
ax man 254

B

back-to-basics questions, 2
    questions about your dreams and aspirations, 2, 9–14
    questions about your P.W.S. (Preferred Working Style), 2, 26–30
    questions that ask you to walk a mile in your interviewer's Cole Haans, 2–9
    questions that blatantly ask you to sell yourself, 2, 15–21
    questions that reveal if you've done your homework, 2, 21–25
background 10
background checks 143
background, financial questions about 173
barriers to employment 62
    clearly, you've got other com-mitments, so... 62, 82–83
    we'd love to hire a man, but... 62, 87–89
    our clients are looking for a certain type of person (not your type) 62, 76–81
    we'd love to hire a woman, but... 62, 84–86

you're too old to work here 62
you're too young to work here 62, 70
Beecher, Henry Ward 200
benefit to the company 7
biggest weakness 34–35
book, favorite 293
boss, female 88, 89
boss, former 36
bosses, best vs. worst 192–193
bosses, several 57
boutique companies 21
boys' club 85

C

career future, five years from now 179
career peak 228
career shrink 39
career-changer 44–47, 51
change, embracing 58, 133, 140–141
childhood, questions about 215
children 158–160, 163–164, 167–168
clients, high-net-worth 118
college awards 73
college education, value of 226
college experience 71–72
college, not finishing 43
commitments, personal 82–83, 140
companies, better elsewhere 57
company closing 252–253, 263

company merger 258
company vision 145–147
company, best managed 92–93
company, leaving 249
company, why did you stay so long 252
competing in the market 25
concrete vs. abstract 184
confidence, breaking 116–117
contract, broken by employer 243
corporate culture issues 54
corporate culture, fitting in with 48–53
courageous actions 115
creativity vs. business acumen 195–196
credentials, overqualified 44
credentials, underqualified 41, 52
credit, taking undeserved 106
criticism, facing 120
cults 81

D

daydreaming 144
deadline, missing a 120
decision, split-second 199
decision-making approach 186–187
department dismantled 256
desert island question 234
disagreements, resolving 35–36
divorce 170

downsizing 253–254
downtime at work 130
dream job, career change 30
dream job, describe your 12, 229

E
Edison, Thomas 200
education, further 71
education, high school only 42
Einstein, Albert 200
electricity 15
entrepreneur to full-time
email 291–326
employee 56
equal opportunity employment
62–68, 77, 80
ethics 9
ethnic barriers 78–79
ex-boss, badmouthing 38, 244
ex-girlfriend questions 213
exit interview 350
expansion, possible 129
experience, too little 70

F
fact-finding skills 196–197
felicity 15
financial firms, popular question 97
fired twice 265–266
fired vs. quit 246
fired, reason why 241
first impression 202
five types of interviews that are

really special situations 328
   informational interview 328,
   336–338
   interviews to keep your job,
   328, 340–351
   one of the bosses never met
   you, 328, 340–343
   phone interviews, 328–332
   the "last interview," 328,
   333–336
flirting, in office 226
free time 17
freelancing 40
frustration with old job 249–250
full-time employee to entrepreneur 230

G
Games Interviewers Play 206
give us one good reason not to
hire you questions 34
   let us tell you your biggest
   weakness 34, 40
   tell us your biggest weakness
   34
   you won't fit in here,
   because... 34
   you'll be miserable here,
   because... 34
   you've jumped ship too many
   times already 34
gender barrier 61, 77–78
gender discrimination of men

87–89
gender discrimination of women 84–86
goals, next ten years 230
goals, setting and managing 14
goals, short-range and long-range 12–13
Good Cop/Bad Cop etiquette 188
Good Cop/Bad Cop questions 178
   defend your job performance questions 178, 186–194
   do you have the right stuff? questions 178, 194–199
   mirror, mirror on the wall (aka self-assessment questions) 178, 200–203
   why us, why now? 178, 204–208
   your philosophy 101 questions 178–185
group therapy 39

H
headhunter 351
heavyweight vs. lightweight 213
heroes, who are your 222
hiring, men vs. women 103
homework on the company 21
hours, long 50
independent working 19

I
ideal conditions 312

if only I had said X instead of Y answers 292
   answers that must be revised due to new information 292, 313–315
   answers that were generic and/or lame 292, 307–312
   answers that you flat-out flubbed 292, 315–325
   answers where you didn't really answer the question (or said too little) 292–301
   answers where you said too much 292, 302–307
impossible questions 92
   pigeonhole yourself questions 92, 108–111
   pop essay questions 92–96
   ethical questions with a twist 92, 101–106
   questions that have no correct answer (but require logic to answer them, anyway) 92, 96–100
   questions that send you to confession (or Oprah) 92, 112–120
independent worker vs. team player 26–27
industry predictions 23
inflexible 111
informational interviews 336–339
insecure, feeling 141–142
interview, best time for 104

interviewing, where else are you 20–21
interviews, packing for 11

J
job, leaving 248
job-hopping 45
Johns, Jasper 118

L
laid off 247
last job, least enjoyable aspects of 134
leadership 125, 127
learning quickly 198
let go 247, 267
level, mid-range 52–53
life lessons learned 220
Longfellow, Henry Wadsworth 200
love, have you been in 221
loyalty to company 114
luck vs. skill 224

M
major in philosophy, preparation for other career 24
managing to not managing 56
managing, up or down 108–109
marital status 153
maturity 74–75
MBA 284
military service 166
minorities 165–166

mistakes made 117, 134, 193–194
money vs. satisfaction 236
morality 9
motivation 27

N
nervous breakdown 261
none-of-your-business questions 152
    questions about the kids 152, 157–164
    questions about your ability to deal with people who are not exactly like you 152, 165–166
    questions about your beliefs 152, 154–157
    questions about your marital/significant other status 152–154

O
optimism 24
optimism vs. pessimism 53–59

oral personality exams 124
questions about how you
filled out the written personality test (or would, if there
were one) 124–128
questions that ask you to take
off your "work mask" 124,
138–142
questions that Freud would
approve 124, 142–149
questions that get you to
reveal your personality (when
you don't realize it's being
tested) 124, 128–134
questions that test your political prowess 124, 134–137
overtime 131

P
P.W.S. (Preferred Working
Style), 26
passions 215–216
performing under pressure 18
personal questions 214, 217
personality style 201
personality test 123, 126
personality test, fill-in-the-blank
126
personality, type A 123, 125
personality, type B 123, 125
pet peeves 145
policy, disagreeing with 181–
182
politics, national 156–157

politics, office 134–137
Pollyanna 57
position, interest in 205
PowerPoint presentation 105
Preferred Working Style
(P.W.S.), 26
pregnancy 161
prejudice 62, 79–80
problems with others 242
problems, anticipating 189–191
products 93
products vs. market 94
promotion possibilities 58, 207
promotion, lack of 36–37
psychiatric counseling 39

Q
qualities in a candidate 3
qualities you admire 203
qualities, unique to individual
149
qualities, unique to job 18
questions from another galaxy
212
questions about life-changing
events 212, 219–221
questions about your core values 212, 222–226
questions that are dimly job
related (very dimly) 212–217
questions that ask you to predict the future 212, 228–231
questions that you'd ask a friend
in a bar 212, 232–236

questions that you should ask, 270

questions about the internal structure and/or job description, 278–282

questions that help you decide if the company's a good fit for you, 283–286

questions that put the ball back in the interviewer's court, 287–288

questions that show you studied the company, 273–276

questions to start the "conversational ball" rolling, 270–272

questions, impossible, 91–120

quit job, 246–247

R

raises, mediocre 102

reason to hire you 8

reference letter, from former employer 38

religion 155

relocating 48

rent 170–171

resigned from last company 259

resources, lack of 55

resume, fact-checking 43

resume, what you left off 6

resumes, false information on 126

retire 228

rewards, career 299

risks 54–55, 264–265

risks taken 112–113

role model 28–29

Roosevelt, Franklin D. 200

rules of life 223

S

salary requirements, low 40

self-improvement class 39

sense of humor 139, 194

September 11, 2001 219–220

7 Classic Interview Don'ts 107

severance package 262

sexual orientation 154

Sneaky Questions about Your Financial Lifestyle 152, 166–173

song, favorite 233

so-you-were-fired questions 240

  are you a big risk? 240, 264–267

  did you see the ax coming? 240, 250–254

  what really happened? 240, 256–263

  why did you quit? 240, 245–250

  why were you fired? 240–244

spare time 142

speech-making 216

spouse's job 168–169

start date 30

stereotyping 76–81

stress, on-the-job factors 22

success, measuring 185

supervisor, clashing with 257

supervisor, previous 37

T

temper, losing your 118–119

tenacity 15

"Ten Worst Companies in the World for a Woman to Work, The" 86

titles, unorthodox 59

Top 3 Things Interviewers Want 4–5

    closure skills 4–5

    people skills 4–5

    problem-solving skills 4–5

traditional interviews vs. behavioral interviews vs. quiz interviews 255

travel required 49–50

trends 19

turning point at old job 251

types of interviews 255

behavioral 255

quiz 255

traditional 255

U

unemployed 266

V

value, what things you 13–14

visionary vs. implementer 109–110

W

what would you do differently? 182–183

work environment, adapting to 111

work group, ideal 204

work philosophy 179–180

workaholic 33

working style 128

ABOUT THE AUTHOR

Vicky Oliver is an award-winning copywriter with experience at brand-name, top-tier advertising agencies in Manhattan. She would confess how long she's been in the field, except that would go straight to her age—something she feels strongly that one should never reveal on a job interview.

Ms. Oliver's articles have appeared in *Adweek* magazine and on *Crain's New York Business* website, and she has been featured in the *New York Times* "Job Market" section and on national radio programs. She has given seminars on job-hunting skills, networking, and the art of branding yourself at *The Writer's Voice* in Manhattan. She is in constant touch with over five thousand recent candidates in all different professions and in all different walks of life: the employed, the unemployed, entrepreneurs, freelancers, retirees, and people returning to the job market.

A Brown University graduate with a degree in English honors and a double major in political science, Ms. Oliver lives in New York City, where she has dedicated herself to helping others turn around their careers and their lives.